£8.95

THE BEGINNING OF THE REST OF YOUR LIFE?

The Beginning of the Rest of Your Life?

A Portrait of Newly-Wed Marriage

Penny Mansfield and Jean Collard

First edition 1988
Reprinted 1988

Published by
THE MACMILLAN PRESS LTD
Houndmills, Basingstoke, Hampshire RG2 2XS
and London
Companies and representatives
throughout the world

Printed in Great Britain by
Camelot Press, Southampton

British Library Cataloguing in Publication Data
Mansfield, Penny
The beginning of the rest of your life?:
a portrait of newly-wed marriage.
1. Marriage
I. Title   II. Collard, Jean
306.8'1   HQ728
ISBN 0–333–44661–5 (hardcover)
ISBN 0–333–44662–3 (paperback)

For my parents (PM)
For Anne Vickery and Valerie Haig-Brown (JC)

'*Marriage, which has been the bourne
of so many narratives, is still a great
beginning, as it was to Adam and Eve,
who kept their honeymoon in Eden,
but had their first little one among the
thorns and thistles of the wilderness. It
is still the beginning of the hope
epic.*'—

Middlemarch,
George Eliot, 1872

'*Getting married is where it all starts. You're not a kid any more,
you're branching out on your own. It's the beginning of the rest of
your life.*'—newly-married husband, *The Beginning of the Rest of
Your Life?* Mansfield and Collard, 1988

'*You cannot plan for the future really. Once you are married . . . you think that the rest of your life is going to be spent
together . . . And then suddenly, whoosh! it's all gone, and there
isn't that safe little world any more.*'—newly-divorced wife, *When
Marriage Ends*, Nicky Hart, 1976

Contents

Acknowledgements

This study is the third research project from the Marriage Research Centre, and, like the other two, it owes its inception to the Director of the Centre, Dr Jack Dominian, who has always had a particular interest in the early years of married life.

Our thanks are also due to the past and present Trustees of the Centre, who have patiently raised the funds for a lengthy study. We are particularly grateful to Xandra Hardie, a former Trustee, who has acted as our honorary literary agent. And we are constantly mindful of the charitable trusts and generous individuals who have given the money which has enabled the Centre to continue in these times of financial stringency. We would like also to express our appreciation of the practical servicing and support the Centre continues to receive from the Central Middlesex Hospital.

A research study such as this one is very demanding in terms of initial planning and fieldwork, and special recognition must be given to Margaret Stoneman and, later, Maggie O'Brien, for their creative participation at those crucial early stages. Other colleagues at the Centre, past and present, also gave helpful advice and support: Julia Brannen, Paul Divall, Maggie Evans, Hanna McCluskey, Alan Tait and Barbara Thornes.

The analysis of the data, and its interpretation and writing up, are entirely our own responsibility, but we are grateful for clerical assistance from Luciana Ballini and Alison Taylor, and the useful review of newspaper cuttings about marriage which was provided by Catherine Taylor.

We particularly want to express our warm thanks to Robert Chester, Research Director to the Centre. His visits always gave us help, stimulation and encouragement. Since we are a very small Centre, we have valued all our contacts with colleagues from other units and agencies and, in particular, George Brown, Peter Chambers, Karen Dunnell, Kath Kiernan, Richard Leete, Michael Rutter and David Quinton.

This research would not have been possible without the friendly co-operation of the various clergy of all denominations who were approached about first-time marriages they had recently solemnised. We are most grateful to them for agreeing to provide the names and addresses of those who later became our research couples.

It is not easy to give adequate thanks to the newly-weds themselves. We hope we have done justice to their warmth, openness and generosity in sharing with us their experiences of getting married and setting up home. Although we were relieved and glad that most of them said they had found it a good experience to talk freely about themselves, we were aware of the inevitable moments of strain there had been for them – they did indeed give us a *total* portrait and not just the 'sunny' moments. They gave us a great deal of themselves, and we have tried both to acknowledge this, and to safeguard their confidences; we hope they will feel their trust in us has been justified.

From a practical point of view, we have been fortunate with our librarians and our secretarial services. Nicky Whitsed, Bridget Farrant and Sheila Cook at the Post-Graduate Medical Library have been a steadfast support and have tracked down even our most obscure requests. Rita Andrews has performed a magnificent task in typing the manuscript of the book, while other secretarial assistance at various stages has come from Louise Derry, Joan Gomez, Theresa Harvey, Wendy Huggett and Janet Johns.

Lastly, we want to acknowledge the help we have received from our own families; the writing of a book tends to take over personal and domestic life. Special thanks, therefore, to Isabella and Sophie Dowden who put up with considerable disruption in their lives, and to Richard Dowden, Catherine Mansfield and Jenny Green who helped to minimise its effects; and particular gratitude also to Chris Collard in Swansea for his uncomplaining acceptance of prolonged absences and preoccupied presences.

London, May 1987   PENNY MANSFIELD
                                       JEAN COLLARD

The authors and publishers are grateful to the following publishers for permission to use extracts from their authors' published material:

Edward Arnold, publishers of E.M. Forster, *Howards End;* *Faber & Faber,* publishers of Philip Larkin, *The Whitsun Weddings;* and Methuen, publishers of Sue Townsend, *The Secret Diary of Adrian Mole.*

Preface

Relationships between men and women have always fascinated people; when we decided to preface each chapter in this book with an appropriate quotation our only problem was one of choice from the examples which abound in literature from the remote past to the present day. A quick glance around the shelves of any newsagent would reveal the strength of current preoccupation with relationships, although today the focus is likely to be on the problems of managing marriages and the effects of divorce on children.

It is not surprising that in recent years, this concern has stimulated research into various aspects of marital disorder and breakdown, but this obsession with marital mishap has meant that little is known about 'normal' marriage, save that it is still popular. Cohabitation is increasing in frequency, but it is often a prelude to marriage rather than a replacement of it; divorce rates continue to rise, although two-thirds of marriages are likely to endure. And this survival has been in the face of the critical reappraisal provoked by the women's movement in the 1960s and 1970s, and the growing awareness of continuing inequalities between husbands and wives. Nor has marriage been outmoded by the struggle for self-actualisation which is the obsessive legacy of the 'me' decades.

It is, however, misleading to refer to marriage as a single concept, since marriage as an institution and marriage as a developmental relationship are, for most people, divergent. The very notion of marriage is still saturated with myth and contradiction: marriage can entice with the offer of companionship, yet be experienced as isolation; it can promise support but prove a disappointment; although it is widely regarded as a passport to adult life, it can arouse the most primitive infantile insecurities. Such paradoxes and contradictions appear to be endemic in contemporary marriage, and present a challenge to explore.

In responding to this challenge it is essential to start at the very beginning of the marriage process, and try to discover what makes people decide to marry, what attracts them about their partner, what is the nature of the experience of adjusting to the married state, and how far it accords with prior expectations. This book sets out to analyse the answers to these questions given by a group of young newly-weds, and also to consider marriage in its current social setting.

We are both sociologists at the Marriage Research Centre, which has as one of its principal aims research into contemporary marriage. A research study was accordingly initiated at the centre, to look closely at husbands and wives in first-time marriages. Interviews in depth were conducted with sixty-five young couples who had been married only three months. The full details and a discussion of the theoretical background and methodology of the study are given in Chapter 2.

The accounts of the newly-weds presented us with a lively and illuminating portrait of 'modern marriage' which dispelled many current myths. The interviews also conveyed the serious intensity with which the husbands and wives grappled with the problems of attaining adulthood through marriage, and achieving and sustaining individual identities while striving to become a couple. It became very clear to us that marriage was, for them, indeed 'the beginning of the rest of your life', since it both reflected, and was fashioned by, their personal orientations to the future. We were fascinated by their differing orientations, and a detailed study of them has enabled us to construct a typology of the various strategies for life.

Our book is in three parts; the first part (Chapters 1 and 2) is an introduction. It relates our study to prevailing attitudes and ideas about marriage, and to other research. We consider also the range of theoretical perspectives which influenced us. We believe that Chapter 1 will be of general interest, but Chapter 2 is likely to be of concern primarily to readers with a professional interest in the study of marriage.

The second part (Chapters 3 and 9) presents a portrait of young contemporary marriage. Chapter 3 investigates various motives for getting married, and explores the climate surrounding courtship. Chapter 4 follows the 'trail' to marriage, while Chapter 5 looks a the wedding itself, with its attendant tensions and doubts. Chapter 6 examines the challenge of setting up and running a home, and is complemented by Chapter 7, which considers the different worlds of work outside the home for men and women. Chapters 8 and 9 relate closely to each other: each conveys part of the total experience of becoming a couple and reveals the inevitable dilemmas of intimacy, disclosure and separateness; and support, disappointment and discord.

The third part of the book is the most interpretative. After considering various ways of looking at people over a lifetime, reflected in the handling of the transition to marriage, we offer our own conclusions. We believe that an important key to understanding individuals' experience of the present lies in their orientation to the future. In this section of the book we show how we have discovered and constructed a threefold typology of people in relation to these orientations: planners, venturers and roamers, and illustrate each of the types with detailed individual portraits.

Our discussion of the typology leads us to consider and pose further questions about differing ways in which men and women can experience and negotiate the marriage relationship, both in terms of orientation towards the future and with regard to gender, and we conclude with a brief Afterword in which we reflect on the basic issues raised by our study.

We value the co-operation of our newly-wed couples and appreciate their trust in talking about themselves so freely. Although individuals may well recognise their own words in the quotations, we have altered all names and places and slightly changed many occupations. Where quotations from individuals are not assigned, this is either to preserve confidentiality, or because we consider the nature of the material to be too intimate.

This book focuses on these husbands and wives as they were after three months of marriage. The same couples have now been interviewed by the Centre a second time, and we are planning to follow this book with a companion volume, in which the experiences of these couples will be reviewed after five years of marriage.

P. M.
J. C.

Part I

A Background

1   Images of Marriage

For this reason, a man must leave his father and mother and be joined to his wife, and the two will become one body. This mystery has many implications, but I am saying it applies to Christ and the Church.
St Paul's Epistle to the Ephesians
Jerusalem Bible

Green on thy finger a grass blade curled,
so with this ring I thee wed, I thee wed,
and send our love to the loveless world
of all the living and all the dead.

Epithalamion
Dannie Abse, 1970

'All I ask,' sang out Ivor, 'is a little peace and quiet; an agreeable wife, a wife who is pleasant to my friends; one who occasionally has the room swept, the breakfast table prepared . . . I am, after all, a fairly easy fellow.'
Me Again
Stevie Smith, 1981

The bourgeois sees in his wife a mere instrument of production.
Communist Manifesto
Karl Marx

We are surrounded by images of marriage, ranging from the mystical through the romantic and the mundane to the ideological. There are our own family experiences and gossip about 'other people's marriages'. We read newspaper articles bewailing 'the state of marriage' and describing the marital difficulties of famous people. Romantic films and great literature portray the ebb and flow of ecstasy and melancholy in the life of a marriage while cartoons and television comedies frequently caricature husbands and wives in petty domestic dilemmas. These are only a few of the sources of marital imagery which can offer useful insights into the relationship between husband and wife. But they are more than that since, taken as a whole, they illuminate a public image of marriage.

Although each marriage is an act between two individuals (and their families) marriage is, by definition, a very public act. When a couple decide to marry they are experiencing, probably for the first time, the full panoply of public action, beginning with the official declaration of their intention to marry and culminating in making vows before a public official (the registrar or authorised cleric) who is delegated by the State to give public recognition to their personal commitment. Of course, the incorporation of the public and private commitment in the wedding is one of its attractions; the public reality corroborates the personal reality.

Although cohabitation has commonly been regarded as the rejection of marriage, recent studies suggest that many currently cohabiting relationships are really informal marriages. Some couples who live together are at some point intending to marry, so for them it is simply a question of the personal commitment having preceded the public commitment of marriage. But there are other cohabiting couples who simply 'don't get round to marrying' or who indeed have chosen not to marry and for them the personal commitment is sufficient.[1]

The main distinction, therefore, is not between marriage and an alternative to marriage, but rather between 'those whose marriages are formalised and those whose marriages are not'.[2] The current incorporation of some forms of cohabitation into marriage (at least in notional terms) is one of the ways in which the definition of marriage is changing – being extended – and is central to its public image. One important way in which the public image of marriage is changing is in the shift in emphasis from the external structure of married life to the private meaning of the marital relationship: the public institution of marriage is being privatised. This may be one reason why some people, though intent on a long-term committed relationship, do not bother to legalise that commitment.

In our inquiry into marriage we will be stressing the importance of understanding what the experience of being married is for the individual (see Chapter 2), but in doing so we are in no way underestimating the influence of the public context of marriage on the course of married life. This context includes existing marriage law, employment practice and the labour market, child-care systems and all the many other areas of social life which relate to marriage and the family. The public images of marriage inspire or constrain the individual shaping of married life. For example, a man and woman who want their marriage to express their belief in sexual equality may be frustrated by the attitudes of the world outside and find that their preferred style of married life is neither supported nor encouraged.

The 65 newly-wed couples whose experiences of marriage form the substance of this book[3] often referred to ideas about marriage which they had absorbed from outside, in addition to their own personal and familial experience of marriage. For some it was clear that external images of marriage posed problems for them – were their own marriages like most other marriages; was theirs a 'proper' marriage? They were anxious to use the opportunity of the interview to try to discover the answers. In contrast, others confidently asserted that they were sure that their marriage *was* different from other marriages. In different ways both these groups of newly-weds were making a similar point about marriage; both implied the existence of a yardstick out there by which marriage could be measured. For the couples who wished to conform, if their marriage measured up well to the standard of modern marriage, their normality was validated and their confidence established. For those who did not wish to conform, their perception of themselves as being different from other married couples was confirmed.

This external 'standard' of modern marriage seems to be an amalgam of a variety of images of marriage. What kind of images are these and where do they come from? How powerful are they in influencing the course of married life? It seems that people hold images of marriage which may differ markedly from their perceptions of their own marriage. A distinction is frequently made between marriage in general and 'my' marriage and yet these two images are interdependent. Any study of marriage must consider first the public context of marriages, the collective experience of marriage. The public interpretations of that collective experience as expressed by the key institutions will form an important part of the context of individual marriages (see Chapter 2), with continual interaction between the public and the private views.

MARRIAGE: THE MAKING OF A MODERN PROBLEM

Although it is often assumed that it is only in recent years that marriage has been perceived as a problem, in fact there have always been those 'moralists who diagnose a diseased present because they worship a past they do not understand'.[4] In the 1960s, Raymond Fletcher published *The Family and Modern Britain* in 'an attempt to argue strongly against the prevailing current of gloom and moral denigration'.[5] A forerunner of the now numerous accounts of the changing face of family life in modern Britain, this book became influential as a textbook. Fletcher argued that many of those aspects of modern family life (such as a higher divorce rate) which were pointed to as signs of instability and degeneration, should on the contrary be regarded as signs of moral regeneration. He concluded that the modern family in 1960 was in a far stronger position than at any period in history of which we had knowledge. How to acquire this knowledge was a major problem, however, for, as Fletcher stressed, it required knowing the facts about family life (past and present), and such facts were difficult to ascertain. In his concern to explain and acclaim the changes in the family, he concentrated on the pessimism of the moral arbiters of family life and overlooked the fact that the public view of the family in decline was closely interrelated with the many private uncertainties and confusions over the conduct of life within marriage and families.

Since the early 1960s there has undoubtedly been an explosion in the information we have available to us about family life both past and present. Greater knowledge about the private lives of our ancestors has destroyed some cherished historical myths, and our increasing awareness of the variation in contemporary family life is shattering some modern ones. We are gradually losing our obsessional lament for the world we *thought* we had lost and are discovering instead a fascination with the world we appear to have found. In the not-so-distant past, statistical evidence which pointed to the declining presence of the 'cereal packet' family (working father, housewife mother and two children) was regarded as evidence that the family was in peril, for at the time this was the explicitly preferred form of the family and any indication that this model was in recession was *ipso facto* regarded as a threat to family life.

Today the evidence of the decline of this type of nuclear family is even greater, but now it is widely accepted that it is but one variety of family living (though perhaps an obsolescent type, rather than an endangered species). It is inevitable, therefore, that the privilege accorded to this particular pattern of domestic living, should now be challenged.[6] In direct answer to such challenges, organisations connected with the family, while readily acknowledging the diversity in present-day family forms, feel it is important to emphasise that large numbers of people today still appear to prefer living in the traditional family unit consisting of mother, father and their children. However, the moral pressure to conform to it has weakened; the issue is no longer one of which model *should* be preferred, but is rather that of which model *is* most frequently preferred in practice. With the acknowledgement of the new pluralism in the forms of family life, a new type of morality appears to be emerging, one based upon statistical normality. Nevertheless, the cereal packet family has not been knocked off its pedestal; it is just that the pedestal is not quite as high as it once was.

As adherence to the traditional rules and regulations of family life diminishes, so the emphasis has gradually shifted from what marriage *should* be like to what marriage *is* like and what marriage *could* be like. People have probably never been more knowledgeable about, and consequently more influenced by, what 'most people do'. We know that today's young men and women are behaving in ways which differ considerably from their parents when they were young: more now choose to cohabit, some as a prelude to marriage and others instead of it; they are marrying at a later age; some are having children outside marriage; a substantial number of those who do marry will divorce and many of these will go on to marry for a second time. However, we know very little about why these changes are occurring.

Experts differ, both about the extent of these changes and whether or not present trends will continue. The overall impression is one of ambiguity; marriage is the same and yet marriage is different: it all depends which aspects of it you are considering. For example, as we have already mentioned, a substantial proportion of young people are now cohabiting.[7] In some cases cohabitation is an extension of courtship; other couples however, may choose to cohabit instead of marry, although in practice the organisation of their lives together often seems very similar to that of a marriage. This leads some people to argue that these sustained 'informal relationships' should in some way be incorporated into marriage, and its definition should be extended to include them. This is only one of the many contemporary issues which make it so problematic to try to define marriage in modern society. We have only to look at the various ways in which key institutions such as the Law, the Church and the State are attempting to arrive at definitions, to realise the confused and confusing public image of contemporary marriage.

The newly-wed men and women whose marriages form the main subject of this book showed evidence of a wide span of influences which had contributed to their image of marriage in general, and to their view of their own marriage in particular. The range of sources was wide: the explicit and implicit definitions offered by existing law and social policy; general knowledge about the marriages of others, acquired both through gossip and the media; the views of marriage experts such as the clergy, counsellors, doctors, and so on; and the newlyweds' impressions of the marriages to which they were closest – usually those of their own parents. Apart from this last group, most of the other images had been disseminated through various forms of the media – a significant public influence upon marriage.

THE DEFINITION OF MARRIAGE

Public images of marriages are in part formed from our general knowledge of the present behaviour of those who are married, and this in turn influences the experience of being married. Even though divorce may never have been experienced personally, the concept of marriage as a life-long relationship is bound to be affected by living in a divorcing society. It is not necessary to be an expert to be aware that today, divorce is commonplace:

> Statistics rarely stick in the mind, yet if you eavesdrop in the pub or at the smartest dinner party, sooner or later divorce will be mentioned, and people will *know* that one in three marriages end that way.[8]

The impact of the statistics that one in three marriages end in divorce has been pressed home relentlessly by the media because it can so easily be made to appear very personal: the one in three 'either means your next-door neighbours – or it means you'.[9] The idea of marriage as an enduring commitment is, therefore, challenged, and it ceases to be a moral image of marriage – 'what marriage *should* be like', and becomes instead an ideal image – 'what marriage *could* be like'. Despite the hopes of all our newlyweds that their first marriage would remain their only marriage, they showed a reluctant but realistic awareness that this might not be so. Some, particularly those who had had a close encounter with divorce, either through their parents or siblings having divorced, were aware that the same could happen to them, and were anxious that it should not.

Katherine Whitehorn has described the way in which knowing 'what other people are doing' in their marriages can impinge on one's own personal experience of being married:

> In a climate where marriages do break up with a fair frequency, there is one reassurance which no man alive can give his wife: the certainty that he will be there for good . . . the evidence is all around her: marriages can and do come to pieces. Divorce is catching, because the more you see

people round you having a second go, and the less you see other couples who've come through the storm and are living it up happily in harbour, the more discouraged you become during your own sticky patches.[10]

Traditionally there was a convention of married life; the rules, both for entering upon marriage and for remaining married were clear. Men became husbands and women became wives; each knew his or her respective identity and the purpose of marriage. In present-day society however, the traditional rules and roles of marriage have become 'little more than a reference point for action'.[11] The less we are inclined to believe in rules for the conduct of married life, the greater will be our anxiety to acquire information about the state of being married which will help us in our individual marital relationships. This is one reason why the public discussion of marriage and of 'other people's marriages' is so important:

> We tend to talk informally about other people's marriages and to disparage our own talk as gossip. But gossip may be the beginning of moral enquiry, the low end of the platonic ladder which leads to self-understanding. We are desperate for information about how other people live because we want to know how to live ourselves . . . .[12]

The 'other people' whose marriages we discuss may be people from our own social networks of kin, neighbours, workmates and friends, but they are just as likely to be the married population in general, or some public figure or even a hitherto unknown person, whose marriage for some reason is suddenly in the public eye. Almost any issue in almost any marriage can become a matter of burning public interest, either because in some way it throws light on the confusion surrounding modern marriage, or simply because it will satisfy our curiosity (and these facets may not be unrelated).

The failing marriage of a 'well-known' person or a well-publicised divorce case can offer us the opportunity to display our beliefs and to air our personal theories about the rights and wrongs, certainties and uncertainties of marriage and family life. We can take as an example the much-publicised pregnancy of the secretary of a prominent government minister in 1983. David Morgan explores the links that are made between public events and more private belief and practices:

> Such events provide the occasion for the deployment, the 'airing' as it were, of notions of marriage, of fidelity, of responsibility, of sexuality, of gender and of countless other topics.[13]

In this particular case, the hierarchy of loyalties of an unfaithful husband were examined and questioned. Was he bound by his marriage vows to remain with his partner in law, his wife, and their children? Or should he (like many of his contemporaries) not feel constrained by such a contractual obligation, especially since his mistress was pregnant? There were several well-argued articles about the case in newspapers and probably innumerably more discussions in pubs, on buses and in works canteens. That particular 'scandal' incorporated all the elements of the modern family drama: the possible abandonment of the older wife and adolescent children; the financial and emotional support of a single mother and her child; who should take responsibility for contraception; the sexual double standard; the stereotyping of vengeful lover, innocent and stalwart spouse, and male cad. As if watching a Victorian melodrama, the audience – the British public – were able to take sides and cheer or boo. The fact that in this particular case, 'political' issues were involved, made everyone feel that talking about the matter was not trivial, but rather a matter for public concern. And so indeed it was, for to all who were interested it gave the opportunity to air their views about marital relationships and family responsibilities without in any way 'getting personal'. The more that we are unsure about the conduct of our own personal relationships, the greater is our need to be able to talk about them 'objectively'. It is only as a result of such deliberations that the variety of theories about modern marriage become revealed.

The impact of such public and private debates affect those institutions such as the Church and the Law, which are concerned with creating and sustaining official definitions of marriage. By taking two specific aspects of the contemporary discussion of marriage we will reflect on the way in which these two institutions in particular are accommodating to them.

MARRIAGE: A LIFE-LONG COMMITMENT?

Most weddings, where the bride and groom are marrying for the first time, still take place in church, and the majority of these within the Church of England, the established religion.[14] For those who marry in church, the service includes explicit commitment to the permanence of their union 'till death do us part'. Yet for many that commitment is 'a timeless affirmation of an existential experience'[15] rather than an absolute commitment. As with so many of the newlyweds whom we interviewed, although there *is* a commitment to stay together, yet accompanying it is the realisation, founded upon the knowledge of what happens to other people, that things may not actually work out that way. Throughout the past half century, the Church of England has, in the face of increasing numbers of divorces, attempted to stand firm on its teaching of the permanence of the marriage vows. Fifty years ago the lifelong definition of marriage was affirmed simply by sticking to the rules and firmly excluding any other possibilities:

> In order to maintain the principle of lifelong obligation which is inherent in every legally contracted marriage service . . . the Church should not allow the use of that service in the case of anyone who has a former partner living.[16]

However, by 1981 the tide had begun to turn strongly, and an increasing minority of clergy were conducting marriage services and services of blessing which involved divorcees. In that year the General Synod carried a motion stating that although 'marriage should always be undertaken as a lifelong commitment' yet 'there are circumstances in which a divorced person may be married in church' and it requested a report 'setting out a range of procedures for cases where it is appropriate for a divorced person to marry in church in a former partner's lifetime'.[17]

Thus the Church of England is accommodating to a changing public image of marriage. In doing so, the image of marriage as a life-long commitment has become an ideal instead of the 'characteristic moral norm of marriage'[18] and this change is explicitly recognised in the terms of reference of the General Synod Marriage Commission, 1975:

(1) To consider the understanding by contemporary people of the place of marriage as an institution.
(2) To report on the courses of action open to the Church in seeking to promote in contemporary society the Christian ideal of marriage as a life-long union of husband and wife.[19]

Increasingly, the key institutions, which offer the explicit definitions of what marriage is, and what marriage is not, are demonstrating an acknowledgement of the meaning this has for the people involved. As with the Church, so also the Law is having to decide on the contemporary understanding of marriage, and in particular whether cohabiting relationships should now be regarded as marital relationships.

COHABITATION: MARRIAGE WITHOUT THE FORMALITIES?

In England and Wales the Law, relative to the Church, is a latecomer to the attempt to define marriage. Before Lord Hardwicke's Marriage Act was passed in the middle of the eighteenth century, the church decided who could marry and how, and since, for the Church, marriage was essentially the exchange of consent between spouses, a variety of informal unions were recognised.[20] Strong objections were made to the Marriage Act of 1753; 'proclamations of banns and publick marriages are against the nature and genius of our people' wrote the *Gentleman's Magazine*.[21] With the formalisation of legal marriage came the promotion of marriage above other relationships, and 'the penalties for non-conformity were ferocious'.[22] Since then the penalties have gradually become less ferocious; for example, the penalties on children born outside marriage have been reduced.[23] However, the distinction between legal marriage and cohabitation has been retained in order to protect marriage:

> So long as it remains public policy to support the institution of marriage, the law must, necessarily distinguish between spouses and those who, whether by choice or force of circumstances, live together without getting married.[24]

The various changes in the profile of domestic life since the 1970s have raised new issues in law and social policy. As more and more men and women and their children are found to be living outside of formal marriage, questions are raised about their respective rights and obligations. There have been changes in the legal position of cohabiting partners during the past decade but they have been piecemeal and 'no clear picture has yet emerged of the true nature of the revolution in the concept of marital and quasi-marital living . . .'[25]

As long as cohabitation was regarded as either the predicament of an unfortunate minority who were unable to marry, or the choice of an exceptional few who were unwilling, it could be argued that the privilege accorded to marriage was justifiable. The recent emergence of cohabiting couples who freely choose to live in every way as married, even though they may not be legally married, puts pressure on the law to acknowledge the fact that many of these couples 'feel' married even though they are not formally married. Those who defend the privileged position of marriage argue that to recognise cohabiting relationships as marriage in this way would undermine marriage. And many of those who eschew marriage reject the notion of the assimilation of cohabitation into marriage on the grounds that it forces upon freely cohabiting partners the disadvantages of marriage, such as the financial dependence of wives. So even those with no desire to use the Law to promote marriage but simply a concern to protect the rights of men, women and children in whatever domestic units they choose to live, find themselves in a cleft stick: the incorporation of cohabitation into marriage appears to undermine *both* marriage and cohabitation.

Interestingly, the debate about the status of cohabitation and the attempts to define it are shedding important light on the invisible and hitherto unquestioned aspects of marital relationships.

CHANGING WAYS IN MARRIAGE

People usually only confront the official definitions of marriage and married life when they have difficulties; for example, during marital breakdown the spouses come up against definitions and interpretations of their behaviour by experts – doctors, counsellors, lawyers, and so on – definitions which may seem quite alien to their personal experience of being married. Because of the natural acceptance of marriage as a way of life, a great many of these definitions are implicit rather than explicit. The law does not state what the specific financial arrangements between married partners should be, yet fiscal legislation and recent divorce legislation are based on assumptions about the financial relationship between married partners; in the former the wife is perceived as a dependant of her husband and in the latter it is suggested that modern wives should have some degree of financial self-sufficiency. The apparent contradiction arises because the former legislation is long-standing and awaiting overhaul[26] whereas the latter results from recent changes based on the belief that modern marriage has changed. First, it is generally assumed that as women's rights within marriage have been expanded (by Married Women's Property Act; Divorce Acts; expansions of employment opportunities; and equal opportunities legislations, for example) so marriage has become a more egalitarian relationship. However, this has yet to be established.[27] Secondly, the freedom of men and women to choose their partners, to choose whether to formalise their relationships and to choose when to end those relationships, is taken as proof that:

Marriage no longer depends on the authority of Church and State, nor in a widespread acceptance of recognised standards and patterns of behaviour, but upon individual choices.[28]

Whatever the real differences, inequalities and asymmetries within marriages, modern marriage is generally reckoned to be more equal than unequal. The overall impression is that marriage can be whatever you want it to be; there are no rules or regulations save that the spirit of equality should be observed. According to the prevailing social wisdom, marriage is whatever a person privately experiences within it, although careful scrutiny of the experience of being married suggests otherwise. The newly-weds' accounts of their day-to-day lives and their plans for the future which form the basis of the second part of this book, show clearly that social and economic structures are still highly influential in shaping the worlds of men and of women and therefore also in shaping the private relationships between husbands and wives.

The public images of marriage offered by the institutions are contradictory, confusing and abstract, so that they offer little practical guidance for the individual. Close inspection of a specific marriage can, however, provide images which may be more coherent, a model of married life which can either be emulated, regarded as a cautionary tale or simply used as a reference point at times of crisis. For most of the newly-weds, the marriage they were closest to which could fulfil these functions, were those of their own parents.

OBSERVING THE PARENTAL MARRIAGE

Most children grow up in the context of marriage – that of their own parents. This is true even today when the divorce rate is high.[29] On a daily casual basis we have all been influenced by observing our mothers and fathers behaving as husbands and wives. Indeed, as many feminists critically point out, girls and boys usually form their identities as women and men according to the socially defined roles of wives and husbands, thus continuing the traditional division of labour by gender. At the same time, in the West, young people are automatically expected to reject most of the values and attitudes of their parents as a crucial part of growing up and 'finding themselves'. Although young men and women may not explicitly follow the marriage styles of their parents, yet the experience of having lived for years alongside their marriages is bound to have profound effects on their own behaviour and attitudes as married men and women.

When we asked the newly-weds in the present study to look back and recall any impressions they had of their parents' marriages, the majority looked blank; most said that when they were young children and adolescents they never thought of their parents as a married couple; 'they were just my Mum and Dad':

'As a small child I think you are oblivious to it. My Mum and Dad never quarrelled. Once or twice I'd catch my Mother crying about something but I never really understood, I just carried on. I didn't really think about it'.

'Don't think I took much notice. I was a bit wrapped up in my own world. Between the ages of 15 and 20 I realised that it wasn't a very good marriage.'

Nineteen of the 130 newly-weds (15 per cent) came from homes broken by divorce; thirteen (10 per cent) had experienced the death of a parent. It was these men and women who were most likely to have considered the marital experiences of their own parents; and for some of the young brides with divorced or separated parents the disruptions in their parents' lives had inspired their decision to marry – they needed to escape (see Chapter 3). The 'failed' marriage usually became a model for marriage by default, a negative model of marriage:

'It made me think a lot – I know we are young people, I'm only twenty-one but I think a lot of young people don't give enough thought to it. I've seen the bad side and won't make their mistakes.'

Obviously, the fact that they themselves were now married meant that none of the newly-weds had been put off marriage by their parents' experience, although several were wary of what they were letting themselves in for.

For the vast majority of the newly-weds, however, their parents had remained married and the comments on these marriages were positive though usually unspecific. Such marriages were considered 'good' because they had been secure and stable and had provided a good setting in which the children had grown up:

'The atmosphere in the home rubs off on you.'

'I suppose it must have influenced me to see them happily married.'

'They seemed to have a nice steady sort of life . . . I knew that some day I would follow . . . get married and have a family.'

'It does help if you come from a family where there is a stable marriage . . . I think I might have thought twice if there had been a split. As it
is, I didn't have to think about it.'

Very few newly-weds were able to articulate any specific aspects of
marriage for which they felt their parents had provided them with a
model, but those who could referred to sharing and companionship
and their fathers having shown respect for their wives:

> 'My Dad always helps Mum. I shouldn't come in and expect my wife to do
> everything for me.'

> 'They put so much into their marriage; they are together all the time.'

> 'They have influenced me a lot because everything they do is to-
> gether – they never go out separately, that's my picture of what marriage
> should be.'

> 'Their marriage has influenced me. I don't hold my father as the shining
> example of a married man, it's just that living with them for twenty-two
> years and seeing them together has affected me. Like the way my father
> behaves to my mother – the way he treats her – I can't give you a specific
> thing, it is just the way he treats her.'

MARRIAGE UNDER SIEGE: THE VIEW FROM THE MEDIA

The fact that marriage is regarded as a problem means that it is
always a good source of copy for journalists. Public images of
marriage are regularly aired by the media and consequently created
by them. The present divorce rate is known so well because it
regularly prefaces articles about some aspect of family life. We were
particularly struck by the references made in the newly-wed interviews to articles which they had read and the authority that such
articles held for them:

> 'Divorce can strike anyone, I know 'cos I read an article about it, it made
> me realise.'

> 'A lot of people of my age don't bother with marriage, there was
> something in the paper about it.'

> 'If ever we had a problem with our marriage I would think seriously about
> divorce. At least, well if we had children I would, you have to think of
> them and it is better for them, isn't it? That's what they say'.

They?

> 'The doctors and child experts. I read about it in one of my magazines,
> there is some research to prove it.'

The media have become the chief source of information about the vital statistics of British family life and in this way they provide 'authoritative' images of marriage. Since the mid-1970s the official statistics about family life have been made more available to the media and are periodically unveiled, thus creating new insights into marriage, and so we took a six-month period of the complete coverage of marriage in newspapers and magazines, and analysed the way in which it was presented and discussed.[30] The period we chose was the first six months of 1983: we wanted to avoid both the lingering romantic aftermath of the 1981 Royal Wedding and the intense, and at times contentious, debate which preceded and surrounded the passage of the 1984 Divorce Bill, so our chosen period was midway between the two.[31]

The most striking discovery was the pivotal role of divorce in the vast majority of articles supposedly about marriage. Not only was divorce taken as the symptom of the problems in marriage, but it also appeared frequently to be the basic inspiration for the discussion of marriage. Two-thirds of all articles about marriage started with a specific reference to divorce statistics, while divorce was mentioned in three out of four.

In the total press coverage, a vast range of issues in modern marriage was examined: legal and financial matters received the most attention (an artefact of the emphasis on equality at divorce), followed by all manner of things to do with children (though principally the rights of parents rather than the process of parenting). Somewhat surprisingly, romantic, emotional and sexual matters (the latter usually considered as problems) were the areas least often covered. After reading some 360 cuttings, the overall impression gained was that whatever modern marriage was or was not, it was certainly under siege.

In a typical article dealing with changes in marriage, the evidence surveyed would almost always be drawn from official statistics: the possible causes of these changes would then be explored, with sometimes remedies being offered and finally a conclusion would be drawn asserting the value of marriage to the society and to the individual.

The way in which the vital statistics of family life are used by the Press deserves some reflection. First, since the mid-1970s the Office of Population Censuses and Surveys (OPCS) has made these statistics seem more accessible by publishing digested and therefore easy to understand versions, called *Monitors*.[32] In the days that follow the publication of these there are always clusters of articles in the Press about the family. In the more serious papers the latest figures for marriage or divorce are recorded, with perhaps some explanation of the reported trends. The more popular tend to use *Monitors* as vehicles for feature articles about the family. The typical formula for such a story would be a lead-in of any particularly striking statistics, with the emphasis on the official nature of the information: 'One in three marriages is breaking up and that's official', followed by a selected real-life experience with a surrounding commentary and opinion, and closing with a reference back to the official statistics, thus leaving the reader with the impression that the real-life example is typical and therefore generally illustrative of the official statistics. In this way, opinions about, say, the causes of marital breakdown acquire authority by virtue of their proximity to official fact. That so many people now 'know' that one out of three marriages ends in divorce is proof of the success of the Press in propagating such information.

It is the notion that 'divorce is catching' and that any one of us can fall victim to it, that has sustained this 'marriage under siege' style in which the changing shape of family life is reported in the British Press. However, from our review, it was very clear that, although marriage was being presented as being under threat, yet the Press were standing firm in defence of it; it was an ailing institution in need of support rather than an irrelevance to be consigned to the scrap heap. The institution of marriage itself was rarely discussed; it was implicitly presented as a good thing: 'Marriage, it never seems to go out of style. And we are just beginning to appreciate it'.[33]

Divorce, however, was presented as a regrettable fashion, and one which hopefully might one day pass away. An example of this 'hope' can be found in a magazine survey of married women, published early in 1983, where the finding that they intended to stay married whatever the problems was linked to the slight drop in the divorce rate and was given as the evidence for reporting 'the happy finding' that 'divorce is dying out'.[34]

Divorce generally got a bad Press. Although there were many first-hand accounts of the traumatic emotional effects it had, and the practical difficulties which ensued from it, yet it was on the whole portrayed as 'the easy way out'. There was very little about the rights or wrongs of divorce, but instead, preoccupation with the 'mess' which it created: the dividing up of property; husbands having to support two homes; the practical and emotional consequences of caring for the children of a broken marriage. These were often highly partisan accounts, with the issues being set out solely in terms of the inequality between estranged spouses, with only a rare mention of the issues relating to the inequalities of married life in general. It is perhaps surprising that the 'marriage-under-siege' approach so often adopted, did not result in much more advice about the avoidance of, or the protection against, divorce. Such articles were few in number and usually consisted of hints for 'keeping romance alive'. The notion of marriage as fragile and in need of defence was so implicit that the publication of a report which stated that most young people still wanted to marry was greeted with ecstatic headlines in the Press: 'The family is alive and well'; and 'The family is fine'.

Sometimes attempts were made by the Press to consider the causes of divorce, but this was usually limited to a journalist choosing to reflect on a few specific marriages and generalise from them. Rarely was any consideration given to the wider context of marriage, so that such basic issues as the nature of the relationship between men and women, or the real reasons why people might want to leave their marriages, were never adequately dealt with. Any explanatory argument was usually over-simple: marriages break down because they are now so easy to get out of, and people want to get out because they are bored, or because the 'romance' has disappeared, or because they expected far too much; or is it all just an inevitable part of modern life?

PARADOXICAL IMAGES OF MODERN MARRIAGE

Marriage is perceived as a problem both in public and in private life. Men and women shift between different and, at times, even contra-dictory images of marriage. Marriages are created by the individuals involved in the relationships but married lives have to be lived and worked out within the context of wider society. In the newly-weds' accounts we found a continual interaction between their images of what marriage should be like, what it could be like and what it probably would be like. In their portrayals to us of marriage, they played with different images and interwove morality, idealism and reality.

One of the attractions of marriage lies in its place within the family; it offers a degree of continuity. Indeed, the permanence of marriage enhances this notion. To follow a tradition of married life is likely to mean adherence to what are perceived as traditional definitions and prescriptions, such as 'men should be the breadwinners', 'wives should be in the home'. For some respondents, the marriage of their own parents was held up by them as representing what is right, a moral formula which had been handed down:

> 'I follow my Dad, the woman's place is in the kitchen. That's the way it should be.'

Consistent with this continuity, however, is the notion that while certain values must be retained, many adaptations are necessary because times change, and women in particular were often caught between their image of a wife as a perfect housewife and mother and their own experience of coping with the competing demands of a job and a home:

> 'Sometimes it gets me down, trying to find time for everything . . . I like to cook and I'd like him to have a proper cooked meal at night but quite often, too often, it's to the take-away or getting something from the freezer.'

> 'When the kids come I want to be home, like my Mum was with us. Then again I can't imagine not having a job or managing on one wage.'

The newly-weds expected that over the years their marriages would come under stress, and possibly even break down, though there were fervent hopes that it would not be so. A general acclimatisation to the extent of divorce combined with their memories of their parents' marriages, gave them realistic ideas about what marriage would be like, and these real images of marriage frequently counterbalanced other, more idealised, images which they held:

> 'Once the kids come along and money is tight, I suppose things will be difficult. People say that and it happened with my parents.'

At the start of their married lives, newly-weds are expected to have romantic images of marriage, of the 'happily-ever-after' variety. In fact, throughout their interviews, very few romantic images were revealed, although many ideal images were offered of what they thought and hoped that marriage could be like: for example, there were many references to hopes of following a sharing, caring, companionate model of marriage, especially from the wives:

> 'I like to think that each of us is the same. That's why we are such good friends. If we could stay that way we'd have a great marriage.'

> 'The usual things – a nice home and sooner or later a family and I'd like our life together to be the most important thing rather than his job.'

'A good marriage to somebody I can *trust*, to be fairly well off, have children and love each other.'

And some of the husbands also shared this kind of vision of the future:

'I want to have our own house, have three kids, have a good life together, share the responsibilities with the children – and retire to the seaside.'

Because marriage was regarded as so natural, 'just part of life', very few men and women spoke about it in any abstract way. When they did it was always with reference to something they had read, ideas and images promulgated by experts but which they perceived as having more authority than their own personal experience. As one woman wryly commented:

'I read somewhere that marriage is all a big con – that it's a way in which men get what they want, you know, clean clothes, food, sex. I had a good laugh. Mind you, when you think about it, men do get a lot. But then so do women.'

Another wife, when talking about motherhood, illustrated the shifting and contradictory images of the relationship between husband and wife. She wanted to share everything with her husband; both of them were to work and share the housework and the care of children. However, she was uncertain about being a working mother, whether it was 'right', since it was, after all, not what her mother did. She thought that men were able to look after children but realised that as they earned more it would be impractical, and anyway, 'it wouldn't be right'. She was confident that if they were free to work things out for themselves, all would be well, yet she recognised that other factors might prevent this:

' "To each their own." Mum was always there when I was little – I'm not saying it's wrong and I'm not saying it's right, there are people who need to work – they are very involved in their careers, more than other women and some women are very content to be at home and their children are their lives. It doesn't mean that a woman who goes to work loves her children any less, perhaps they love them all the more, but I think from a child's point of view, I can look back on my upbringing and my mother was always there . . . and that's nice, I could count on my parents being there . . . '

Do you think a woman should be more involved at home?
'No, not at all.'

So what about a husband staying at home to look after the children?
'If a woman was in the position where she could go out and earn more than a man, yeah. Mind you, I don't think it's right because I think men have a

bigger ego than women and I don't think it would do the man's ego no good at all. I don't think it would be right but I believe a man can look after a child as much as a woman . . . Mind you, if we were working for ourselves [which they hope to do] I'd like to work and look after a baby and he [husband] would do the same, we'd share it. If we could work it that way that would be the best.'

Marriage has now become something of a riddle: its public images are confused and confusing, and the world of private example is equally perplexing and paradoxical. We are constantly seeking clues about marriage, and about other people's marriages, because we want to be able to understand our own, but everywhere we are faced with contradictions. It is no wonder, then, that newly-married people, who are grappling with this mixture of confusing images, are uncertain about their image of 'my marriage'.

2 Exploring Marriage

All down the line
Fresh couples climbed aboard: the rest stood round;
The last confetti and advice were thrown,
And, as we moved, each face seemed to define
Just what it saw departing: children frowned
At something dull; fathers had never known
Success so huge and wholly farcical;

The women shared
The secret like a happy funeral;
While girls, gripping their handbags tighter, stared
At a religious wounding. Free at last,
And loaded with the sum of all they saw,
We hurried towards London, shuffling gouts of steam.
Now fields were building-plots, and poplars cast
Long shadows over major roads, and for
Some fifty minutes, that in time would seem

Just long enough to settle hats and say
*   I nearly died,*
A dozen marriages got under way.

The Whitsun Weddings
Philip Larkin

Other people's marriages exist in obscurity and that is their fascination. The world of marriage is a complex area for exploration; although we are all close to some marriages in everyday life (our own, our parents', our friends', our neighbours'), 'married life' still remains an unknown territory. These hidden worlds of 'other people's marriages' are neither clearly expressed nor easily understood. This is partly why, despite the fact that it always has been, and continues to be, a significant part of our social experience, marriage has for so long been overlooked as an area of serious sociological enquiry. The result of this is that there has been a relative absence of any strong tradition of theory and of critical evaluation.[1]

We 'know' marriage too well, yet at the same time we do not expect to 'know' other people's marriages at all, because they are considered to be part of that private world, which is hidden from public gaze. We catch a glimpse of the secluded world of 'other people's marriages' only when difficulties or problems are revealed. However, such revelations apparently legitimate public scrutiny of what is essentially 'a very private matter'. It is fascinating to take the lid off married life, although to do so is certain to reveal and confirm that a great deal of married existence is routine, unremarkable and commonplace.

Every research study needs to be set in a context; it is important to explain the origins of the study, to show the contemporary state of knowledge about the subject and to relate it to existing theories and research report findings. At times the usual academic preamble to a research seems to be there in order to demonstrate the credibility of the researchers rather than to allow the reader to understand the developing spirit of enquiry. The undertaking of research, like any other activity, can only be fully appreciated in terms of the inspiration and aspirations of those undertaking it. Moreover, it is particularly important for an enquiry into marriage, such as the present one, initiated in the late 1970s, to be placed within an historical context.

The shaping influences of this research project were not simply the theoretical perspectives which inspired the original research choices which were made. The research idea was formed concurrently with a rapidly unfolding awareness of change in the statistical profile of the modern family, a growing literature of research and (as we have shown in Chapter 1) a widely debated public image of modern marriage. These three sources of influence were, of course, inter-related, and it is important to consider the nature of these interrelationships, although they are complex to fathom. The images of marriage which are purveyed in the media are frequently annexed to recent statistical evidence of research findings. But at times of rapid change, it is particularly important to remember that official statistics and research findings are never in synchrony; by the time the results of any enquiry become accessible to the public, they are already out of date. To undertake research at the beginning of a period of rapid social change, in an area which was previously grossly under-researched, is at first bound to result in many enquiries being coincidentally replicated, and may be further compounded by a sequence of publication which may prevent the findings from one study being available to influence the shape of another.

A decade has elapsed since the idea of the present study of marriage was first formed and it has proved to be a critical one for the study of the family. In 1976, as part of a series called 'The Changing Face of Britain', *The Times* published an article on marriage with the headline 'Never more popular, never more risky'.[2] At that time the key trends to be noted were the high divorce rate and the continuing trend to marry young. According to *The Times*, the important social revolution of the 1970s – the changed and still changing status of women in society – was leading to a 'changed relationship' between the sexes, making it 'inconceivable that the institution of marriage will not be drastically transformed'. There was little evidence to show what changes were already taking place. For example, at that time there were no official statistics on cohabitation (although the Family Formation Survey had collected information from women aged 16–49 that was not reported until 1979).[3] The General Household Survey (the continuous survey of a sample of private households in Great Britain, which was started in 1971) did not include questions about women's fertility outside their current marriage until 1979 and that report was not published until 1981. The reasons for this omission are, in themselves, an interesting reflection on the changing attitudes towards marriage and family life:

> Prior to 1979 it had been judged that an expanded Family Information section might put response rates on the GHS at risk. For example, it was not known whether remarried women (or their husbands) might resent being questioned about a first marriage. Nor was it known how older informants who were not currently married would react to questioning about such topics as cohabitation and childbirth histories.[4]

At the same time, academic thinking about the family had been developing, and the sociology of the family was beginning to gain prestige. In his recent book *The Family, Politics and Social Theory*, David Morgan explains why it had to be a sequel, rather than a revised edition, of his 1975 critique of contrasting theories of the family:

> The main grounds for preparing a completely new book are chiefly in terms of the changes that have taken place since 1975. The enormous growth of feminist literature and theorising is the most obvious one . . . Few areas of sociological work, including the practices of sociologists in their various institutions, remained untouched by these developments . . .[5]

It is not our purpose here to provide the reader with a summary of the total range of theoretical perspectives available to the family sociologist. These are better located and provided elsewhere.[6] However, it is necessary to reflect broadly on the theoretical perspectives and the research findings which were available in the late 1970s and which shaped the particular course of this research, up to and including the fieldwork. Before doing so, though, we need to distinguish between the period before the collection of data and the post-fieldwork period. Once fieldwork is completed, and the analysis of the data has begun, the researchers begin to modify old perspectives and incorporate new ones, while at the same time they have to take account of the changing scene in society and in the research world. Most importantly, the data itself issues challenges to understanding, which may not be able to be answered solely in terms of the theoretical influences initially used. In any truly exploratory study, the researchers must expect to be confronted with subtleties of meaning which they did not expect, and they therefore have to search for more diverse sources of explanation and interpretation. The shaping influences discussed in this chapter will only take us up to the first interviewing stage in 1979. For those which influenced the analysis and interpretation of this research, the reader must turn to the second stage of the research account in the first part of Chapter 10.

SHAPING INFLUENCES

The original idea for a study of marriage in the early years grew out of a previous research study at the Marriage Research Centre; a survey of divorced men and women, *Who Divorces?*.[7] As its title suggests, that survey was based, like many others in the 1960s and early 1970s, on the notion that divorce was dysfunctional and that certain individuals, because of social and psychological factors, seemed more prone to divorce. In that survey a substantial number of the divorced sample reported that their marital difficulties had arisen in the early years of marriage and many located them in the first year in particular. This finding resonated with clinical observations made by therapists working with couples who had sought help with their marital problems.[8]

Although such a finding was of considerable interest to therapists, it was not clear what it actually indicated (unfortunately a common problem with findings from large surveys). Does the presence and nature of difficulties in the early years of marriage make it possible to identify at that stage couples whose marriages may later end in divorce? Or do all marriages experience strains in the early years, but only those whose marriages later break down, retrospectively identify these as a source of the eventual breakdown? And after all, we must never forget that people describing their past marital experience are very likely to reinterpret it to fit in with their present knowledge; namely, that their marriage has failed.

The most obvious way to try to clarify the finding from *Who Divorces?* was to construct a prospective study; one in which a group of marriages could be followed from the beginning for a period of several years. Regular interviewing of these couples would surely generate material whereby marriages which had broken down could be compared with those that had remained intact at the end of the chosen period? However, such longitudinal research would have involved an expensive long-term fieldwork commitment, which relatively few institutions can undertake, and it was certainly not feasible for the Marriage Research Centre to do so. The first task for the research team newly-appointed to the study, was therefore, to reduce the original research aspirations to fit the available research resources. The decision finally made was to interview newly-married husbands and wives for the first time shortly after their weddings and then re-interview them once again at a later date.[9] The present book reports the findings from the first interviews, three months after the wedding; the second interviews with the same couples five to six years later will be the subject of a sequel to this book. While such pragmatism has to be practised by most researchers (that is, research has to be designed within what are, usually, slender means), its critical role in research decision-making is rarely acknowledged. Nevertheless, in deciding what it is possible to accomplish, the researchers are not simply practising expediency; they are also declaring, albeit indirectly, their own preferences and prejudices both as social scientists and as people.

WAYS OF LOOKING AT MARRIAGE

The way in which a researcher looks at marriage will be evident in the type of information which is sought and gathered, in the method used to record that information and, finally, in the explanations and interpretations offered for what has been discovered. The different ways of looking at marriage are systems of ideas which have been theoretically developed both as a basis for reasoning, and for forming explanations for people's attitudes and behaviour. We therefore began our study with an examination of those systems, in order to see which offered the greatest potential for our task of exploring new marriages, at a time when family life was in a state of considerable flux.

The most influential perspective used by family sociologists up to the 1970s was one which stressed the functions of marriage both for those who were married and for society in general.[10] Within this *functionalist* perspective, marriage is regarded as a central source of stability and harmony in society; it provides a highly structured way of life in which spouses can behave according to the socially scripted and biologically determined roles of husband and wife. In this way a stable environment, conducive to both the emotional and physical well-being of the married couple and their children, is created. It is one which provides a sound basis for the inculcation within the next generation of those values and general precepts regarded as vital to the smooth running of society. In this model of society, the relationships between the various institutions which make up society and between the individual and society, are all-important. The emphasis is upon the adaptation of family members to the constraints imposed upon them by society and upon their personal behaviour, rather than on their having the potential to create their own personal life story.

Until the 1970s, research into marriage was dominated by the overwhelming influence of this functionalist way of regarding family life: men and women were seen as gaining their identities through their family roles; the man through the instrumental role of provider – the anchor of the family in the outside world, and the woman through the expressive role of housewife – the anchor of the family within the home. Research which stemmed from this perspective was highly descriptive, predictive and problem-orientated. Later on, by the time that feminist critiques appeared which challenged this view of the relationship between the sexes, these functionalist approaches to the study of marriage were already in eclipse; research findings were beginning to confirm that there was much more variation in men and women's perceptions and interpretations of family roles than that perspective had allowed. And despite attempts to incorporate within the fundamentalist perspective a limited degree of flexibility for the individual in working out family roles,[11] it still remains too rigid to be of contemporary use as a paradigm for understanding the complex and often ambiguous processes involved in contemporary family living.

Another cluster of important perspectives on marriage in the 1970s (and one which is found in several different approaches) regarded family relationships, especially marriage, as being essentially full of conflict.[12] One version of the *conflict* approach holds that this is basically so because the marital relationship is, first and foremost, an economic one. Marriage in this way is seen as simply a minor version of the whole network of inequality between men and women which exists in the wider society; so that, for example, the dependence of wives in marriage both creates and sustains their relative powerlessness as women in a man's world.

Another depiction of this 'conflict' approach to marriage rests on the premise that since marriage is a relationship of partners who have different and contradictory values, conflict is inevitable. According to this view, the story of any marriage becomes an account of the avoidance, regulation and resolution of conflict through constant negotiation and bargaining. The more powerful partner, the one with greater access to and control over resources, has the greater influence in the relationship. To see marriage in this way, as the outcome of inherent tension between the spouses, is very valuable. It reminds us that each marriage consists of two individuals who have come from different pasts, that each experiences the present differently, and that they are both making different assumptions about the 'shared' future of their marriage. All these differences are inextricably linked to the wider society.

However, it is still not the whole story; the inspiration for getting married and the commitment to staying married involve much more than conflict and tension. A sense of co-operation, of mutuality and a common purpose are also required, though these will not consistently be achieved. The marital relationship, like all other personal relationships, is in a constant state of flux, and the participants move in and out of conflict, negotiation and agreement. Certain moments in a marriage may be outstanding in one or another dimension but for most of the time the differences are coexisting rather than being resolved; as soon as one issue has been negotiated things change. Furthermore, while there will be points in a marriage when a particular issue confronts the couple, for most of the time their relationship will consist of many issues, some of which may be able to be resolved in the short term, some of which will lie fallow, while others may perhaps be acknowledged by only one of the partners.

Much of the study of marriage to date has been preoccupied with the investigation of marital roles, men as husbands and women as wives, in various situations and contexts and at different stages of their married life. Whether they are viewed from a conflict or a functionalist perspective, certain definitions of marital roles have been accepted and enquiries have then tended to be confined either to the content of the role or the performance of it.

In our exploratory study of marriage we wanted to move beyond the notion of roles. We required a way of looking at marriage which would enable us to discover how people come to 'choose' marriage, how the transition from being single to being married is made and experienced, how married life is defined and linked to other parts of living and then relate all these aspects to a particular cultural and temporal context. Above all we required an approach in which flux, uncertainty and change would be regarded as central to the understanding of human behaviour. We were looking for a way of incorporating into our study the processes through which men and women perceive and construct their lives as married partners. We were therefore drawn to a perspective which rested on an image of individuals creating their own lives, making choices such as the decision to get married because it made sense to them to do so. Fundamental to such an *interactionist* perspective are the beliefs that the understanding of any aspect of human behaviour requires knowledge of the definitions and interpretations of the situation by those involved; the recognition that change is continual and that the constant flux is accompanied by a constant challenge to redefine, and reinterpret.[13] According to Alfred Schutz, who has written extensively about interactionist thought:

> To a certain extent, sufficient for any practical purposes, I understand their [fellowmen] behaviour if I understand their motives, goals, choices and plans originating in their biographically determined circumstances.[14]

In an era of rapid change in marriage it is particularly important to discover how married people define and interpret their existence as married people. This is not to say, however, that the reported experience of married people is all that should concern us. The tendency of researchers who use an interactionist approach is to fail to 'ask questions about the social material with which people construct their marriages' and has led to some incomplete pictures of family life.[15] Each marriage is different and, moreover, each partner in a marriage has a unique perception of that marriage, but all these 'marriages' exist within a common social landscape.

Nevertheless, sociologists are not mere chroniclers of their own times. Although they deal in other people's narratives, they then offer their own interpretations; it is the job of the sociologist to make sense of others 'making sense'. The creativity of the individual must be acknowledged but the sociologist is in a position to recognise that the individually created meanings are often shared, and may, indeed, be shaped by similar experiences, similar pasts and similar plans for the future. Moreover, the sociologist is in a position to relate collections of narratives to *public* images, definitions and beliefs:

> Seldom aware of the intricate connection between the patterns of their own lives and the course of world history, ordinary men do not usually know what this connection means for the kinds of men they are becoming and for the kinds of history-making in which they might take part. They do not possess the quality of mind essential to grasp the interplay of man and society, of biography and history, of self and world.[16]

In 1964, Peter Berger and Hans Kellner published an essay on marriage and the construction of reality, in which they argued that it is through relationships with other people that the individual validates his personal identity and that:

> Marriage as a social arrangement . . . creates for the individual the sort of order in which he can experience his life as making sense.[17]

According to Berger and Kellner, the individual turns to the private world of home because it seems to have been shaped by himself, in contrast to the 'immensely powerful alien world of public institutions which have resulted from the industrial revolution', which he experiences as a world which has shaped him. 'Getting married' is a transition in which 'two strangers come together and redefine themselves'. Mainly through conversation, the partners form a new understanding of the world which results in a sharing of future horizons, thus stabilising for both of them their sense of 'who they are' (the self images of the spouses). And in this private world, not surprisingly, the marriage partner becomes 'the most decisive cohabitant'.

This essay by Berger and Kellner was regarded as a classic exposition of the interactionist perspective and as such it provided a starting point for several studies which were initiated in the 1970s.[18] It focuses on four aspects of marriage which were of critical importance to our study: the nature of transition; the concept of a relationship in process (the continual interaction of two individuals attempting to settle on a level of co-operation); the ways in which individuals make sense of present experience with respect to their past lives; and the assumptions they hold about the future. Until that time much of the theoretical and empirical consideration of transition had centred on the change in role; the abandonment of one social identity in exchange for another within the clear ritualised structure of the courtship career (boyfriend/girlfriend; to fiancées; to bride and

groom; and finally to husband and wife), with consequent reverbera-
tions and reordering for any other roles held (for example, in work or
family of origin). As part of the family life cycle approach, marriage
was regarded as only one (albeit highly significant) transition in the
typical sequence of life: and the emphasis was on the departure from
one stage of life and entry into another rather than on the experience
and meaning to the individual of the process itself.[19]

Berger and Kellner offer an important reflection on both the
nature of transition and the process of marital interaction, although,
as later studies show, their view of marriage is a partial one. They
focus on a particular type of marriage, and an *ideal version* of that
type. Indeed, as they themselves admit, their view of marriage is
based on marriages entered into at a 'normal' age in urban, middle-
class, Western society. They justify their selectivity by saying, that
what the urban middle-class Westerners do today, the rest will do
tomorrow (or maybe the day after). When you compare Berger and
Kellner's portrayal of marriage with the marriages described in
subsequent research studies, it is clear that this type is simply one
variation. However, it is an influential one; it is the model of the
caring, sharing, highly communicative 'marriage of good friends' that
is taken as the prototype of 'modern marriage' (see Chapter 1).

As a view of marriage it can, however, also be accused of being
male-centred. Berger and Kellner refer to the confirmation and
stabilisation in marriage of the personal identity of the partner who
finds in the home 'a world in which he is somebody, perhaps within its
charmed circle a lord and master'. The other partner is probably the
type of wife who features in many family studies which emerged in
the late 1970s and early 1980s; a 'captive' housewife, oppressed by
the home, trapped by the demands of husband and children, lacking
autonomy and low in self esteem.[21]

Implicit in this perspective on marriage is also the notion that as the
main source of stability for men and women, the marital relationship
is unproblematic. Various writers have since pointed out that the
dilemma for modern spouses is to find a balance between the
constraints on individual freedom which marriage imposes, and the
recommendations by society to pursue that freedom in order to
enhance personal identity.[22]

SOME RELEVANT RESEARCH FINDINGS

The research portraits of 'normal' marriage available to us in the late 1970s were not very satisfactory since they had been based largely on samples of white, middle-class, college-educated men and women in the United States. In addition to the unrepresentativeness of the men and women whose marriages were studied, these studies were unsatisfying in other respects also since they provided only a fragmented picture of marriage. And although there were studies of who married whom, and of various aspects of the behaviour of husbands and wives and their reported satisfaction with these, there were almost no overall views of married life.

One notable exception, however, was *Blue Collar Marriage*, Mirra Komarovsky's small but inspired portrait of working-class marriage in the United States.[23] This was a real attempt to capture the experience of everyday married life, to examine the different experiences and perceptions of married men and married women, and to test out the prevailing prescriptive model of modern marriage (as an intimate, highly verbal relationship) on marriages from a 'culture' different from those on which the original model had been based. Komarovsky showed that there were marriages in which intimacy and verbal communication were low on the agenda of priorities for a satisfying relationship; she demonstrated that husbands and wives often inhabited very different worlds and opened up the theme of 'his' marriage and 'her' marriage which was taken up by others during the 1970s.[24] In many ways this study was seminal to our developing research plans, and it strongly influenced the choice of themes around which our enquiry was based.

At the time we were beginning our research, there was little empirical material which specifically related to the transition to marriage, and marriage in the early years. Most family researchers seemed to have been more interested in courtship than in marriage. There is a vast literature on choosing and acquiring a mate; it has constituted a major part of family enquiry for half a century.[25] The concept of the courtship career which has evolved, although useful for following the development of relationships, is typical of the rather conventional ways of looking at marriage; a neat and tidy picture of premarital interaction emerges but it is one which is largely unconvincing because it gives an over-rational account of how people come to get married (see Chapter 3). The important questions of the context in which these relationships were formed and any recognition of the merging of two independent biographies in such a relationship are completely overlooked. It is as if there has been an obsession with *who* people choose to marry and one which has totally neglected the crucial question of *why* people opt for marriage at a particular moment in their lives. Overall it seems that perhaps biographers and novelists have in the past made a better job than sociologists of understanding the process of getting married.

Studies of newly-wed couples were rare and those that had been undertaken had concentrated on two main themes. First, in some studies, done from a functionalist perspective, getting married was viewed 'as one of the many "normal" but significant *critical transitions* from one social status to another in the life cycle of the individual in his family and work contexts'.[26] The process of moving from being a single man or woman to being a spouse was described as a psychosocial transition, and the 'work' of coming through the critical transition was conceptualised as a series of tasks 'that punctuate the flow of life'. The concept of transition as a role-change was dominant; newly-wed marriage was seen as a time when marriage novices were fitting into the role-image of husband and wife for which society and their families had spent years preparing them. The chief issues in marriage in the early days were seen as the adaptation of the spouses to being husbands and wives and the successful negotiation of the interface between these roles and other roles.

Second, and related to the first approach, researchers were also looking at the ways in which newly-wed couples developed mutually by moving from independence to interdependence; and the 'couple' was seen to be more than simply the association of the roles of husband and wife. If the 'work' of newly-wed marriage was accomplished, then there would be marital success and, apparently, marital satisfaction.[27]

However, studies of family life in general were beginning to suggest that these roles of husband and wife, which newly-weds had to learn, were becoming less distinct; the modern marital relationship could be described as one in which the traditional structure of male breadwinner and female homemaker was beginning to break down and change into a more egalitarian partnership. The fact that married women were increasingly to be found working outside the home was taken as evidence of the evolution of a 'marriage compact', one which involved two roles for the wife, as wage earner and homemaker, and the same two roles for the husband.[28]

In the mid-1970s, the strict distinction between traditional marriage and modern marriage began to be challenged on two fronts. First, social historians were challenging the notion that the housewife role was the sole traditional role for women and second, inspired by the growth of the literature and theorising of feminism, sociologists were beginning to report findings which offered little support for the idea that modern marriage was a truly egalitarian relationship. It seemed rather to be more a variation on the old theme of housewife marriage.

A cluster of small studies which concentrated on the issue of the division of labour in the home offered some important methodological issues for consideration, such as the way in which conventional research approaches had always suppressed the revelation of gender differences in the experience of various aspects of everyday married life. Ann Oakley in particular, provided a useful discussion of several of those issues.[29] Although such studies as these highlight an interest-interesting discrepancy between the 'ideal' image of modern marriage, one where both partners share the domestic responsibilities, and the 'reality' of most marriages, where wives still take the major responsibility for housework and childcare, they fail to account for the meaning this apparent inequality has for the married couple. According to a strict quid pro quo definition of marital equality, the majority of contemporary marriages would appear to exploit wives, and yet further evidence suggests that many wives do not see the situation in that way. It is, therefore, clear that it is crucial to explore the explanations and interpretations of their ways of living which husbands and wives can give, since otherwise vital clues towards the understanding of modern marriage are missed.

INQUIRING INTO MARRIAGE: SOME PROBLEMS

Treating marriage as a process

Unless it is possible to follow individuals from birth, the researcher has to enter the biography of the respondent at a chosen point. Nevertheless, the individual's past up to that time will have enormous bearing on the present (see Chapter 10) and is the context in which present actions take place. The past is, therefore, essential to the meaning and understanding of present action and experience and is far more than simply the backdrop to the present. However, caution must be exercised when listening to the story, since any narrative of the past is liable to be influenced by inaccurate recall and retrospective interpretation.

When married people, even very recently married people, discuss their courtship, they are bound to be affected by the knowledge that they are talking about their own route into married life. Thus, for example, when a bride remembers a disagreement in the early days of courting, her account of it is almost certain to differ from the one she would have given nearer the time it actually happened. In similar fashion, her story of a disagreement with a boy she was only dating will be very different from one about a disagreement during courtship with the man she actually married. And this is not simply a matter of selective memory operating through rose-tinted spectacles, although this will be part of the process. The meaning for her of these events is bound to be coloured to some extent by their different contexts: it is a fact that retrospective experience *is* different from current experience. Even had the data been collected before marriage, the problem would still not have been solved; it would merely have shown that the meaning of any event for a person is inevitably bound up with its context.

Not taking things for granted

The very ordinariness of married life can become a pitfall for those who wish to explore it. It is only too easy to overlook or ignore important clues to the understanding of marriage. The research interview is frequently complicated by the interviewer's understandable anxiety to gain rapport, to make the person being interviewed feel relaxed, and to give the interview the feel of a conversation. Accounts of the mundane and routine activities which go to make up so much of married life are frequently punctuated by the respondent with the phrase 'you know what I mean?' The interviewer is often tempted to give or imply assent, in order to affirm an understanding of the respondent's experience, and also encourage or enhance rapport. However, to do this may not always be helpful, since it can mean that subtle explanations and meanings which may underlie the easy 'plea for agreement' may be lost. In order to avoid this, it may at times be necessary for the interviewer to become 'anthropologically strange', to ask a seemingly obvious question, or to probe a respondent's answer in a way which will make it quite clear that there are no implicitly shared assumptions or meanings. The respondent is, therefore, pressed to say what he or she means.

However, such an approach must be used with care, since to require further information in this way is often only fully acceptable if the questioner is a bona fide stranger, someone genuinely foreign to the situation. If this is not the case, then the interviewer must be aware that he or she is running the risk of appearing to be 'not one of us', with the possible result that the respondent may become suspicious and unhelpful.

Nevertheless, despite the risks involved, to 'take nothing for granted' can yield dividends. An example of this is when the newly-wed husbands were asked the question, 'Do you think there will be a time when you cease work for a while?' Their wives found this a completely 'normal' question, and were able to answer easily, with 'Yes, when I have a baby', as the most common reply. In contrast, some of the men had to ask for the question to be repeated, or needed to ask what it meant: 'You mean when I retire?'; 'If I get the sack?'; 'Get made redundant?' Others brushed it off as a 'daft question'. However, although (obviously) no man gave the reply most usually given by women, some used the question to reflect on the pressure on them to stay in work, not being able to step off the the assembly line, and they pondered alternatives, and the constraints on their future experience as fathers.

Questions about the seemingly obvious can be risky, yet sometimes they turn out in practice to be of great value, since they can reveal false assumptions that could have been made between the interviewer and respondent. They can also highlight and clarify some of the accepted ambiguities of married life. We think it is an essential technique to consider when exploring the relationship of husband and wife, particularly since there are constant changes in marriage, both within itself, and in the ways in which it is perceived and portrayed by society as a whole.

Implicitly offering a definition of marriage

People who have just been through a transition are likely to be anxious to demonstrate that they have changed in some way. In the case of newly-wed husbands and wives there was often keenness to show the interviewer that they were 'proper' husbands and wives. The researcher therefore, needs to be aware of any conformity to a 'proper' model of marriage which may be implied unconsciously in any of the questions. Questions which are specifically designed for 'husbands' or 'wives' rather for 'people who are married', can imperceptibly define roles for men and women in marriage, and may thereby block the revelation of hidden meanings.

On occasion it may seem strange to the respondent if he or she discovers that men and women are being asked identical questions. For example, in order to discover 'who does what in the home', if the interviewer asked wives one set of questions based on traditional notions about their domestic behaviour, and their husbands a different set, also in accordance with traditional expectations about *their* domestic performance, then it might be thought that the interviewer shared the assumptions that certain tasks were always performed by women, and others exclusively by men. However, if the researcher takes the view that in every household there is a total set of basic domestic tasks that have to be regularly undertaken, and then simply asks each partner who most recently performed any of this range of tasks in their home, the question phrased in this way cannot imply that any particular task is the special responsibility of either a husband or a wife. It was hoped that this approach would preclude automatic responses in line with traditional views.

Nevertheless, despite all our precautions, hidden assumptions and definitions on the part of the researchers were still found in unexpected places – or were believed by respondents to be there. The subtle nature of this was revealed by the responses which some of the couples made to the (in our eyes) straightforward request for the husband and wife to be interviewed separately, although simultaneously. This was challenged by some of the couples on the basis that they felt our request indirectly suggested a bias on our part toward perceiving them as two separate individuals rather than as a married pair, an issue about which we discovered they had a high degree of sensitivity, as we shall reveal later in the book (Chapter 8). The very unexpectedness of reactions such as this can prove to be very fruitful for the research, since it can provoke a new awareness of the nature and strength of some contemporary norms about modern marriage.

What happened versus 'what should have happened'

To enquire about what usually or generally happens in everyday life is not at all the same as asking the respondents what actually took place on a specific occasion. The latter should evoke a description of something that actually happened, whereas the former is liable to produce an answer coloured to some extent by attitudes about what *should* or *could* happen. Confusions of this kind are likely to occur when there is a great deal of public discussion over the nature of marital relationships. We have already referred to the concept of marriage as egalitarian and symmetrical,[30] and young married couples, therefore, may be anxious to demonstrate that their marriages conform to this 'sharing' model. Moreover, when asked general questions, it is likely that respondents will reply largely in terms of what they *believe* happens, and then later in the interview they may well contradict this by giving an account of what *actually* took place. This perhaps helps to explain the frequently large gap between belief about what marriage is and marriage in practice, and it shows how crucial it is for researchers to be sure of the exact nature of their data.

His and her narratives: versions and perceptions

If both spouses are interviewed individually about their marriage this results in two different accounts, which may often be highly inconsistent with each other. The researcher may then try to compare these two narratives, and, rather like a judge, try to determine what the 'story' of the marriage really is. At times it is clear that one partner simply mis-remembered. In general, men tend not to concern themselves with complete accuracy about dates, time and sequences (see Chapter 3); it is more often their wives who seem to be expected to 'care' about and 'hold' such information, and to be the biographers of the marriage.

However, the experiential reality of events may at times have actually been quite different for each partner. This is particularly clear in some of the accounts the newly-weds gave of their courtship, where the pace of the courtship was differentially experienced because the *meaning* of the same events was quite different for each partner. And similarly after marriage, the identical issue may be described by each spouse so differently that it can appear to the interviewer that each is referring to a completely different issue. This highlights the paradox we so often found, that it can appear as if there are two different relationships cohabiting in the one marriage.

THE NEWLY-WEDS' STUDY

To capture the texture of an experience, as opposed to merely cataloguing the details of it, requires a particularly sensitive and flexible mode of enquiry. The research interview has been aptly termed a conversation with a purpose, for it is intended to provide an atmosphere which is as natural and normal as possible, and a structure within which individuals are enabled to review and reveal particular aspects of their own experience in their own words. Such interviews take time and demand considerable interviewing skill, so that the quality of the interview takes precedence over the number of interviews, and the interviewers need to be closely involved in the research, not merely hired hands who execute the task. For this reason, all the interviews in the newly-weds' study were conducted by the research staff who had designed the interviews and who expected to be involved with the analysis.[31]

In a qualitative study such as ours far fewer people can be interviewed than in a large-scale survey. However, large-scale surveys of family life have never been able to provide any understanding of processes within the family, and this inadequacy has led, in the past two decades, to the rise of the small-scale qualitative study.[32] Such studies have demonstrated the way in which small but intensive enquiries can yield valuable data in terms of the subtle and ambiguous meanings that attach to and influence the choices made by individuals.

However, the decision to undertake a study in depth with a small group of respondents also means accepting that the findings and interpretations from it, however great their value qualitatively, cannot be regarded as samples of the general population in any statistical sense. In any exploratory research of this kind, the focus is on what happens to that particular chosen group of people, rather than on whether or not the patterns and processes discovered in the group are representative of society as a whole. Nevertheless, this does not mean that the selection of such a research group need only be arbitrary and that the findings have no relevance outside those particular individuals. The fact that a group cannot technically be described as a representative sample does not automatically define it as unrepresentative. When the group of newly-weds was selected, great care was taken to avoid the more obvious sources of bias, so we hope this study can be accepted as a portrait of contemporary marriage.

In order to be able to detect coherent patterns and processes in the group, we needed to obtain respondents who were reasonably homogeneous, and we therefore decided to exclude those whom we regarded as atypical of British newly-weds at that time. We had decided to choose marriages where both partners were marrying for the first time because we wanted to study a group of people who were going through a similar transition: their first marriage. Since the vast majority of all such brides and grooms are under the age of thirty on their wedding day, we excluded those who were older, on the grounds that by marrying later they were atypical; they would be historically more experienced, and perhaps part of a different generation of newly-weds.[33]

Our concern with homogeneity also led to the exclusion of marriages from cultures which were distinctly different, for we knew that such marriages would need to be understood within their own strong cultural traditions.[34]

Marriage and social class

As sociologists, we were already primed to be alert to the differences in attitudes, values and behaviour patterns between working-class and middle-class marriages. The influence of social class on individual experience has long been the subject of debate in the social sciences, and there are a variety of explanations for the ways in which it operates. From our point of view, therefore, it seemed reasonable to expect that social class would predicate the material conditions of married life, such as housing conditions and amenities, income, and security of employment. We also expected that certain styles of living would be associated with, and reinforced by, social class. There had been earlier research which suggested that there were certain class differences in marriage; working-class marriages had been found to be more likely to follow traditional patterns, with the emphasis being on the segregation of the lives of the husband and wife, while middle-class marriages had tended to correspond more closely to the joint lifestyle regarded as the epitome of 'modern marriage'.[35] Since we wanted to be able to make comparisons between our findings and those of other researchers, we decided to try to obtain equal numbers of middle-class and working-class couples.

However, the definition of the relationship of two individuals in terms of social status is an extremely complex matter. Although the conventional method has always been to ascribe the marriage to the social class of the husband, this assumes that the social position of the wife is that of her husband, an assumption that has been widely criticised.[36] On the other hand, if each spouse is considered separately, how can the social class of a marriage be defined? The problem is further compounded by women's jobs being concentrated in certain occupations; according to the most recent national survey of women in employment, over two-thirds (69 per cent) of women who work full-time are in jobs which would put them into a non-manual and therefore middle-class category. The vast majority of our newly-wed wives who were working full-time were in non-manual occupations such as typist or shop assistant, whereas only 60 per cent of the husbands were, and both spouses had the same social class in only three out of five marriages.

Although we considered other methods of assessing the social class of the wives, none would have overcome the basic problem of assigning the *marriage* to a social class. In the end, in common with other researchers at that time, we decided that whenever we wished to assign the marriage in terms of social class, to use that of the husband. However, as it turned out, social class did not appear to account for any of the main differences we observed in the experience of the newly-wed marriages: in practice, gender proved to be a more influential divisor.

The selection of the couples

Our original intention had been to draw our group of newly-weds from the total number of first-time weddings which took place during a given time-period in the churches and register offices in one registration district in the Greater London area. In order to do this, we required access to the marriage notices, the public declaration of the intention to marry, but the Registrar General felt unable to give us permission to obtain the names and addresses of prospective newly-weds in this way. We then approached the Church authorities, who hold the notices (banns) for all the church weddings in the area, and were successful in gaining their co-operation.

We wondered if limiting ourselves to weddings in church would bias the research in any discernible way; we were already aware that, at that time, two out of three of all first-time weddings were celebrated in a church (or chapel). Additionally, although we could speculate that there might be some differences between those couples who chose to marry in church and those who opted for a civil ceremony, there were no clear characteristics which appeared to differentiate the two groups; for example, those who married in church could not necessarily be regarded as religious. We therefore decided it was acceptable to conduct our research solely with couples who had had a church wedding.

We ourselves imposed certain further constraints on the selection of couples for the research by our requirement that both spouses must agree to be interviewed, and interviewed separately; the style and intensity of the suggested interview (2–3 hours in length); and by our intention, stated at the outset, that we hoped to return at some time in the future to interview the couple a second time.[38] For these and other reasons, some of the couples who were initially approached were either unwilling or unsuitable to be part of the research group.

Some couples were precluded because they were willing to take part only if they were interviewed together, since they felt strongly that they wanted to be regarded as a couple. We also had to exclude marriages where one partner, invariably the husband, refused to be involved, even though his wife might have been enthusiastic. It was clear that the prospect of being personally interviewed at some length proved daunting for many men; several asked if they could answer a written questionnaire instead, while others said they did not have the time. Although a certain degree of reluctance to be interviewed was displayed by many of the husbands, we found that an outright refusal was more likely to come from those in semi-skilled or unskilled occupations.[39]

The prospect of a second interview at some time in the future was also a deterrent for some of the couples. And our own wish to safeguard the possibility of a second interview by limiting the future erosion of our research group, meant that we had to assure ourselves more firmly of the commitment of those couples who did agree to take part, than we would have done had they been going to be interviewed once only.

Where the couples lived

We made contact with all the clergy in the area, and in most cases visited them in order to set up our system for collecting marriage notices from them. Two adjacent registration districts in London were chosen, areas which were neither inner city nor outer London suburbia, although there were features of both in each. Our visits to the clergy provided us with glimpses of the great contrasts in this urban setting; on the edge of one borough a visit was made to the clergyman in his graffiti-covered house next door to his church, and surrounded by huge ugly blocks of flats, built before the last war, along straight streets with names from a distant colonial past. The next visit was to a vicar only two miles down the road, but a world apart: he took us through the centuries-old lychgate into a churchyard covered with spring flowers, to his office in his picture-book church.

The marriage notices provided the addresses of the bride and groom prior to the marriage and, since we had agreed to wait until after the wedding before we made any contact, this meant that those pre-marriage addresses had to be visited in order to establish the address of the couple after marriage. This meant that by the time the interviewing got under way, many of the couples were no longer living in the area where they had married, with several having moved out of London and the Home Counties region to towns in areas as far away as East Anglia and Cornwall. Nevertheless, except for two couples who had to be interviewed in the Marriage Research Centre, all the couples were interviewed in their new locations.

The design and timing of the interviews

During a test run of pilot interviews prior to the eventual fieldwork, we had experimented with different interview designs: interviewing husbands and wives together; interviewing them separately but simultaneously; and separately on different occasions. We had also tried out interviewing the couples at different points in the courtship/marriage sequence. Some test couples were interviewed in the courtship period, some just after their marriage and others three months after the wedding. The 'couple' interviews (both together) proved to yield consensus accounts in which one spouse took the lead (sometimes throughout the interview, sometimes only in specific areas) and then sought confirmation from the other. After discussion and consultation between them in front of the interviewer, the different meanings and perceptions which had been held by each of them merged into an 'official' version, which was not at all what we wanted. In those couples where the interviews took place separately but on different occasions, it was clear that the partner who was interviewed last had already been primed by the other, with the unsatisfactory result that those interviews had the feel of prepared statements. In the interviews with couples who were on the verge of marriage, or who had only just married, there was considerable diffidence and a heightened anxiety, both of which adversely affected the interview.

From all the preliminary styles and timings of interviewing, we concluded that the optimum for our purposes was to have a separate interview with each spouse, conducted simultaneously by two interviewers, in the couple's own home, some time around the third month of marriage, and this was the pattern we consistently used. However, this style of interviewing meant that we were sometimes faced with practical difficulties: for one thing, we had to find private locations within the newly-weds' homes for two separate interviews to take place at the same time, which led to some bizarre situations, such as one interview being conducted with the interviewer perched on the side of a bath! A second problem arose through the impossibility of synchronising the length of the two different interviews – one interview almost always lasted longer, typically by fifteen minutes. However, there were certain occasions when one spouse had finished the interview in two hours while the other continued for a whole hour more. Such occasions tested the ingenuity of the interviewer with the less loquacious partner, since the spouse who had already finished was often anxious about the reasons for what appeared to be the prolonged interview of the other, perhaps fearing undue 'revelations'. In such circumstances, the interviewer had to suggest plausible reasons why the other interview might still be continuing, and sustain a chatty conversation.

Such incidents apart, the experience of interviewing the newly-weds in their own homes greatly enhanced our appreciation of the variety of physical settings for (new) married life. In one home, we were taken on a guided tour by the couple, to inspect the DIY handiwork – they had practically rebuilt the interior of their 1930's semi-detached house. The next night one of us interviewed a young bride sitting on the bed in the bedsitter which she shared with her husband (he was interviewed in the communal kitchen), and spent the first fifteen minutes watching her proudly demonstrate some of the kitchen gadgets she had received as wedding presents. Although we did not attend any of the sixty-five weddings, we felt as if we had – we were shown dozens of wedding photographs, from family snapshots to albums that played the theme from *Love Story* when opened. The enthusiasm the newly-weds had for their new homes, however meagre they were, reflected their hopefulness for their future together.

The style of the interview

We wanted the interviews to provide the newly-weds with a framework within which they could recount their immediate past and accurately describe and convey their present experience. They needed sufficient freedom to be able to raise issues that were relevant to their own understanding of their lives, but also they had to offer us sufficient basic material to enable us to make comparisons, both between the partners in a marriage, and between all the newly-wed marriages in the group.

We therefore chose a flexible style of questioning – the 'non-schedule standardised interview'.[40] In this type of interview questions are not rigidly worded, nor is the specific sequence of questioning decided in advance. Instead, the interviewer relies on a list of the topics and information required, and has to judge in the interview itself when enough material about a particular aspect of behaviour has been obtained. It is, therefore, essential to be certain in advance about what it is hoped will be discovered, and the interviewer must continually be sensitive, ready to probe for more information should there be insufficient detail about any topic. This kind of interviewing has, paradoxically, been described as a questionnaire to the *interviewer* and indeed, it can prove very taxing to administer.[41]

Additionally, and particularly in an exploratory study such as ours, the interviewer must be constantly receptive to the unexpected, and always be ready to probe further whenever the respondent indicates, however indirectly, that there is more to be said. One important advantage of this kind of approach is that the interviewer does not have to adhere to predetermined questions and is therefore free to pick up the vocabulary of the person being interviewed. Once the meaning of such words for the respondent has been established, questions can then be phrased in his own 'language'. To do this is, after all, the essence of any conversation. However, since the interview is a 'conversation with a purpose' there has to be a clear contract between the interviewer and respondent about the nature of the exchange in this situation: on one side the respondent narrates, and on the other the interviewer listens and poses questions.

What the interview covered

The interview followed a chronological sequence: it started with a review of the previous year, based on a schedule of life-events[42] designed to provide a catalogue of recent events and changing circumstances (health; employment, family and friends, and so on), all of which formed the background and context of the marriage.

The next section concentrated on the story of the courtship, starting with some biographical details and ending with the wedding. The rest of the interview took the newly-weds in some detail through their day-to-day married life, and enquired into their housing situation; their domestic routine; the management of their money; their employment and leisure; their physical and psychological intimacy with each other; and their disagreements. In addition to this, each interviewer also explored with the newly-weds their expectations of parenthood, their hopes and their worries about the future, and their general experience of marriage so far. And finally, they were asked what they thought they would do if they were ever to experience any serious difficulties in their marriage.

The analysis of the data

Each of the 130 interviews was tape-recorded, and the analysis was based on full transcripts of these. In addition, the interviewer had made thumb-nail sketches of each respondent, and also noted any conversations outside the interviews, as when waiting for the other partner's interview to finish.

The initial task in the analysis was the somewhat daunting one of having to sift through the information contained in some seven thousand pages of transcript. We applied the original interview schedule-guide to the transcripts, so that the basic information could be clearly and systematically recorded in order to provide a series of descriptive outlines.

Following on from this, we then looked in detail at each section of the interview, gradually building up analytic categories as we went along, and applying these in turn back to the complete set of interviews. This was a painstaking and time-consuming procedure, especially since we had decided wherever possible to retain verbatim quotations rather than make an edited précis, in order to remain as faithful as possible to the language of the newly-weds, for, as we have already suggested, we felt that this was the only way that the richness and subtlety of the material could be fully exploited. It was especially important to do this in our study, since ambiguity and contradiction were so central to the experience of early marriage.

As it turned out, this method of analysis, though very demanding, bore unexpected fruit, since it alerted us to the ways in which the whole lives of the newly-weds could be characterised by their differing orientations to the future.[43] The more we became immersed in the data, the more connections began to emerge, and these demanded a range of explanations for attitudes and behaviour which went far beyond any with which we had started out.

In the end, however, for any analysis of qualitative material to be really successful, the researcher must move beyond description, interpretation and reinterpretation of the data, and become open to the impact of the interview *as a whole*, responding to it with an intuitive awareness which is difficult to articulate. This awareness seems to be a coalescence of observations, concepts and theoretical hunches, and can perhaps be best described as a leap of the sociological imagination.

Part II

A Portrait of Marriage

3 Ready for Marriage

She felt that she had entered a new world, some unknown planet entirely different from anything she had known and loved; everything in her life and thoughts was upset. This strange question occurred to her; did she love her husband? He suddenly appeared a stranger who she hardly knew. Three months earlier she had not been aware of his existence; now she was his wife. What did it all mean? Why should one fall into marriage so quickly, as into an abyss suddenly yawning before one's feet?

A Woman's Life
Guy de Maupassant, 1883

Unlike their ancestors, today's young lovers are said to be free to marry whoever they choose, whenever they choose. Indeed, the concept of marrying for love symbolises the very spirit of individualism which characterises modern Western society. According to some family historians, marriage in the past was a union founded upon social and economic considerations, whereas modern marriage is simply a love match. More recent writers have contested this polarisation and pointed to a strong thread of continuity linking lovers of the past with those of today:

> As soon as one gets close to the more ordinary people of former centuries, the myth of their different mentalities starts to evaporate and one begins to find them curiously modern. As soon as one starts to analyse the feelings and motives of modern couples, on the other hand, the rationality of their decisions, the 'good sense' of their falling in love with one another can be equally striking.[1]

Marriage fulfils certain functions in society and public attitudes to marriage at any one time are reflected in the ways in which people enter marriage. Thus, in former times, when marriage was primarily regarded as a means of establishing a new economic unit, the emphasis was on being 'able' to marry and the 'right partner' was someone who would facilitate this. To be 'in love' was not then regarded as essential, although to like each other was an advantage. Today this emphasis is reversed; the most important consideration for potential spouses is that they should love each other, but at the same time it is recommended that they should be mindful of certain practical considerations. Romance and reason are, therefore, both significant motives for marriage, but the prevailing public attitudes may determine the priority given to one over the other. In present-day society, the domination of the motive for marriage of romantic

51

love often conceals the 'good sense' of falling in love, whilst to give recognition to other factors, such as wanting to leave home and to have security, appears to profane the very notion of romantic love. In Chapter 2 we reflected on the difficulties encountered by people in articulating the process of getting married. Newly-weds, when recounting the unfolding of their courtship, may be attracted to explanations which make sense of the past. Romantic love is the simplest and most socially acceptable explanation for choosing to marry and there is a whole vocabulary available from romantic literature for describing courtship, so that other motives can easily become obscured. We may lose sight of the fact that in present-day society as well as in the past, marriage is an important cultural symbol. It is through marriage that most people achieve and demonstrate the civil responsibilities which comprise adulthood: setting up a new household and raising the next generation. In this way marriage becomes a boundary marker and a means of organising the rest of life; it concludes the growing-up part of life – a time of dependence and limited autonomy, and offers a clear structure for adult life, a normal and secure future. People may fall in love at the moment when they are ready to focus on the future.

It is essential to be aware of the motives, goals and choices of the characters involved in a courtship if we are to attempt to understand their behaviour. To do this we have to examine their attitudes to marriage within the context of those events and circumstances which accompany their decision to marry: in other words we need to explore their motives for *that* marriage at *that particular time in their lives*.

MOTIVES FOR MARRIAGE

The 1979 General Household Survey confirmed a trend which had been widely debated in the 1970s, that a significant number of men and women were living together 'as man and wife'.[2] The increasing popularity of cohabitation, coupled with a very high divorce rate, has stimulated a public concern (and media obsession) with the survival of marriage. It is argued that if many young lovers are choosing to live together as husband and wife without bothering to legitimate those titles, and at the same time, if those couples who opt for the marriage ceremony are failing to achieve the objective of a life-long union, then marriage as it has been known is obsolescent. However, cohabitation is a behaviour which occurs in different contexts: some cohabiting partners may be renouncing marriage but others may not be free to marry or are simply waiting to marry.[3] There is evidence that for many cohabitees, living together is a preliminary to matrimony rather than a renunciation of it. Rates of first marriage have been in decline since the early 1970s, but this trend appears to reflect a shift in the timing of marriage rather than a decline in its popularity.[4] Young people may be delaying marriage but on present trends the vast majority will marry at least once; and the increase in the remarriage rate suggests that for a substantial minority getting married will not be a singular experience. Cohabitation is fashionable and divorce commonplace, yet marriage still remains attractive.

Perhaps the enduring attractiveness of marriage lies in the fact that it continues to provide the *most obvious and natural means of validating adulthood in our society*. Of course it is not necessary to marry to be regarded as an adult, but the marriage contract brings with it a package of rights which guarantees a quick and effective transition to adulthood.

'Marriage is inevitable'

'I suppose I accepted it as being inevitable because I suppose 90 per cent or whatever it is of the male population in this country is married. I suppose I accepted it as inevitable that I would marry.'

Nearly all the newly-weds accepted, like this husband, that marriage was inevitable. Because most people do marry it is normal to marry, and therefore by marrying one's normality is confirmed. Busfield and Paddon, in a study of fertility in post-war England, point out the reinforcing effect of normality and inevitability:

Much of the pressure to marry comes from the simple fact that being married and having a family are regarded as proper and normal conditions. The argument might sound circular as if we are back to asserting simply that people marry because they are expected to do so . . . It is not that people marry because they are expected to marry, but that by marrying they come to occupy roles that are socially acceptable and legitimate. Marriage slots people into their rightful places as adults in society.[5]

Marriage incorporates a set of adult roles and identities which are clear and distinct, a scheme for organising the rest of one's life:

'I just thought marriage was something that was going to happen. As far back as I can remember I've always imagined myself leaving school, getting a job, you get married, you get a house, you have kids – and basically I just followed from there. I never thought "I'm going to be single for six years, I'm going to do as much as I can in that time" . . . time just seemed to have passed and all of a sudden, I'm married.'

Because marriage is regarded an initiating a sequence, it subsumes other decisions concerning the future. It is thus easy to see the lure of the happily-ever-after myth, a myth particularly seductive to women, who have traditionally been forced to submerge their legal and social identities into those of their spouses.[6] Women are subject to the greater pressure to marry since female identity is still predominantly defined in terms of marriage and motherhood. Marriage can appear to offer them a haven from responsibilities, with husbands shouldering the main burdens of life. One bride, who at the age of twenty-six was older than most of the other new wives, was able to compare her attitude to marriage when she was twenty with the way she felt now:

'Between 18 and 20 I thought I must get married before I'm 20, but by the time I was 20 – 21 I didn't want to marry until later.'

Why?

'I went to work and I loved work but it is still something that you had a routine and you had to do – I think it was just opting out for a lazy time and thinking that marriage was just a time for having children and sitting back and I didn't realise the implications.'—*Mrs Wilson*

Generally it was the younger brides who referred to the protective functions of a husband:

'Well a woman has a lot more to cope with, housework and everything, but that is not hard, you get used to that, and obviously you must always have helped your mother at home, but a man has got more responsibility. He's got a wife and a home and all the bills as well to keep up with. — *Mrs Butcher*

'He takes on a lot more responsibility – a lot more worry . . . before it didn't matter but now he's got a wife to look after, a home to keep. — *Mrs Browning*

The pressure on husbands to accept responsibility for their wives, and eventually for their children, was not resented by them because they considered such responsibility demonstrated maturity; it emphasised the identity of the man as breadwinner and symbolised that they were 'men in their own right'.

'A place of one's own'

The transition from dependent adult-in-waiting to autonomous adult involves a process of dislocation and relocation, both physical and psychological. This is why 'a place of one's own' is of such significance, both as a means and an expression of the transition which is being made.[7] It is still uncommon in our society for young, single people to live independently. The 1981 Census revealed that in the age group 20–24 almost four out of five single men and seven out of ten single women were still living as children with their families of origin.[8] This was certainly the case with the newly-weds, for two-thirds of the grooms and nearly three-quarters of the brides had lived with their parents until their wedding day. Interestingly, satisfaction with the new home was often given as one of the main pleasures of married life. Material ownership of a home demonstrates adult status, but more importantly it provides privacy and a personal domain in which to exercise the newly-acquired autonomy of adulthood. As it is usually a novel experience for both spouses, together they share a taste of freedom:

What sort of things about being married do you like?

'Coming home after work and sitting in me own house – giving the orders – I'm not being told what to do, I can decide what *I* want to do, when and how – Heather can decide the same.'—*Mr Allen*

'Privacy is nice – I never thought I'd want privacy. As I say, I've always got on with my parents and I love to be with them but to come home and just sit with Nigel is lovely.'—*Mrs Browning*

'As an adult – as well as a married couple – you know we've got our own home and we've got our own views and we've got our own way of doing things and we've got our own front door, you know, and what we say and do behind it is our business.'—*Mrs Brothers*

The following account from one husband highlights a potential dilemma for those newly-weds who achieve independent housing through marriage – individual possession versus the sharing ethos of the couple:

Has anything given you special pleasure in the last year?

'Getting married. Being able to get married I think – self-satisfaction.'

When you say being able to get married . . . ?

'Well, being able to afford to get married – it's not an easy step to take nowadays. Having something of my own – like this place – that's very satisfying . . . yeah, I think everything that comes with being married really pleases.'—*Mr Allen*

'An individual in my own right'

The strain for young adults of 'living in someone else's home' (their parents' home) was relieved by marriage, even for those couples without a place of their own who had to 'board' in the groom's, or more usually the bride's, parents' home. In spite of the comic tradition of embattled in-laws and newly-weds, tension between the generations did not feature much in the description of post-wedding relations. Moreover, the acknowledgment of sons and daughters as husbands and wives usually improved the parents' relationships with their offspring. A new, respectful and more distant relationship was often established; one which clearly recognised the status of the new family unit:

'I can't explain it . . . when we go round there or they come round here they seem different – they seem to welcome us differently and *treat us as if we are different people*. Although I'm still their daughter I'm married now, you know – that seems to make a difference to them.'—*Mrs Neath*

'We get on much better now than we ever did before . . . we didn't get on very well at all but since we got married he treats me more *as a man in my own right*.'—*Mr Kirkham*

'I think getting married made them finally realise that I was an *individual in my own right*. They always tended to be fairly protective parents which I've had to fight against a little bit . . . now we've got a very good relationship.'—*Mr Turner*

This young husband, unlike most of the grooms, had lived independently of his parents while studying at university, but he had nevertheless found it difficult to untie the parental apron strings. Marriage aids and abets emigration from the world of the parents because it bestows the right for another (the spouse) to displace them as the next-of-kin. The newly-weds offered some powerful accounts of this experience. In a few cases the hostility between parents and the future spouse helped to force the break, and so crystallise feelings of commitment. When Mr Gunter started courting his wife they saw each other every night and 'although we didn't think of marriage, I thought one hell of a lot of Christine'. This intensive courting meant that he only went to his parents' home after work for a meal and went straight out to his girlfriend's, returning home in the early hours of the morning. As he was keen to point out, his parents had not objected to this behaviour when he was unattached, but once they became aware of the existence of his girlfriend they 'decided to get funny about it':

> 'It was terrible, I think my Mum and Dad thought Christine wasn't good enough or they didn't like her. My Mum and Dad are terrific but they have always been very possessive. I think what really got up their nose was that *I was placing Christine before them at that stage.*'

How did Christine feel?

> 'She felt that I *should* place her before my Mum and Dad.'

In the end, 'it got that bad' that Mr Gunter left home. Having to move out of his parents' comfortable and protective home made Mr Gunter realise 'if I can put someone in front of my Mum and Dad – I suppose it didn't really click before that – I love the girl'.

Adults-in-waiting

The enthusiasm for married life displayed by the newly-weds high-lights the difficulties of being single in a society which offers little validity to that state despite demographic changes which demonstrate that people are remaining single for a longer time.[9] However, since most men and women do marry, and the vast majority by the latter part of their twenties, it is realistic to expect that being single is a temporary circumstance, an ephemeral phase, defined only by its boundaries; the end of childhood and the start of married life.

Single men and women, unfettered and unmarked by the responsi-bilities of 'real' life, receive society's sanction to dedicate their time to 'seeing the world', being 'footloose and fancy free' and 'having a fling' before the serious business of settling down. These phrases were offered by the newly-weds to describe the period prior to settling down: they had been asked to give an ideal for marriage and to justify their choice. For most of them, twenty-five years of age was the watershed, and by this time (the 'end of youth' according to one young man) this free-living period should be abandoned in order to settle down into marriage. Public recognition of 16–25 as the 'travel-ling years' is perhaps neatly symbolised by concessionary fares to the under-26s.[10] Certainly, the reasons offered by respondents for wait-ing until this time to settle down reveal an almost socially prescribed life style for young, single people:

> 'I was going to see the sights and have a good time and then I thought I would settle down about 25.'

'When I first started university I had every intention of being footloose and fancy-free.'

'I wanted to have a good time and see the world before I got married.'

'25 seemed a good age – you'd been around.'

Yet a feeling of unrealised intention is indicated by the fact that the great majority of those who gave an ideal age range (93 per cent of men and 88 per cent of women) had relinquished their freedom prematurely – indeed, a quarter of women had married as much as five years or more before their ideal age. Furthermore, some of those who had married earlier than they had expected said they did so because of a 'conversion to marriage'; that is, they came upon 'the one for me'. Most simply said they felt 'ready' to marry: that is, *ready to cease being single*. The conflict between wanting to make the most of the opportunity to remain uncommitted, and the need for security, was well expressed by Mrs Moncrieff who had favoured a late marriage and yet became a wife at nineteen:

'I was totally against marriage.'

Why?

'It's very hard to explain; I sort of made myself like that. I was hell bent on exploring the world and having lots of adventures, and marriage was just out of the question – it seemed such a boring thing to do. It was strange when I met Ian – it was a total conflict within myself. I couldn't quite shake him off. I used to try and create arguments so he would say, "Right, I don't want to see you again" and make it easy for me, but I couldn't bring myself to say, "I don't want to see you any more", because I did.'

How do you feel now that you are married?

'I feel I have admitted something to myself. I've admitted the fact that I need security because I've always had it and I couldn't do without it . . . and I think that's about it.'—*Mrs Moncrieff*

There is a dilemma between the need to be an adventurer, even if the adventures amount merely to being 'one of the boys (or girls)' and the yearning to bring to an end a state of anticipation which is recognised as inherently unreal and insecure:

'I wasn't one of these Roger Moore types – the sort of character he plays . . . I appreciated in time it [marriage] would come along . . . sort of twenties . . . '

'I didn't fancy growing old singly . . . on your own . . . and nobody at all . . . no children . . . it's horrible'.

'Thought of myself as an old bachelor. I'm on the shelf and I'm staying there – it did bother me to a certain extent but I didn't let it get me down'.

It was evident this was not too difficult a dilemma for these newly-weds to resolve since they expressed little regret over the exchange of a phase of freedom and exploration for the encumbrances of marriage and (subsequent) family life. Responsibilities may 'tie you down' but without obligations you have no right to a status and, therefore, to an identity. In the world of the 'just married' the status of being a husband or wife, of being 'an individual in my own right' and 'having a place of my own', is equated with independence. The newly-weds appeared as yet not to have encountered any conflict between individual identity and what Berger and Kellner term the 'maritally defined identity':

> [at marriage] there occurs a sharing of future horizons, which leads not only to stabilization but inevitably to a narrowing of the future projections of each partner. Before marriage the individual typically plays with quite discrepant daydreams in which his future self is projected. Having now considerably stabilized his self-image, the married individual will have to project the future in accordance with this maritally defined identity.[11]

Being ready to settle down

The desire to be recognised as a normal, independent adult and to secure the future, appears to be the most common motive for marriage. However, while this accounts for the potency of marriage, it does not explain how the individual determines his or her readiness for it. Conventional wisdom holds that we will know when Mr or Miss Right comes along. Theories about mate selection suggest that this knowledge is founded on both conscious and unconscious estimations of mate suitability. It is curious then, if readiness for marriage is determined simply by the chance appearance of an eligible partner, that there should be so much uniformity of age at first marriage, so that alternative explanations appear to be necessary.

Consideration of the factors which contributed to the ending of previous serious relationships provides some clues about readiness for marriage, since a major cause of premarital separations cited by the newly-weds in their romantic memoirs was their own feelings of not being ready for marriage to anyone at that time:

How did the relationship finish?

'We finished it because I wouldn't get engaged'.

Why?

> 'I felt I was too young – I didn't feel ready in myself to think of being tied down and the responsibility of running a home and going to work – I just didn't feel right you know, I felt too young.'—*Mrs Neath*

So, as far as the respondents were concerned, many of these early 'serious' relationships could perhaps have developed into marriage had things been different; that is, if either they or their lovers had been ready for marriage, or if circumstances and events had fostered or promoted marriage at that time:

> 'That's why I think I called it off – because I didn't want to – I mean I'd been going out for a year and a half and I was serious but I didn't really feel ready enough – old enough – to get married.'

Do you think if you'd met him later you might have married him?

> 'Yes, I think I would have. Apart from being boyfriend–girlfriend, we were very friendly as well – we used to talk – very similar to what I am to Brian (husband).'—*Mrs Butcher*

About two-thirds of the brides and grooms had been involved previously in 'serious relationships'. These relationships had been serious in that they were characterised by a frequency of meeting and length of contact which distinguished them from casual 'going out with' acquaintances. Varying degrees of open-ended commitment were described, but within these relationships marriage had been seriously considered by half the men and two-thirds of the women.

It is relevant here to note two sources of distortion in these retrospective accounts of such 'failed' relationships. From the vantage point of a recent marriage, a relationship which at the time had seemed promising is likely to be reinterpreted as having been fatally flawed:

Were any of those relationships more serious than others?

> 'One, only one and that was infatuation, but that wasn't serious, looking back.'

And how long did you go out for?

> 'About seven months I think – I can't really remember.'

Did you ever think of marrying him?

> 'Yes I did at the time – it wouldn't have survived five minutes if I had . . . '

And how did it finish?

'I found out that he was married . . . .'

Were you very disappointed?

'At the time, yes – but now definitely no.'—*Mrs Dawson*

Mrs Robertson had previously been engaged for seven years; she and her then fiancé had bought a house and were about to get married but then 'everything fell through':

What caused the break-up?

'He was very moody, wanted everything his own way, you know, things didn't work out.'

Was it a mutual decision?

'Yes.'

Did you find it upsetting?

'At the time I did but you know they kept saying, "You'll get over it" and funnily enough you do and think to yourself "Oh I couldn't bear to be stuck with him all my life . . . '. It was the best thing that could have possibly happened that we didn't get married because if I had married him I would have been divorced soon.'—*Mrs Robertson*

This account highlights a second source of distortion: there are two sides to every story and for these early 'serious' relationships we have only the one account. There is a great deal of discrepancy in the reports from newly-wed respondents of such relationships and the differing accounts from men and women suggest widely different gender perceptions of what goes on between a man and a woman. Just as the pace of a relationship which concludes with the marriage vows may be stage-managed by one partner with a vocation for matrimony, so also the termination of the earlier liaison may have been similarly contrived. In this way, the would-be spouse who was enthusiastic about settling down may have experienced the break-up as a drifting apart because the other party was unready for responsibility, and therefore unresponsive to moves to push the relationship in the direction of marriage.

'Drifting apart' was in fact the most often cited explanation for the demise of previous involvements. Such relationships appeared slowly to peter out without any dramas or mutual decisions, or even, in some case, goodbyes:

'it just dwindled'
'grew away – growing up'
'we just saw less of each other until we didn't see each other any more'.

In the same way that courtships which led to marriage found their own momentum in that they flourished simply because they did not die, so many of these 'serious' relationships had expired simply because they did not survive. However, a range of explanations for the ending of previous serious liaisons was offered: the arrival of a third party; the realisation that the other party was not suitable spouse-material; the revelation that the lover was already married, and so on.

Consideration of the factors which contributed to the ending of earlier serious relationships, together with those which appear to have some significance in the successful outcome of the courtship with the spouse, suggests that the potential for marriage in any heterosexual relationship is a combination of the lovers' attitudes to marriage *at a particular time*, within a climate of events and circumstances. A specific climate may foster, provoke or hinder matrimony. This process, therefore, both offers an explanation why the newly-weds successfully arrived at the altar, and also why their partners in earlier serious relationships did not.

Meandering courtships

The way in which attitudes to marriage at a particular time combine with a relationship climate which fosters or promotes marriage is demonstrated by six couples whose courtship waxed and waned. The progress of these courtships had been usually interrupted because of the unreadiness for the marriage of one or both partners.

Mr and Mrs Emery had met when they were both at school, when she was fourteen and he sixteen. After four years when 'we used to row every so often and split up but always got back together again', the couple decided to get engaged. He was then in his first year at university and she had just reached eighteen. According to Mrs Emery:

'When I was quite young I thought we would get married. I was engaged at 18 and I thought I'd be married by the time I was 20.'

So Mrs Emery saw their engagement as a prelude to marriage, whereas Mr Emery had not even considered marriage at all:

'I had got engaged because it was the done thing, that's the way I intended to look upon it. I got engaged but the idea of marriage hadn't crossed my mind then, getting engaged was great, but marriage, no, it hadn't crossed my mind'.

Their differing perceptions of engagement became clear to each other when Mr Emery announced his decision to get a loan for an expensive new car. The disagreement which ensued, and which resulted in Mrs Emery throwing back her engagement ring, was, according to him, rooted in her disapproval of borrowing money. However, as far as Mrs Emery was concerned this was not so: the spending of savings on a 'very expensive car' was to her a sign that he was not saving to get married and therefore she delivered an ultimatum 'well, it's me or the car'. Mr Emery took the car. In the following three years, Mrs Emery got involved seriously with two other men; the first relationship finished because she discovered that the boyfriend was married, and the second affair ended because she had been reunited with Mr Emery. None the less she admitted that she would have liked to have married this second boyfriend had she not discovered that he was going out with another girl:

How did that relationship finish?

'I went back with Alan and I decided to settle there really.'

The decision to 'settle there' was reinforced by her parents who didn't like the boyfriend and preferred Mr Emery.

By now, Mrs Emery was twenty-three and Mr Emery twenty-five and both were still hopeful of marriage. The previous ups and downs in their relationship had engendered wariness on both sides. Their mutual attitude was 'either we get married or we forget it . . . we get married or else – and so we had to make a determined effort'.

It appears that the first engagement had been broken because Mr Emery declared, albeit indirectly, his unreadiness for marriage *at that time*. Several times in his remarks about marriage Mr Emery stressed that 'you need money to get married . . . I could never conceive getting married without buying my own home'. Interestingly, just three months before his reunion with his future bride, he heard of the death of his grandmother and that he was a beneficiary in her will. He was candid about the way in which the advent of this legacy coincided with his readiness for marriage:

'I was left some money which went towards the home, which is one of the reasons why I decided to get married'.

All the couples with meandering courtships broke up and were reunited (one couple as many as four times) before finally consolidating their courtship with marriage. At times of disruption, one partner had always been more ready to settle down than the other, but finally the climate was right for matrimony.

THE COURTSHIP CLIMATE

Obviously, if one or both partners in a relationship is reluctant to become committed it is likely that the relationship will founder. However, conversely, the mere fact that both are open to marriage and now feel ready to settle down may not in itself be sufficient.

Circumstances which promote marriage

In the description of the Emery's tortuous courtship, we showed that Mr Emery's ultimate readiness for marriage was closely associated with an improvement in his financial status. Circumstances which offer the instrumental means to marry can prove crucial in directly promoting marriage. Improvement in occupational and economic status and the availability of marital accommodation are often deciding factors in the progress of courtship. However, other events and circumstances may also promote marriage, albeit more in-directly. For example, a pregnancy scare is suggestive of marriage because the discussions arising from it inevitably raise the issue of getting married, as one wife explained:

> 'My periods are usually very regular and I was about two weeks late and we started to worry. I had two pregnancy tests which were both negative which eased my mind a lot, you know, but it was very worrying . . . I started thinking. But Ian said he would marry me if I wanted to and I started to think about it'.

A forced separation during courtship, most usually a holiday, which interrupts the cycle of relationship, can stimulate an examination of commitment. Mr Trist described himself as 'falling in love quite early' soon after meeting his future wife, but she was uncertain about making any commitment:

> 'I told her about how I felt and she said " . . . don't hurry me along, otherwise you will ruin it".'

Months later when Mr Trist was about to go abroad for a holiday with friends he was surprised and delighted to hear that at last his feelings were reciprocated:

> 'The day before I went on holiday, I phoned her up from the airport and she says, "I'm catching up with you" – that was her sort of thing – she was catching up . . . you know I went on holiday feeling pretty well.'

However, most typical of all the conditions which may raise the issue of marriage may well be simply the awareness of time passing:

> 'Well probably – it didn't really come about like, "Right, we'll get married". It just sort of came about really, you know it just seemed to be a natural progression. I suppose it took about two and a half years. I think we got engaged after two and a half years.'—*Mrs Browning*

The realisation of time passing aroused in some respondents (mainly women) anxiety about their age and the contracting opportunities for marriage:

> 'I was on my own then and I had quite a lot of girlfriends in London – the problem is people tend to get married and then you find, well, "I don't want to go round to them because they are married" – and people move away. But I had a good time . . . I did want to get married a bit before Trevor [spouse]. I thought about it – well not necessarily getting married but I thought I ought to be doing something. That's why I've always been a bit job conscious, I thought I ought to be doing either – if I wasn't going to get married then I wanted to have an interesting job: or I wanted to go abroad – I was really wondering what I wanted to do, what I ought to do.'

Circumstances which provoke marriage

Events which appeared directly to provoke marriage were less likely to be articulated by respondents as contributing to the progress of their relationships, but to the observer, the coincidence of such events with crucial stages in the relationship was often most striking, as the following examples demonstrate.

Mr Linden started dating his future bride, a girl whom he had known for several months, when his mother, who had just remarried, was on her honeymoon. He described his relationship with his new stepfather as a 'bumpy ride' which improved once he had left home to get married. Mrs Pitt, the youngest of six children of an elderly widow, decided to marry her future husband at the same time as she discovered her mother was terminally ill with cancer. Mrs Robertson had been involved in a serious accident which had resulted in a broken leg; as soon as she recovered from her injuries she felt 'very down' and went to a dating agency where she met her future husband to whom she became engaged two weeks later.

Getting married could in part, therefore, be a reaction to an event which had in some way stimulated a fresh perception of oneself, perhaps by having accentuated the need to relinquish the adult-in-waiting period of life for a more stable status. The death (or expected death) of a parent, or the aftermath of an unhappy love affair, especially where a child had been conceived, could all make marriage an appealing haven. It is also interesting to note the tendency for young women, and sometimes young men, to topple into the marital courtship shortly after the concluding traumas of a previous affair. One bride described how she had become pregnant after a two-year affair with a boy who was 'a bit of a Jack the lad'. She decided to have her baby adopted and shortly after this she met up again with a previous boyfriend who later became her husband. She believed that getting engaged to her eventual spouse 'changed me to a totally different person':

> 'It was being loved, I think – I remember when I got engaged all the girls said "Let me see your ring" – I know a ring means nothing, but it shows that someone loves you – a different kind of love obviously from your mother and father and so on – security as well should be.'

For as many as two-fifths of the newly-weds, an event of the type described above coincided with critical stages in their courtship.

It is generally acknowledged that the unexpected conception of a child before any declared commitment to marry is a common trigger to marriage. However, with young brides in particular, an 'unexpected' pregnancy is often only one part of a total set of circumstances which conspire to make marriage an attractive proposition, since getting married means leaving home.

Escaping into marriage

Marriage bestows the expectation, although not always the facility, of having 'a place of one's own'. In certain instances it was impossible to disentangle a marriage which was a *means* of leaving home from a marriage which was an *outcome* of leaving home. Particularly for some very young brides, their parents' marital difficulties or the intrusion of a step-parent had provoked the need to escape, and refuge had usually been found in the parental home of the current boyfriend. The following account is an example of the build-up of events which may result in a young girl needing to find a sanctuary in her boyfriend's home. She had come home one day to discover that her stepmother had walked out taking her children with her, and the house was 'an empty shell':

> 'I sat down and thought, "What am I going to do?" and I went round to my friend's house to ask because she is very good about giving advice and said, "What am I going to do because I've got no mummy" [laugh] and she said "You've wanted to leave home, now would be as good a chance as any".'

On her return home to collect her belongings she was confronted by her father who tried to pressure her into staying to look after him. After a heated discussion 'he started to get a bit nasty' so in order to pacify him she agreed to stay. Later, with help from some friends, she managed to remove most of her things before telling her father that she found it impossible to stay with him:

> 'I said I was sorry I couldn't stay and if there was any way I could help him I would, but I couldn't stand being alone with him.'

Her father 'got really funny about it and started to get violent', so she ran out and went to her friend's house for the night. The friend's family said that the arrangement could only be temporary:

> 'I said I knew that and shot off. I decided, you know, that I would go to Jimmy's mother'. [Jimmy was the boy she had started dating a week earlier.]

A year after leaving home she and Jimmy were married, and at the time of the interview they were still living with Jimmy's mother.

Escape attempts of this type have been detected clinically by Lily Pincus in her work with adolescents:

> Where adolescent difficulties have been particularly severe, courtship or marriage may be a desperate attempt to deal with the conflicts about dependence or rivalry. The partner may be important as an instrument, rather than in his own right as a person to love; as offering an opponent to the parents, or a way of escape, rather than as a life partner. Many of the very young couples who reach helping agencies seem to have married out of conflicts with their parents rather than from any real feeling for each other. . . . [12]

But it is not only strife-ridden homes which need to be escaped from. Several respondents described their struggles to break free from loving parents who suffocated their independence. As the example of Mr Gunter quoted earlier demonstrates, the rivalry between parents and future spouse, in externalising the conflict over independence, may help the young person to flee an unduly protective home.

The marriage seekers

Although marriage had been on nearly everyone's agenda for life, some newly-weds (about one in five) displayed an almost vocational commitment to getting married and can appropriately be described as 'marriage seekers'. With the expectation that female identity is firmly rooted in marriage and motherhood, it is not surprising to find that among the newly-weds it was the women who were usually the most zealous in their pursuit of a spouse in this way. For the marriage seeker, becoming engaged is a goal which must be realised sooner rather than later, and courtship is, therefore, a very serious business. The more fortunate marriage seeker was able to pursue her (or his) very first serious relationship through to marriage, but the less fortunate were at first deflected from their goal, as the pattern of one serious relationship failing and being swiftly replaced by another demonstrates. (Of course, for a few people this 'in-and-out' conduct of serious relationships did not reflect an avid pursuit of marriage but rather the reverse, a retreat from commitment and an uncertainty about getting married.) The most assiduous marriage seekers did not flit from one relationship to another, but purposefully sought out a suitable mate, one who would reciprocate their inclination for marriage.

Mrs Dawson exemplified one such marriage seeker; she had finished a previous serious relationship reluctantly because her boyfriend had not felt ready, 'he did not want to settle down'. According to her husband, her seriousness about their present relationship had been clear from the start:

> 'When I first met her I remember the famous words she came out with, "Are you serious about me?" '

Mrs Dawson defined her own seriousness; as a matter of course she assumed that Mr Dawson felt the same:

> 'It was serious because I never went out with anyone else all the time – and I know he didn't, and it was just him and I and we used to go out with our friends separately and I think we always knew it was serious and it was taken for granted – all our friends thought we'd end up together.'

Mr Dawson had broken a previous engagement only five months earlier; he had ended that relationship because 'I didn't want to get married and I didn't know what I got engaged for really.' Aware of this recent experience, Mrs Dawson kept reassuring him that they were 'just good friends':

> 'Because he'd just got out of one relationship and he wasn't going to break his neck getting into another.'

After about two years, and on return from a holiday, the couple got engaged because, according to Mrs Dawson, 'We realised that that was "it".' However, her husband experienced it differently:

When did you decide to get married?
> 'When did *Julie* decide we'd get married?'

Did Julie propose to you?
> 'No, I don't think *I* even proposed – it was funny, we just got engaged . . . We went along . . . then we bought the place and she said "Well, we ought to get married".'

The response to the seeker by the partner is all-important to the outcome of the courtship, since it requires two to make the marriage vows, even if one does most of the orchestrating. One wife reported that her decision to marry coincided with their engagement; however, her husband says that he did not decide to marry until sixteen months after their engagement! After an earlier unsuccessful engagement, it was clear that he still felt unready to settle down. He expressed alarm at his fiancée 'having her hooks' into him and attempted to combat the pressure from her by constantly delaying the wedding date still further in an already prolonged courtship. He reported, with some glee, that when he finally could no longer delay booking the church for the wedding he deliberately chose a date considerably later than that agreed with his fiancée and justified this (to us) by explaining that he needed to delay things 'as long as possible'.

Brides are more involved than grooms in the wedding plans, so it is usually they and their parents who are more concerned to set the date:

> 'Well, we got engaged July last year and I suppose it was about September I said, you know, "We'd better set the date."

So you didn't have a date in mind?
> 'No – we said within two years and then a couple of months went by and I said, "Oh, I can't wait two years" and I said to Stephen about setting the date.'—*Mrs Leeming*

Mrs Leeming's husband had intended to marry much later and the interviewer asked him what had changed his mind:

'She did.'

In what way?
'I don't know, she changed me mind [laugh] and that was it.'

In spite of their overwhelming influence on the process of courtship, all marriage seekers must not be considered to be devious manipulators; their 'victims' are usually willing conspirators who are hopeful of marriage *at some time* but who may simply lack the impetus to organise their commitment.

Setting the pace of the courtship

Manipulation by one partner intent on marriage is one way of raising the pace of the relationship, the climate of the courtship may also prove influential in shaping its progress. A courtship may be promoted or hindered, for example, by the availability or non-availability of suitable accommodation. For some respondents, the possibility of an alternative to living at home may make marriage more desirable, as was the case with the husband whose parents' decision to move away made him bring his wedding forward:

'My parents were talking of moving to Shropshire, which meant I had to find somewhere else to live – I was sort of looking around for a job and couldn't get a job which had accommodation – don't get me wrong, don't think I *just* got married for that because I didn't.'

The partner with the greatest inclination to marry is likely to exercise more power in respect of the pace of the courtship. Conversely, the pace of the courtship may be restrained by a reluctant spouse-to-be; while a wife might initiate and maintain the momentum for marriage, a husband's uncertainty may be influential in counteracting her efforts. Indeed, those who were genuinely reluctant to marry did usually effect some delay in the progress of courtship, although as we will show later with Mr and Mrs Hill, delays in courtship may be differently perceived by the two partners. The cultural stereotype of the elusive groom, who settles down only when he has finally run out of excuses, is neatly summarised in the old saying 'He chased her until she caught him'. But a different implication of that old saying is that men and women experience their shared courtship differently.

Gender differences in courtship

Women are generally expected to have a greater identification than men with the ritual processes of courtship, and their more accurate recall of the crucial dates in the process demonstrates that this is so. Men were usually vague even about more formal stages such as engagement, whereas the women 'never forget'. One husband, when asked for the date of his engagement, ruminated:

'Yeah, '78 – beginning of last year – or half way through last year – I don't actually know the date – she does but I don't.'—*Mr Hatch*

In contrast to men's uncertainty over dates, women were often able to be extremely precise:

'Actually, I started going out with him on 6th January and on 4th February he asked me to marry him – I'll never forget it.'—*Mrs Rudd*

Thus it is women who are custodians of detail and so tend to be biographers of relationships. However, although women are more accurate about crucial dates, they tend to be less revealing about certain aspects of their relationships. When discrepancies between husbands and wives in reporting sensitive issues such as the start of the sexual relationship were examined, it was nearly always the woman who stated that the relationship was well advanced chronologically before sexual intimacy occurred. Schofield, in his study of the sexual activities of young men and women, remarks that women may say that their relationships are more committed when sexual activity starts simply because they appear to reach commitment sooner.[13] On the other hand, Huston and his colleagues noted that men seemed to reach high levels of commitment in courtship earlier than women, although he points out that this may merely reflect the fact that overall the male has more control over the course of the courtship.[14]

If discrepancies between newly-wed partners over the decision to marry are examined, equally as many men as women reach commitment before their partners. Obviously, marriage seekers (who are most usually female), are likely to reach the decision quickly, and generally before their eventual spouses. Among the rest of the newly-weds, however, the only pattern detectable was that, where the decision to marry was made around the time of engagement for both partners, men had usually made this decision a month before the engagement, and women not until the engagement itself or even a month later. Interestingly, although there were very few instances of the formal marriage proposal *per se*, this pattern of deciding to marry uncovers the vestigial traces of the traditional roles of male proposer and female accepter.

Two views of the same courtship

A person who is keen to marry, and attempts to accelerate the pace of courtship, may provoke such anxiety in the 'spouse-to-be' that she or he attempts to restrain the progress towards marriage. We have already seen how one husband covertly delayed his wedding because he felt his wife, a marriage seeker, was rushing their courtship. Mr Hill was not a marriage seeker (although he did want to marry) but he was 'dead set on getting engaged that Christmas' which was only a few weeks after he met Mrs Hill. According to him:

> 'Christmas was the time when we *both* wanted to get engaged. Circumstances had it that we didn't, and we got engaged the following Christmas.'

Mrs Hill, however, felt uncertain about committing herself and her 'infatuation' with somebody else convinced her that she was unready for marriage:

> 'Well, we were going to get engaged the following Christmas.'

You said you were going to – you didn't?
> 'No, we didn't. It was all very idyllic at the beginning; it was fine for a while and then I had a crush on one of the people at work and he asked me out. Andrew knew about this; we often talk about how we got over that stormy period of our lives.'

So that put off the engagement?
> 'It did; I felt definitely that I wasn't ready; I felt in *no* way am I ready to get engaged if I can feel what was obviously an infatuation for someone else . . . for quite a long time I was chopping and changing – I didn't really know what to do – I felt I was still very young.'

It was this continuing uncertainty which, according to Mrs Hill, resulted in the wedding being delayed:

So you got engaged; did you decide on the date of the wedding then or not?
> 'No, we thought at first it would be a year, but it went on.'

Why did it go on?

'For the same reason why it went on before we got engaged. I think it was a feeling of this is really it; you feel this is really it when you get engaged, but at least there is that feeling that it is not quite so definite. I felt it is such a big step, I wanted to be so sure.'

However, once again, Mrs Hill's husband attributed the delay in getting married to 'circumstances':

'I don't know, we changed our minds quite a bit about when; it just slotted in. It was time and money and circumstances which prevailed and the wedding just slotted in at that time. Beforehand it just wouldn't have been practical for a number of reasons so I think we just waited until the time was right.'

THE TRAIL TO MARRIAGE

For people marrying for the first time, marriage provides a unique means of acquiring identity, and, through the acquisition of identity, for settling the future. As in all good fairy tales, marriage marks the end of courting (which has often been a stimulating yet harrowing period spent fending off the challenge of uncertainty), and the beginning of the more tranquil ever-after. It is, therefore, not surprising to find most of these newly-weds placing the significance of their married status above that of the quality of their conjugal relationship. However, such a finding contradicts the notion of the courtship career, which implies a developmental process of increasingly intense and intimate relationships in the build-up to marriage.

The courtship career may simply represent an idealisation of what advocates for marriage would like the build-up to be. If contemporary young lovers were able to approach marriage through such a process, marital success might be more certain. It is, therefore, attractive for those who have got married to perceive everything left in the wake of marriage as having led them to their goal. Such a holistic and tidily developed picture of courtship can only readily be drawn from the vantage point of marriage. The evidence from the respondents suggests that it is more realistic to construe modern courtship not as a *career* but as a *trail* which leads to marriage – a trail which, as can be seen, may for many have been quite haphazard.

4 The Trail to Marriage

Tuesday, 20th November 1731, Wilhelmina's wedding day arrived after a brideship of eight months; and that young lady's troublesome romance, more happily than might have been expected, did at last wind itself up. Mamma's unreasonable humours continued, more or less; but these also must end. Old wooers and outlooks . . . they lie far over the horizon; faded out of one's very thoughts, all these.

Frederick the Great
Thomas Carlyle

Traditionally, courtship was regarded as a period of waiting; waiting for the 'right' spouse to come along and then waiting for a wedding to be arranged. Modern courtship is different. It is regarded as a time of preparation, an opportunity to explore and test out various relationships and finally, *the* relationship which will be marriage. The prelude to modern marriage is influenced by the requirements for careful pairing which that style of marriage requires,

> 'Dating provides an opportunity for trial and error selection. In our affluent, consumption-oriented society so much is expected of marriage that consummate skill in personal interaction is required to fulfil those expectations'.[1]

The changing legal status of engagement demonstrates this. One of the reasons for abolishing the right of action over breach of promise was because it was considered that engagement was no longer a pledge to marry but rather a trial commitment which might end in marriage. So, in contemporary courtship it is expected that commitment to marriage follows from, rather than precedes, a developing personal relationship.

A MODERN COURTSHIP

The trail to wedlock began early for most men and women, starting at around fourteen years of age when they first went out with a member of the opposite sex. A few people had not gone out with anyone before their spouse, while others went out with many different dates on a casual basis; most people had at least a couple of casual relationships and about half the newly-weds had been involved in at least one 'serious relationship'.[2] Getting involved too young (under 18) was generally disapproved of and, indeed, it was given as the cause of the demise of many serious relationships. Men painted a picture of having to avoid and deter women who were intent on involvement:

How many girlfriends did you have before your wife?
'What, serious? None. Not serious.'

So they were just going out for the odd evening?
'For the odd evening. Perhaps a fortnight; *that* was a lengthy romance, you know. I just wasn't interested.'

Why?
'Normally we'd be about ten blokes and eight girls and one of them would want to go out with me; I'd take her out for the night but I never wanted to get involved at all.'—*Mr Slater*

However, in contrast, by the age of eighteen most of the women had started dating the man they eventually married and he was usually her senior by about two years. The decision to marry and the engagement were closely associated with motives for marriage within that particular courtship climate and have already been discussed. Different motives and different climates contributed to a range of courtship styles, but the most frequent pattern was for the couple to reach their wedding day within two and a half years of dating. However, there were variations, with some shorter courtships of six months or even less and a few very protracted ones of over five years.

It has been suggested that the length of courtship can be used to predict the likely success of a marriage; for example, hasty marriages have been perceived as risky on the basis that there will have been little opportunity for the potential spouses to get to know each other, and, conversely, long-drawn-out courtships are thought to be indicative of lack of commitment on the part of one, or both, of the spouses-to-be.[3] When the sequence of the significant moments in a couple's trail to marriage, such as deciding 'this was it', deciding to get engaged and deciding to move in together, is considered in the context of a particular courtship climate, a view of individual motives emerges which has complications beyond the decision to marry. When we examined the courtship strategies of the newly-weds we found we were able to distinguish a typology of future orientation which is described in detail in the final chapter of this book.

Getting engaged

Only four couples said they did not get engaged, and although the legal contractual obligations of engagement have been abolished, getting engaged was still perceived as an important personal and social declaration of commitment. There is no accepted etiquette, so that for many couples, once the decision to marry had been made, an engagement followed quickly, frequently coinciding with a family occasion or anniversary, which bestowed extra significance. However, some engagements had already lasted a long time before the fiancés agreed when to marry, whilst other couples delayed the engagement for several years until they were ready to initiate their actual wedding plans. Engagements can, therefore, be described as either active or passive, in that the first type marks the start of the wedding process itself while the second simply signifies the end of the preliminary courtship period.

Passive engagement usually occurred sooner rather than later in the courtship and signified a moratorium on sexual activity other than with the partner. The wedding itself was probably not mentioned but the couple were defined as, and perceived by others to be, 'an engaged couple'. In contrast, *active engagement* marked the starting point of the prelude to the wedding; such couples were on course to marriage and would be seen by others as people who were 'getting married'. Mrs Inver met her future husband when they were both sixteen years old and their courtship lasted seven years. They did not get engaged until the last quarter of the courtship, twenty-two months before the wedding (an 'active' engagement). In her account she makes it clear that in the period up to the engagement both had been free to 'date' other people (a 'passive' engagement would have precluded this):

So when did you actually come to the decision that it was something serious?

'Just sort of drifted into it really – after that amount of years, you just get used to someone and then. . . . '

So you just went on going out together and . . . ?

'We did and then like a couple of years ago he wanted to get married, so I said, "Well, not until you're absolutely sure, because I'm not going to push you into anything" – you know. When I was younger my idea was to get married as quickly as possible but then I sort of thought it's not a good idea because men feel trapped – just sort of make sure that he definitely wanted to and it was *him* that said so and not me influencing him in any way.'

So when did you get engaged?

'About two years ago.'

But you'd decided it was serious before then?
'Oh yes, yes for a long time we'd always thought because neither of us used to go out with anyone for a particularly long time, apart from these two other guys.'

Sex and the unmarried couple

In *Family Formation 1976* Karen Dunnell wrote:

> Whether or not there was under-reporting among older women in the survey, there is little doubt that the frequency of pre-marital sexual relations for women in successive marriage cohorts has been increasing. Three out of four of those marrying between 1971 and 1975 reported such relations.[4]

Only three of the brides in the newly-weds group said that they were virgins on their wedding night, which implies that a full sexual relationship has become an accepted part of the courtship process. A recent MORI poll suggests that while both men and women are increasingly likely to have a sexual relationship while unmarried, a woman's first sexual partner will most likely be her eventual spouse.[5]

Of the newly-wed couples who reported having a sexual relationship prior to marriage, 45 per cent of the women had had that relationship exclusively with their eventual husband, in comparison with 29 per cent of the bridegrooms in respect of their wives. Among the brides, just over half had had a sexual relationship with someone else as well as their spouse, whereas almost two-thirds of the husbands had done so. The newly-weds were asked when they started having a sexual relationship with each other and over half the couples reported that they had started sexual relations before 'committing' themselves in any way, with about a further third stating that sexual relations started at or after the decision to marry or get engaged (whichever came first). The partners in seven couples gave discrepant reports and in six of these it was the husband who said sex occurred before any commitment while their wives said it was after. One of the wives in this group, who had decided to marry within weeks of dating her eventual spouse, was clearly committed earlier than he was. However, in nearly all the other cases of discrepancy, the partners agreed about stages of commitment. Three of these wives later in the interview gave information which showed that they had earlier misled the interviewer: it became clear that they were trying to present the sexual relationship as having developed out of explicit commitment rather than as having pre-dated the commitment (the latter appeared to have been the actual case.)

In general, however, all questions relating to the sexual behaviour of partners, both before and within marriage, were answered easily and without embarrassment. The section was deliberately placed towards the end of the interview when rapport was well established. The attitude to sexual relationships offered by the newly-weds suggests that the old standard of the bride waiting until the wedding night to consummate the marriage is out of date:

'It would have seemed strange to me if after all this, well, no sex till the wedding night. You know, I don't think that holds any great virtue. I think, years ago when no one touched anyone until their wedding night and it was a big thing to save up for – maybe that was OK then, but now it would seem rather strange, you know.'—*Mr Vaughan*

About how long after you had known each other did you start a sexual relationship?

'Not long after – that was one thing in our relationship I regretted – because at the time I'd had – it was after a disco and I had had quite a lot to drink and he persuaded me, and afterwards I used to say to him "You won't respect me" but I think in this day and age – as stupid as it sounds – unless you let a man make love to you, you almost don't keep them because they can get it somewhere else.'—*Mrs Leeming*

Do you think it's important to have a sexual relationship with your future husband?

'Well I would think so, I think it's advisable because for a start, it just gets so ridiculous if you were engaged for even, say, six months before you get married you wonder why you're waiting – I mean, I found that. I found that when I first started going out with Ian you would get to a certain point and I would just say "No" and I didn't know why I was saying "No", and I said "Well, okay", and that was it.'—*Mrs Moncrieff*

For most couples the sexual relationship started early on in courtship with about three-quarters of all couples having sex for more than a year before the wedding, and 40 per cent for over two years. One-third of the couples said they had started a full sexual relationship soon after meeting. In most instances getting involved sexually was just a natural part of courting; there had been no clear decision as such to do this:

Do you think it is important to have a sexual relationship before marriage?

'No, it just sort of came, it started off with kissing, sort of heavy petting and it led to it. You've got to experiment. If you don't like each other, there's no point in getting married.'—*Mr Slater*

Testing sexual compatibility

Sexual intimacy before marriage was particularly valued by the couples because they believed it allowed them to test their sexual compatibility. In their view, compatibility was a static component; you either were or were not compatible and it was important to discover this before marriage if possible. Two husbands used the analogy of testing a car to explain this:

> 'Like buying a new car – you wouldn't buy it unless you had driven it.'

> 'Sex is part of married life, you can't buy the car without looking under the bonnet.'

Implicit in these accounts of sexual compatibility is the notion that suiting each other in bed may be a protective factor against marital breakdown.

> 'Well I think you should find out before you get married if you can enjoy one another's bodies or not. I mean, once you're married if you're not suited in bed then it is quite difficult, you know you're married then – that's when affairs begin to start'.—*Mrs Strong*

> 'Well I don't think you should go around with everybody and anybody but I think if you both feel – you know – close to each other, it's a way of finding out. I mean if you got married and found out that neither of you agreed with each other, he didn't arouse you or you didn't arouse him, it would be wasted. You can find out more about each other – before we were married, lots of times we just sort of laid down and talked about and discussed what we liked and what we didn't like and what we felt about things, and so we found out a lot before we got married – so it helped us in a way'.—Mrs Klein

Although in most instances couples justified their pre-marital intimacy on the grounds that they were testing their sexual compatibility, in a couple of cases there had been a deliberate decision to experiment:

> 'We both felt that perhaps it was better if we both sleep together once or twice before we got married, just to make sure that part of our marriage was going to be OK because for all we know I might – he might – just not turn me on at all in bed, you know, and it's not much being married to a man who you can't make love to – you know it is a part of marriage anyway. It's better that it's a good part than being a bad part.'

Did you make love once or twice before . . . ?

> 'After we first made love it was ages – we sort of never done anything after that for a long while – then just before we got married, we started to make love because then we started to sleep together in the same bed.'—*Mrs Norden*

But more usually, once established, the sexual relationship was maintained, although it was often difficult to find comfortable and private locations. The car, usually a young man's first possession, was a popular place for conducting sexual activity. So although most of the brides and grooms had sexual experience with their partners (and some additionally with others) over quite a lengthy period, the constrained circumstances of sexual behaviour conspired, as will be seen later, to make this premarital relationship very different from the sexual relationship within marriage.

Honeymooners have traditionally been regarded with affectionate amusement, because it was always supposed that they were sexual novices whose principal task was to discover 'what it was all about'. One young husband, who had been persuaded by his wife to start a sexual relationship half way through their courtship, expressed the ambiguous feeling of wanting to delay sex with the spouse until the wedding night in order to make it special, yet at the same time not wanting to go through the agonies of a disastrous first night on the honeymoon:

> 'Before we were married – when it was coming up to getting married – there were no definite thoughts on it but it occurred to me that it was a disappointment that we didn't have this peak occasion to look forward to but we talked about it and she put forward the point of view when we were talking that she was glad because there is enough things to worry about when you are getting married without having to worry about sexual performance. And the more I think about it – and since we've been married – I agree with her.'

For those women (and the few men) who had no previous sexual experience with anyone apart from their spouse, there was relief that the wedding night had not been the 'first night' in terms of sexual intercourse, since their actual 'first night' had been tense and uncomfortable:

> 'I don't think I would have liked to have just come back to this flat on the first night and be like the time I was the first time we made love, because I was so petrified I did not enjoy it one bit.'

Living together – the final phase of courtship

According to the most recent figures, about one in four spinster brides who are marrying bachelors will have lived with their future-husband for a period before the wedding.[6] All the evidence points to an increasing trend for first marriage to be preceded by a period of cohabitation and the length of the period of premarital cohabitation is getting longer. Research in Scandinavia demonstrates that this trend has become the normal pattern for premarital relationships there, and Jan Trost concludes:

'We can now say that, far from being deviant, cohabitation has become a social institution.[7]

Widespread and open cohabitation is relatively recent in British society and therefore it is difficult for both researchers and their respondents to define. It seems likely that in some research enquiries respondents may have denied that they had cohabited simply because they did not recognise the definition implied in the wording of the question. Questions on cohabitation were included in the General Household Survey for the first time in 1979. Women were asked 'Before you and your husband actually got married, did you live together as man and wife, or not?'[8] The phrase 'man and wife' implies a kind of cohabitation which masquerades as marriage, so it is likely that several women who had lived with their husbands *as a prelude to marriage* would answer the question negatively.

The prevailing social attitude towards a behaviour affects the level of reporting about it, and where people have to conceal their living arrangements from significant others, such as families and neighbours, there is usually under-reporting. In view of this, the present study made use of a range of questions in the interviews with the newly-weds, asked at different points in the interview, in order to maximise the possibility for the brides and grooms to reveal the behaviour that they themselves had or had not defined as 'living together'. For example, when a question about residence immediately prior to the marriage was asked, a card was offered to the respondent listing a range of answers which included 'living with spouse'. In this way, at least cohabitation by propinquity could be established and then further probes were able to elicit more details.

In addition, all newly-weds were asked if they had considered living together, and their attitudes to it. This technique proved successful in identifying two women who were reticent about admitting that they had moved in with their husbands some time before their weddings. However, there were still problems, since in several instances the discrepancy between spouses over whether they had lived together was not due to the women's attempts to deceive but to discrepant definitions of living together: three men who had regularly 'stopped over' in their girlfriends' flats overnight had reported this as living together, whereas the women concerned had not.

'Stopping over'

Where one member of a courting couple is living independently of parents it is likely that the couple will spend most of the time there. Since parents are more tolerant of (and less anxious about) their sons than their daughters staying out at night, it is not surprising that of the eleven women in our study who before marriage were living independently of their parents, seven had lived with their future husband and four were used to him stopping-over regularly. The following descriptions are provided by two husbands, one of whom considered that he *had* lived with his spouse-to-be, while the other did not:

Did you consider living together?
> 'Well we did [live together] because although I was living with my parents and Sandra was in the hostel, when I finished work I would go to Sandra's and I wouldn't bother to go home.'

The second husband had a different view about a similar living arrangement:

Can you tell me where you were living just prior to your marriage?
> 'With my parents – oh, hang on – well as she had the house and it was winter we – er – I wouldn't call it living together, but I was staying there, having breakfast and going to work . . . '

Did you consider living together?
> 'Living together with our two families as they are would not have been on.'

Why?
> 'Not acceptable – well I don't believe in it either – you either do or you don't, but I suppose what I just said sounds like we were living together – it was just that you watch the midnight movie – and it's midnight – and you are in a warm place and you don't want to go home, so I'd stay there.'

Moving in together

Just before marriage, if the marital home has already been arranged, it may be possible for the couple to move in together with parental acceptance. Moving-in together in this way was tolerated by the newly-weds' parents because it was not regarded as a blatant defiance of convention. Once again, however, while the husbands defined this as having lived together, their wives did not:

> 'Well we lived – no we – it was only when the flat came up that we

decided to move in – because Steve had a flat in Cricklewood and it was ridiculous, so we moved in here about six weeks before we got married but of course we stayed at our homes the night before [the wedding].'

Did you consider living together?
'No, I didn't want to, really – I thought, well, if he wants to live with me he can marry me.'—*Mrs Roberts*

'Well, just before we got married I was living with Rosemary – I sort of got up and went home for a clean shirt every now and then and said "Hello" to my parents, but you know, basically I was living here.'— *Mr Oliver*

Living together in the parents' home

Women who felt they had to get away from difficult circumstances at home, and men who usually through study or work were living a long way from their parents, were those most likely to move into their current boyfriend or girlfriend's parental home. Most of the couples who did this considered themselves to have been living together before marriage, although occasionally it was difficult to determine the difference between simply residing in the future spouse's parental home and living *with* the future spouse in her parents' home.

Only two of the seven couples who lived together in this way made it clear that they were living together in the home of one of their families, and they had parental acceptance if not approval. One young bride whose boyfriend's family lived in Cornwall said that when her boyfriend moved in she had been unsure of marriage; in the end, her parents's feelings about the arrangement contributed to her decision to marry:

Were you actually living together?
'Yes'

And that worked out all right with your parents?
'Yes'

Was there any particular reason why you decided to get married rather than continue living together?
'At the time we were living together I was still quite against the idea of marriage and I thought, we'll live together – there seemed no dif- ference – I don't really see the difference.'

So why did you decide to marry?
'Because it would please me deep down – I felt it would please me, and if we didn't it would upset my parents and other members of the family.'

In the other instances the couples and their parents appear to have conspired to keep the arrangement vague:

> 'I'm not too sure whether Kathleen's Mum actually knew she was sleeping with me – I think she probably did but she never actually brought it up.'

This last remark demonstrates the way in which parents were protected from any certainty of knowledge of premarital sexual activity, a reason perhaps why 'stopping-over' stopped short of 'moving-in'. Even with couples who had set up house together for a substantial period before marriage, the reality of the cohabitation was often concealed from the parents:

> 'Every time mother came over I had to put all my things in the back bedroom to make out as if that was my room and that was Tony's . . . she was quite nosey when she came over – I think she knew but she didn't want to be told'.—*Mrs Castle*

There seems to be a distinction recognised by the couples themselves between living together prior to marriage and living together as an alternative to marriage; the latter was regarded as being an attempt to live as a married couple without any clear intention of marriage. One young wife who had moved into a flat with her future husband ten months before their marriage explained this distinction:

And where were you living just prior to the marriage?
'Here.'

And your husband?
> 'Here as well . . . we didn't live together – sleep together. We lived together and slept separately because there are two bedrooms . . . I don't see the point of living together and just not doing anything about it, just living and carrying on . . . I didn't want my parents thinking about it. I told them – they knew all about it, I asked them if they would mind and they said no. I still would probably have done it but I just wanted them to know about it rather than behind their backs . . . I was quite surprised [at her parents' reaction] – my father said he was all for it . . . I thought he'd say "no daughter of mine", etc . . . He said "You know, if you've got any problems you can find them out there and then before you commit yourself". I just didn't want the label you can get when you live together.'

Not surprisingly, those couples who declared that they had lived together were usually positive about the experience, for it provided an opportunity to get to know each other 'warts and all', an experience not available to the traditionally defined courting couple. Mr and Mrs Castle moved in together after their engagement about a year before their marriage, and here Mrs Castle discusses the benefits of living together:

'Yes, I think it was something we both benefited from – let's face it, when a chap takes a girl out for two or three evenings a week – you might think they know each other but you don't until you are actually living under the same roof as somebody else – share the same bed – doing all his washing – fight for the bathroom in the morning and it's all the funny habits – you know, individual habits each of you have got and also your moods – Tony tends to be quite – well he used to be very moody and if things didn't just go quite as he wanted them to he would just go very quiet – very moody – if he knew you wanted to go out shopping he would go out deliberately and start digging the garden over or something like that – so it would keep you waiting – but he's not now – not so much.'

Being able to put the relationship to the test could be both a benefit and a disadvantage of premarital cohabitation. As one young wife explained, getting married meant that she could relax:

'When we got the flat it came at the right time [six months before the wedding] – so we were going to get married anyway and I personally felt happier when we got married. I must admit I felt as though I was taking a deep breath, whereas when we were living together I found we were more on edge because we were always too wary of what the other one was doing – that is another thing that changed for the better when we got married.'—*Mrs Mead*

In coming to a decision about which couples were to be defined as having lived together before marriage, it was decided to include only those who lived independently of parents, with the exception of the two couples who made it very clear that they had been accepted as 'living together' in the parental home. This means that 'stopping-over', however regularly, has not been included in our definition, although 'moving-in' together before the wedding has. Based on these criteria, seventeen couples, (26 per cent of the newly-weds) had lived together before marriage. Over a half of these had lived together for a year or more, and only four of the seventeen said that they had started to live together prior to any commitment to marriage. Only one couple had lived together for a substantial period without any decision on either side of getting married.

In general, however, the newly-weds were not in favour of living together and about two-fifths of the brides and a third of the grooms said they had never even considered it. Although about a quarter of the grooms and brides expressed negative views about living together, none the less, in general, more of the grooms were in favour of it. Parental disapproval was the most frequently given reason for not living with the spouse:

Had you and Helen considered living together?

'We discussed it . . . we didn't because we were lucky in that we had a fair amount of freedom at home. We had a lot of time to ourselves if we wanted it . . . I think we would have soured a few parental relationships if we had.'

Any particular parental relationships?

'Both [laugh] . . . we thought about it, we always thought we'd be getting married by a certain time, so we always had the goal of getting the house, so the fact of living together prior to that didn't seem too important.'

Occasionally, women expressed the fear that moving-in with the boyfriend might remove an incentive for marriage, and this was particularly the case for one marriage seeker, 'I never considered it; I thought if he wants to live with me he can marry me first.'

From our data, although sexual intimacy in courtship was widely accepted by courting couples (and even their parents) as natural, and beneficial to marital happiness, cohabitation prior to marriage was still generally not accepted by them. Even though a quarter of the newly-weds lived together before marrying, they did not regard this as an alternative to marriage. For the remaining three-quarters of newly-weds (and especially their parents) the idea of living together was unacceptable, even when considered as a final phase of courtship.

The scene set for marriage

Once a couple feel 'ready for marriage' a momentum for marriage is set up, a momentum which can either be accelerated or broken by the circumstances of that particular courtship. The couple recognise that a commitment to each other has been made, and they then become caught up in the intricacies involved in the actual process of 'getting married'. Sooner or later the commitment between them becomes public (either formally or informally), and this marks a further stage in the process of 'getting married', a process which is not at all the same as being 'ready for marriage'.

5 Getting Married

Oh, let us be married
too long we have tarried.
But what shall we do for a ring?

The Owl and the Pussycat
Edward Lear

The relationship between a man and a woman before their wedding provides a background history to the marriage; it may also furnish clues to its success. Predicting which marriages will endure and which will flounder in order to develop a formula for marital happiness has long been a preoccupation of social scientists, particularly in the United States. Tests were developed which were founded upon the theory that the outcome of a marriage depended upon choosing the 'right' partner (someone like oneself) and that very little or no conflict in courtship indicated that the couple were likely to continue to get on well with each other, after marriage.[1]

In view of our high divorce rate, it is understandable that those who are particularly concerned with marriage, such as the clergy and counselling agencies, will look for ways of preventing marital breakdown, by attempting to use the premarriage period as a time for preparing the couple for married life and, by implication, enabling them to test out the suitability of their match.

Can it be said that certain marriages appear to be divorce-prone, with the seeds of their destruction already having been sown in courtship? It does appear that highly disturbed and disrupted courtships are more likely to feature among couples who eventually divorce, but such disruptions can be associated with a variety of factors: stresses and strains arising from social and environmental disadvantage; or personalities marrying who have difficulty in forming and maintaining close relationships. In practice, a certain amount of disruption in courtship is no more than a normal part of adjusting to the transition from being single to being married. And even breaking up and reuniting may be a ritual feature in the process, while quarrelling can be a potent form of communication between the couple – a way for them to get to know one another and break down the false, romantic images which are part of 'falling in love'.

STAGES IN MARITAL COURTSHIP

When a couple decide that the relationship is serious it is the beginning of a new stage in the process of getting married. Although retrospectively the marital courtship may seem to be simply the time between deciding that the relationship has the potential for marriage, and the actual day of the wedding, in fact it consists of a sequence of unfolding stages.

'After deciding this is it': stage 1: post-commitment

For most couples, their commitment, their decision to marry, was formally ratified by getting engaged, although, as we have shown, there are two types of engagement, active and passive.[2] The post-commitment stage usually begins when both partners realise that their relationship has a future, and for many this was the moment when they got engaged (passive). From this point on there was a tacit understanding between the couple, of which other people were probably also aware,

> 'He used to refer to me as his Mrs and so did everybody else'— *Mrs Monkhouse.*'

Once the relationship has moved on from 'going out with' to a relationship with 'a future', changes take place, although they may sometimes be hard to detect. Mrs Monkhouse described how she and her husband-to-be went through some 'difficult times':

> 'We had difficult times . . . very difficult times . . . we went through a stage where we argued an awful lot; we couldn't walk home without arguing – we used to keep the subject at "dogs" and still end up arguing. We even argued about which dog we were going to have when we got married.'

The newly-weds reported more quarrels at this stage of the courtship than later on. Once the seriousness of the relationship had been admitted, an increase in conflict could be expected: each partner probably relaxed, tentatively unveiling the 'real me' to each other, so that habits and personality characteristics were revealed and their acceptability to the future spouse thus tested out. This was usually an unconscious form of marriage preparation, although some couples said that they deliberately went away on holiday together or moved in with one another in order to get to know each other better:

> 'We went away on holiday together – somebody lent us a caravan – and my mum had to come with us because Mick's parents didn't think it was right to do that sort of thing – they're very old-fashioned but it was more

to get to know each other than to be near each other – just what it would be like to stay with him all day and every day. It was only for a week in August and after that we decided to get engaged.'

At this stage of the courtship, quarrelling is primarily an opportunity for establishing limits. The fact that almost any discussion can now frequently turn into quarrelling may indicate the inexperience of the couple in handling such matters – they do no yet know each other well enough to anticipate each other's reactions:

So after you decided to get married until you did actually get married, did you ever have any difficulties or quarrels in that time between the two of you?

'We didn't have an argument for over a year – most surprising. When we did have an argument, I used to argue worse than Maggie, I used to be able to beat her every time. In the end – about six months before we got married – she used to agree with everything I said and, all of a sudden, I thought, "That's wrong, she can't agree with *everything* I say – we're not that much alike", and I phoned her up one evening and I said "What are we playing at, you're supposed to have an opinion of your own", sort of thing, "You might have to say something I might not like – in fact, I'll probably shout at you for saying it but", I said, "you might as well say it because otherwise I'm going to walk all over you".'

Quarrelling can be highly provocative and stimulating – the lover's tiff is part of the ritual of courting because the response to it confirms commitment, and this seemed to be especially so for women, as two of them showed:

'I handed his ring back I think about twice – over silly things but it developed into a terrific row – I sort of just lost my temper and gave him the ring back – I never left him – although I'd handed him the ring back – we had an argument in the car and he got so hysterical that I couldn't leave him – I was frightened that something would happen to him.'

'Yeah, I used to row with him – but the next night I used to think "Oh, I don't know" and that was it – I used to say, "I don't know but I might put it all off, Steve, and all this, and he used to get on his knees and in the end say "Oh no, no, please don't".'

But such quarrelling is often more than conflict between the spouses; it may also be the result of conflict within the individual who is trying to come to terms with the demands that the relationship is making – and will increasingly make – on his or her personal privacy and independence. One woman recognised this very clearly:

'It was a total conflict in myself. I couldn't quite shake him off. I used to try to create arguments so he would say "Right, I don't want to see you

again" and make it easy for me, but I couldn't possibly bring myself to say
"I don't want to see you any more" because I did. Something within
myself kept saying "get rid of him or you are going to get more and more
fond of him".'

Why do you think you didn't want to get more fond of him?
'Because I wanted to have lots more adventures.'—*Mrs Moncrieff*

As we saw in the meandering courtships described in the previous
chapter, it was often just at this stage that those relationships
foundered. A couple broke up because one or both of the partners
realised that he or she was not yet ready for all that marriage meant:

'I felt like I was probably getting a bit bogged down so we sort of stopped
for a bit and then . . . '

And how long after that did you get back together again?
'I think it was about – it wasn't very long – a couple of months, and then I
think we were going for another couple of years and then we split up
again – I think we were both getting to the stage where we thought "Well,
we either get engaged or we think about getting married or we *don't*", and
I sort of bottled out – I sort of got cold feet really and we stopped doing it
and then Debbie became quite ill really.'

It is interesting that the 'serious relationships' which many of the
brides and grooms had had earlier with other boy and girl friends and
which had not led to marriage, had also usually broken up at this
post-commitment stage. Although several of the newly-weds had also
felt unready for marriage with their marriage-partners at this same
point, the difference was that this time they had not wanted to break
the commitment to the relationship altogether. They had needed to
declare some sort of moratorium, and so, by means of quarrelling and
'mock' break-ups, they skilfully and effectively managed to adjust the
pace of the relationship, while enabling it still to carry on – ultimately
to marriage. The post-commitment stage was thus extended and the
pre-wedding build-up to the marriage delayed. This technique was
particularly noticeable in couples where one partner was a marriage-
seeker:

'I said I can't stand just drifting with our relationship – I just felt "What
the hell's going on" – we went on for a time when I think I liked him more
than he liked me and I became aware of this – I am not the type of person
who says "All right, that's it", you know "You don't like me as much as I
like you" [laughs] – I'm much more a person who perseveres and tries to
make things work out . . . '

Another major source of conflict was the response made by the
parents of some couples to the announcement of the couple's

commitment. Although some parental disapproval (from at least one set of parents) was expressed over almost half of the forthcoming marriages, it was not always possible to establish any specific objection: often there was just a general expression of concern. Sometimes the parents were disappointed over the choice of the future spouse: he or she wasn't 'good enough', or came from a very different background:

> 'Well, Robin's mother and father aren't very friendly, I don't mean they're not – they're just that way inclined, they don't say "come in and sit down and have a cup of tea" and make you welcome – I'm used to being treated in a friendly sort of way and I didn't like it and they had a better house and I had the feeling that they didn't like me, they didn't think I was good enough for him, but he said it was just the way they gave that attitude but I don't know, it didn't seem that way at first.'

There were also parents who were over-protective and simply resistant to the idea that their child was old enough to marry, or who were wistful about lost educational and career goals which would now be abandoned because of marriage:

> 'At first when my mum and dad knew that we were getting very serious, they didn't like it. They had known that I had all these ideas about university . . . and somehow thought that Mick was stopping me from doing that, no matter how I explained it to my dad. And also I think he looked on me as his little girl and nobody else's and it was very hard. So we had a bit of a rough time . . . my dad probably thought that he was letting me slip through his fingers.'

In some other cases, however, parents had expressed a clear dislike or disapproval of the future spouse, although rarely did they attempt to interfere directly with the progress of the courtship. One bride had nevertheless felt very aggrieved:

> 'I took an instant dislike to his dad when he called me a tart because I had once been pregnant, but they didn't seem to remember that their own daughter had had an abortion when she was fourteen – and they didn't take into account the fact that I was twenty – I was a lot older when it happened to *me* – *she* was fourteen. I was "not nice" for their son – and they said this to Richard.'

More frequently, it was the prospective husbands who felt criticised:

> 'They didn't like me – the way I was dressed [as a Teddy Boy] . . . but as soon as I started wearing flared trousers and changing my hair, we got on all right.'

> 'Her father thought we were too young and he didn't get on with my family – but I didn't care – I married *her* not her family and she married *me* not the family.'

The most negative attitudes towards the prospective marriages were apparently expressed by the parents of the men, and especially their mothers. However, it could be that men were simply more likely than women to report such hostility. Since our interviews took place only three months after the 'rosy glow' of the wedding, it would be very understandable that some respondents may well have overlooked or even suppressed earlier negative reactions from their parents. It was also remarkable how many of the respondents who had complained of earlier criticism from in-law parents, later reported a complete transformation of the relationship by the time the wedding took place.

'Getting close to the big day': Stage 2: the pre-wedding stage

When the 'active' engagement period starts, the relationship changes gear once more, and the plans for the wedding start in earnest. The whole marriage sequence begins to get under way: the vicar is visited, deposits are paid and the world outside acknowledges that a wedding has been arranged. Pulling out from the marriage at this stage seems less of an option, and our respondents reported less quarrelling and few break-ups in this period. Interestingly, for some couples the quarrelling they had experienced in Stage 1 of the courtship even began to reap benefits: the couples felt they knew more about each other and were more skilful at communicating. Mrs Monkhouse described how untypical for them the extent of their quarrelling in Stage 1 had been:

> 'We pulled ourselves out of it [post-commitment period of quarrelling and one break-up] . . . we realised that we had managed to get through a stage and we looked back and saw that Shirley and Bill [husband's sister and brother-in-law] went through exactly the same . . . you know, her engagement ring got lost, she threw it back at him so many times . . . we realised that those two are particularly hot-tempered, whereas we don't like arguing a lot. We only argued about little things after that.'

Another factor which may have led to the decrease in quarrelling in Stage 2 was that its effect would have been far more disruptive as the wedding day got closer. As the web of commitments which comprised the wedding plans drew tighter, so it was increasingly important to be cohesive. The main sources of 'friction' (this was the word most frequently used to describe conflict at this stage) in the pre-wedding days, were things directly concerned with the wedding itself: whether to have 'the works' or restrain it to a small wedding; who would pay for what; and who was to be invited.

By this time the couple tended to be leading a much more settled life, staying in more because they were saving for the wedding and/or a home of their own. This made some husbands feel that they had been stranded at home too soon before actually being 'tied down', so that money featured strongly in pre-wedding disagreements:

> 'Financial things – getting on edge – it was getting close – we can't afford this and that – we almost had an argument about what she was going to wear.'—*Mr Wilson*

> 'Jonathan likes going out – at the weekend he does like his little night out if he's worked all the week – and at one point I got so uptight about spending money . . . in the end we sorted it out – we put so much money away then what we'd got over we spent . . . *Money* – I think a lot of people argue over that.'—*Mrs Klein*

> 'Just the normal sort of rows – over the marriage – her dad wanted to get highly involved and I didn't want him to – the wedding breakfast and all this caper . . . all *I* wanted was a buffet with free booze and that's it – and a band.' [In the end the bride's father gave them £600 to 'do what you want' and they decided to do it the husband's way because his sister had married in July and had had that sort of wedding.]—*Mr Monkhouse*

Parents' negative feelings towards the marriage frequently became channelled into disputes over the wedding, and even some of those who had previously felt positive began to create difficulties over practical problems. Usually, however, this was a symbolic expression of the tug of loyalties which any marriage, in initiating a new family group, can easily cause:

You said your father wouldn't come to the wedding?'
'Well, he wouldn't give me away.'

'What was his objection?
'Well, he said it was because we were living together – we lived together before we got married for about five months to sort of just give it a try – so that if either of us changed our minds we wouldn't have all that legal binding sort of thing, and I think that's the excuse my dad used – but . . . there was a lot of bitterness at home [her parents had only recently divorced] . . . he had said he would give us £100, and then when he found out that we were moving in together – I mean I didn't lie to him – I could have told him I was here on my own and try to get round it that way, but I didn't. I just came straight out with it and told him that we had moved in and he called me all the names he could lay his tongue to and just said that he didn't want anything to do with it and that he

wouldn't give me away and wouldn't even come to the church and he
wasn't going to give us any money – and we ended up having a big
argument.'

In addition to some fathers like this one, who refused point blank to
'give away' their daughters, there were also other families where
parents threatened not to attend the wedding, or not to contribute
financially to it. One wife referred to the glowering rivalry and
complications which threatened to arise over the problem of who was
to pay for the wedding:

'There was all the hubbub about who was going to pay for the wedding
reception – oh God – it was terrible . . . '

Who did pay?
'They went halves in the end.'

What – both sets of parents?
'Ronnie and me paid for the wedding but *his* parents, Vic and Kath, paid
for the reception – all the drinks and that. The week before the wedding
Vic and Kath said they weren't going to come because – I don't
know – there was all the hullabaloo about the money and "who" was
going to spend "what" on "which". Vic is like a sergeant-major you know,
and he wanted everything done his way because it was his son. My parents
weren't going to get a look in at all. Then Ronnie said to me – and we had
an argument about it – "*Your* parents aren't interested – they don't want
us to get married." I said "It's not that – it's just hard for them to come by
the money to pay for it." Well, it sorted itself out. I said to Vic and Kath
"Right, I don't care – it's us that's getting married – we don't need you at
the wedding." But it all turned out for the best.'

And in fact, despite the earlier difficulties, this bride found her actual
wedding an unexpectedly reconciliatory experience as far as she and
her own stepfather were concerned:

'At the wedding I had my dad *and* my stepdad, and I saw my mum – I
know it might sound stupid – but I saw my mum and my *dad* dancing
together, and then my mum and my *stepdad* dancing together and it just
looked so right for my stepdad to be with my mum – and now I'm married
I think I realise more what she felt for him, but I used to be so horrible to
him – it's unbelievable – yet he's given up – what – fifteen years of his
life to look after us, when he didn't have to . . . and he's been really
fantastic to me since I've been married.'

Although at this particular wedding everything had been satisfactorily resolved, the respective roles of a bride's father and stepfather
can present a real problem.[3]
Generally speaking, those parents who had at Stage 1 of the
courtship been negative or even hostile to the forthcoming marriage,

had, by Stage 2, come round to accepting it. Nevertheless, the glowing clichés which some prospective husbands used in their interviews to describe the transformed relationships they now had with their in-laws, did not sound entirely convincing:

> '. . . now we get on like a house on fire.' [From husband who had earlier been banished from the house]

> 'we had that stinking argument . . . but since then she [wife's mother] has been as good as gold.'

> 'now – everything in the garden is lovely, shall we say?'

> 'ever since that row – we've been the best of friends.'

There was, however, once instance where a mother-in-law really did appear to see her son-in-law in a completely different light. Mr and Mrs Brothers had had a meandering courtship, which had started when they were both teenagers. At that stage, Mrs Brothers' mother had considered Mr Brothers unsuitable as a boyfriend for her daughter, had actively sought to break up the relationship, and had succeeded. However, her daughter then became involved with another boy (he also was later considered unsuitable) by whom she became pregnant, had his baby and had it adopted. Eventually, Mrs Brothers met up again with the first boyfriend, whom she decided she now wished to marry. The second time her mother met him she regarded him quite differently – as a fine prospective son-in-law, since she now perceived him favourably in relation to the unsatisfactory nature and behaviour of the previous boyfriend. As Mrs Brothers explained:

> 'I think after what happened previously she was pleased to see me with somebody that had settled. George, by that time, had grown up a lot and was a lot more sensible than when she knew him when he was 15–16 . . . she was relieved to see that he was steady and that *I* could lean on *him* because this other fellow had a tendency to rely on me.'

Mrs Patmore also was a bride with problems. She had run into difficulties with her prospective in-laws just before the wedding, although up to then her courtship had been fairly trouble-free. She was dismayed to discover that her potential husband's family had involved him heavily in the traumas of the pregnancy of his unmarried sister, and she was particularly concerned that he had said nothing about it to her. As it turned out, Mr Patmore found that his sister was not pregnant after all, and this then became his excuse for him not having told his fiancée. However, as far as Mrs Patmore was concerned, this incident had revealed two aspects of her relationship with her husband which continued to worry her: she was unhappy about the continued dependence of his family (particularly his mother) upon him, and she was also upset because he himself had excluded her from the situation since she 'wasn't yet one of the family':

> 'He didn't tell me so I got rather upset about it to think that I was the last one to know anything and we had a few arguments about that, but it turned out she wasn't pregnant anyway and it was a big thing about nothing, but it did hurt me to feel that he didn't tell me about it and we had an argument about that – that was when I sort of had a go at him, saying that his mother would have to learn to – she would have to go to his father – you know, she couldn't keep coming to Keith all the time. She'd not even told his father about the pregnancy, so everything had fallen on Keith.'

At this pre-wedding stage, very few of the quarrels concerned the habits and personality characteristics of the spouse, although we were given a few instances of bridegrooms 'behaving badly' as part of an attempt to savour the final taste of freedom. One of these husbands admitted:

> 'The month in between when we said we were going to get married and the actual marriage date, I suppose I *was* taking extra liberties – you know – drinking . . . she was going to call it all off . . . I think she might have – I was a bit of an alcoholic – well not an alcoholic but a bit of a heavy drinker – "What are you going to be like when I marry you?" I'm not really that way – I didn't even realise I was making the last of my freedom, but every time I met somebody it was "Come and have a quick one" and you just get involved. And she said "Either you give the drink up – cut it down and calm down or . . .".'

For some men this urge for a final fling was legitimised and excused by saving the 'bad' behaviour for the eve of the wedding – the stag night. In general, however, rather the opposite seemed to be the case: most husbands-to-be were perceived by their fiancées as having been transformed by the forthcoming wedding into ideal partners! As one wife described it:

> 'It was quite funny – it's hard to explain – going out with him before and then him being what he was like during the actual run up to the wedding – you know, going out and buying his suit and his shoes – he looked quite a different person – *he's back to the old one now* but . . .'

In what way was he different?

> 'More caring and – I don't know – I can't really explain it – but he was really proud that he was getting married. If you had known Patrick before that it was totally out of character.'

A WEDDING IN CHURCH

Since all the newly-weds interviewed had had the choice of where the wedding was to take place, they were asked why they had decided to marry in church. Most people were able to say why they had opted for an occasion which would, on however modest a scale, make considerable demands on them in matters of expense, preparation and organisation. However, one (or quite often both) of the partners believed that to have the wedding in a church would offer them direct or indirect benefits which far outweighed the cheaper and less complicated option of the register office ceremony.

The brides and grooms were also questioned about their own and their parents' denominational allegiances, and their own curent religious practice (if any) in terms of church attendance. Denominational allegiance, both for the couples and for their parents, appeared very rarely to be of more than nominal significance. Two-thirds of both the men and the women said that they now never went to church, with a further quarter going only at festival times: Christmas, Harvest Festival, weddings, and so on. The very few (six) who did attend church regularly, included two couples whose religious beliefs clearly influenced many of their decisions in addition to that of being married in church. The husband of one of these illustrated this when he told of how he and his wife had, from the very beginning, been aware of a sense of divine guidance in their relationship with each other:

> 'The very day we started to go out Gwen had to go back to college at Islington, which is no distance, as you know, from Hackney. So I took her up in the car, and we were going straight there, but every single traffic light was red, so we thought, "Hello – what's this all about?" We found a back street and went and prayed about it and decided it was right to go and see Gwen's parents, so we popped in to see them that day. I was holding Gwen's hand, which I suppose indicated that we were doing something, but I didn't really mean to say we were going out or anything like that.'

'We're not deeply religious but. . . . '

Despite their apparent lack of religious adherence or practice, on the whole the newly-weds displayed a surprisingly marked awareness of a spiritual dimension; they had a notion of the sacred, a sense of the numinous. A wedding in church was chosen for its spiritual and transcendental associations by almost a quarter of the women and well over a tenth of the men. They revealed this in the way they said that 'nothing else would do – I think marriage is sacred', or 'I don't practise but I do believe in God'.

And one woman was particularly emphatic:

> 'I thought I would never feel properly married if I didn't get married in a church; we're not deeply religious either of us but I do believe in some kind of Being, and so in a way it was like a public pledge that we take with the little blessing of somebody else.'

One man implied his belief in a deity rather more obliquely:

> 'I suppose we are religious in convictions if not in actions – we believe in good and evil and all that.'

He went on to recount how during the wedding there was a storm, with a loud clap of thunder at the very moment they were pronounced man and wife, and the curate had said, 'That's a message of approval from God.'

Several newly-weds referred to the importance to them of being married 'in the eyes of God' or of having their weddings blessed, even though in the next sentence they might hasten to disclaim themselves from being 'sickly religious'. One such woman said:

> 'I'm not a regular churchgoer but I do believe in God – I don't think you have to go to church to believe in Him and I thought it was much nicer to have His blessing – especially if you had been troubled.'

(Her father had died a few months' previously and she had been distressed about that, as well as being concerned about marrying and leaving her mother on her own. All this had caused her considerable tension about her forthcoming marriage.)

'More sort of binding'

The reasons given most frequently by the newly-weds for having their wedding in church suggested a belief in the marriage service as offering some kind of symbolic affirmation of their undertaking, an acknowledgement of the serious import of the occasion. Some had a wish to make the marriage a special and binding public commitment 'more of a seal on it', coupled with, for others, the recognition of the uniqueness of the event. Additionally, a small number also mentioned the need to have and cherish memories and photographs of a special occasion, 'a day to remember':

> 'I think it is partly tradition but also to me it's more sort of right – it's more sort of binding and I think it's nice for – I mean that it's the bride's

day . . . the one thing in her life that she wants to look back on – and especially if you have children – they are going to want to see the photographs – the couples that I know that have got married and had no wedding photographs or nothing, they miss them – they are things you can't get after – you know – it's there once and gone.'

One woman who earlier 'wasn't really bothered whether it was a church or not', now said that she was glad it had been a church wedding:

'I think it gives you a lot more to remember . . . I think when we went to see the vicar and we went over the service . . . I'd never really listened to the words of the service before, but you really understood what you were saying. I think it was . . . a nice sense of occasion and it's something a lot of people could share because we had a lot of people there in the church.'

Wedding rituals, such as the bride's father giving her away and the final procession of the newly-weds followed by the mother of the bride, arm-in-arm with the groom's father through the assembly of family and friends, seem more 'natural' when co-ordinated by a clergyman within a church setting. As one groom explained:

'I'm not religious but I must say the Church does it all so well. You might feel silly doing all those things, I thought I would . . . saying the vows . . . but it all seems right. You go in as you were and come out different – as a real married couple.'

These ritual actions may appear strange and irrelevant in modern times, yet they are performed with surprisingly little self-consciousness by thousands of people every year. They form part of a 'symbolic grammar'; when men and women conform to such displays of ritual they are recognising the breaking of old ties and the forging of new relationships which are implicit in marriage:

'symbolic grammar is a language to express the meaning of relationships – their purpose, expected pattern of interaction, the framework of assumptions about the world in which they fit.'[4]

'The Register Office – over in ten minutes'

Some of the most revelatory comments about the significance of the church wedding were given by about a fifth of both men and women, who made spontaneous but disparaging reference to the idea of a register office wedding. The register office ceremony was variously described as 'not an occasion', 'just signing a bit of paper . . . not a marriage', 'no atmosphere', 'like going into an office' and 'very, very cold – all sort of cut and dried, bleak and miserable'.

When one man had gone to a register office to get the form for marriage, he found it a disappointing place: 'It hit me that it seemed just like getting a car tax disc or something like that – no solemnity.'

The newly-weds felt that the ceremony in the register office failed to acknowledge 'the biggest occasion of your life', or the 'important step of marriage'. One woman said she felt very keenly that her wedding was:

> 'A day in our lives that we always want to remember, whereas in the register office it is all over in ten minutes and you just don't feel married . . . the service is so short . . . it just wouldn't feel the same [as in church], with the ceremony and having the vicar to do it and bless us properly – it made it all seem worthwhile – it was one special day and we're going to be together for ever and ever.'

Not only was it the shortness of the register office ceremony that was the deterrent; one bride admitted that part at least of the reason why she and her husband had chosen to marry in an Anglican church was because of its age and its romantic setting:

> 'We knew what the register office looked like and where it was, and it was such a nasty looking building – concrete – one of those new modern concrete blocks with bits and pieces round it – it wasn't romantic enough to me [laugh] and of course we both liked history, and the church round the corner is fairly old . . . and the graveyard is beautiful and it's so nice round there.'

'A wedding with all the trimmings'

The idea of white wedding, a 'proper wedding' had a strong appeal for the young couples, and was mentioned by almost half the women and a third of the men. One couple, interestingly both atheists, were fully aware that they were going to 'use' the church, but they wanted to 'have all the trimmings'. Since the traditional image of a wedding is of a bride in filmy white floating up the aisle, it is hardly surprising that it was so popular. For some women it was clear that the traditional fairytale notion of a white wedding had been a long-cherished dream:

> 'I think all girls dream of a big white wedding and all the rest of it.'

> 'That's what I had really set my heart on – getting married in church – every girl does – you know – want a big wedding.'

In many ways a wedding is regarded as a fantasy, so it is hardly surprising that the chance to live it out should be welcomed. In addition, a wedding is one of the very few occasions in contemporary life where special dress and traditional behaviour can still obtain, and the opportunity for 'splendour' strongly visual and choreographic as well as social, had a very strong appeal, and not only to women. As some men admitted:

> 'I like the flamboyance of it, to be honest.'
> 'I suppose [I like] the show of it all.'
> 'I want to wear a top hat and tails . . . I am a bit of a big-head'

And another man spoke enthusiastically of:

> '[The] pomp and ceremony – the general atmosphere . . . it makes people a lot happier – the build-up to it . . . to buying the dress, getting people ready – the surroundings of it.'

while his wife felt it was splendid because of:

> 'All the glory . . . the register office isn't the same, you don't have to dress up [there] . . . with a church there's so much about it – all the people and dressing up and everything – it's lovely.'

Two of the women, one premaritally pregnant, the other already having a child, both expressed ambivalence towards a white wedding. They had wanted one and felt they 'deserved' it but had had some reservations about wearing the traditional white dress: in the end they decided to compromise and wore cream.

'A great big fuss and palaver'

There are always those who are uncomfortable with any kind of formality, and it is likely that, increasingly in the future, such people may well choose not to have any ceremony of marriage, let alone a wedding in church.

Among our group, however, even those least happy with the ceremonial had agreed to it, although in their interviews they expressed their personal dislike of the 'big fuss and palaver' and 'all the paraphernalia of the traditional wedding'. One man complained vigorously:

> 'My wife wanted to get married in church . . . but *I* would have walked into a register office and signed the register and given the bloke his money.'

He went on to say that whereas he had wanted a register office wedding and a small reception:

'*She* got a church wedding and a *big* reception – but it's give and take on your wedding day – really it's your wife's day and that's it – nothing you can do – all you can do is say "yes" and "no" to the vicar – "three bags full sir".'

As many as two out of five grooms in the sample claimed that they had only married in church because of their wives, and that they themselves would have preferred to dispense with the ceremonial. Several wives also stated that they were impatient with the fuss, and one 'couldn't bear the thought of all these bridesmaids and everything', and that she would feel very self-conscious with everyone's eyes on her. She had finally agreed to a church wedding, but compromised by marrying in a 1940's style dress which was 'not a wedding dress' as such, and with no bridesmaids.

'Mostly for the parents really'

A substantial minority of the newly-weds (28 per cent men; 20 per cent women) said their parents' wishes had strongly influenced their decision to marry in church:

'I knew that would please my mum because of her going to church.'

'Mostly for the parents really . . . I wouldn't say I would have liked a register office, but it would have saved me an awful lot of money and I'm not one for a lot of fuss . . . but I'm glad we did have a church wedding.'

One husband was still disgruntled over their having acceded to the wishes of his mother-in-law:

'We were going to have a register office wedding . . . I went down to arrange it but her mum and dad wanted a church wedding.'

For some women, the fact that they were the only child or only daughter reinforced their own decision to marry in church:

'Being an only child it [the church wedding] was how my parents wanted it as well – it was their only chance.'

And, occasionally, the fact that a sister or other family member had *not* married in church persuaded a bride to do so:

'My sister's divorced and she never had a white wedding . . . and Barry and I both wanted it for our parents . . . it's a big day in your life to remember and I think it's nice to have a good start.'

Perhaps a church wedding was perceived not only as an assurance for the parents but also as a talisman, something of benefit to their own marriage. A few brides wanted to continue in their family tradition by having their own wedding in a particular church, one which held strong personal and family memories for them, as was the case with the woman who said, quite simply: 'This was my church – just opposite my house – I'd always gone there – been christened there.'

Another woman said that her parents had been married at the church she married in, as well as she herself having been christened there, and a third one spoke of the 'tradition in our family to marry there'. Even one husband was aware of his wife's family ties: 'nearly all her sisters and brothers got married in that church and she wanted to carry on the tradition'. However, in contrast, one or two of the newly-weds seemed to consider that a wedding in church had been simply an inevitability for them in the light of their upbringing: 'Something I was brought up to do – christening, confirmation and getting married in church.'

DOUBTS ABOUT THE MARRIAGE

Since marriage was such a serious undertaking, it was not surprising that in more than half of our couples (thirty-eight) one or both partners admitted to having had doubts before the wedding, with little difference between men and women. Even in those marriages where no definite doubts were recalled, several husbands believed that their wives may have entertained some, although 'she never actually *mentioned* any'.

Wives seemed to be considerably more adept at picking up their husbands' uncertainties about the marriage than their husbands were about noticing theirs. However, neither husbands nor wives were particularly good at it, since, in those marriages where *both* spouses in their separate interviews had admitted to doubts, in only one third was there any awareness that the other partner also had had misgivings.

'Everyone must have some doubts'

To have some doubts before such a major event in your life as getting married was seen by many of the newly-weds to be very normal: 'Everyone must have *some* doubts'; 'just nerves'; 'nothing serious'; 'only the usual'. And one husband vividly conveyed the common panicky flavour of pre-wedding nerves:

'I think you do [have doubts] – all of a sudden – it was two weeks away you know, and my panic button started to go a little bit . . . and I thought "Christ – what am I doing . . . ?" '

For others, the feeling of some degree of doubt was considered either an inevitable stage in the *rite de passage*, or part of their own ritual teasing and testing process:

'I think we both [had doubts] but when we pulled ourselves out of it we realised that we had managed to go through a stage.'

'We used to say to each other "I don't want to get married" . . . I don't think we meant it . . . probably always intended to marry Susan.'

'Am I doing the right thing?'

Concern over whether or not they were doing the right thing in getting married accounted for the largest number of both men and women who were unsure:

What about Roger – did he have any doubts?
'No – I think he was a bit panic-struck when we actually said the day because it sort of happened so quickly . . . . '

More persistent doubts were expressed by one husband who admitted he had done his best to mask his misgivings:

'Deep down I did [have] although I wouldn't admit them to myself.'

Why do you say that?
'Well, I think I was trying to put on a front almost like that I was sure what I was doing and that I was right – to sort of convince everyone else that I knew what I was doing but . . . you obviously think twice – am I doing the right thing? Although it isn't necessarily for the rest of your life, it is what you hope and you want to make it right the first time if you can.'

Did the doubts go away?
'They went and came back, and went and came back.'

Did you have them right up until you got married?
'Yeah, I think so. I think even now, occasionally, I still think "Well, it's all right *so* far", but you know, we'll have to see how it goes – we've been married no time – it's only three months and we're still getting to know each other.'

One bride, who was already pregnant before the wedding, recalled her very mixed feelings about getting married, both the night before and even on the day itself, when she almost panicked as she walked up the aisle:

'Even on the way down the aisle I said to my dad, "Stop – I want to go . . . I don't want to go on . . . . " I was sort of giggling and crying at the same time.'

Did you mean that?

'Yes, well, up to the minute I was getting married I thought Jeremy was marrying me for the wrong reasons – I was marrying him for the wrong reasons and it was because of the baby that we had to get married. First of all I had wanted to get married *after* the baby was born; I still felt a bit dubious about getting married.'

Did you talk to anyone about it?

'My mum, and she said, "Oh, you always get them when you're getting married and it's only nerves", and I thought to myself "It's not nerves – I know I'm doing the wrong thing", and then when the day came – even walking up the aisle I thought, "Oh, what am I doing . . . what am I doing to Jeremy?" It was always in my mind what I was doing to him. And then when I got there and stood beside him, that was it.'

She went on to speak of the confusion and uncertainty she had also felt the night before the wedding:

'I told him it was all off – I said, "I can't marry you" and he just sat there and said, "You're joking". I said, "I'm not – I just can't go through with it – I don't love you, I don't need you, I can do it all on my own" [so I thought]. He says "Don't talk so daft – so daft – do you love me?" I said "What is love?" and he said "I don't know – do you feel you want me there?" and I said, "No – I don't need you" and I really believed that I didn't need anybody – I was Miss High-and-Mighty and I didn't. It really upset him, and I thought, "Oh, you bitch" – 'cos I didn't really mean to say it – I just didn't know what I wanted.'

A somewhat happier instance of misgiving about the marriage is found in a couple where both partners were aware of each other's doubts and had discussed them to a degree of resolution. The wife attributed her uncertainties to her personality, and considered she had lots of doubts and kept changing her mind 'because I'm that sort of person anyway'. Her husband viewed it slightly more seriously:

'We did have a problem . . . Joanna went through a stage . . . like a mental thing . . . she wasn't sure whether she wanted to get married ever or whether we should call the relationship off. There was no reason – we hadn't argued or anything like that, nothing to pin it down to. She went to the doctor about it – it was depression, that's what it was . . . nothing we'd done wrong to upset the apple-cart . . . I hoped it would sort itself out and it did.'

Later on this husband referred to his own doubts, although he was unable to specify their exact nature, and he said he and his wife had discussed their doubts together and spoken of her fears:

'We both talked . . . Joanna used to ask herself a lot of questions about whether she was doing the right thing . . . she likes to be free to go out – to do what she wants and I think she was afraid deep down of losing that . . . and it wasn't because I don't particularly do a lot. Women have a lot to lose by getting married – which she probably thought she would – but she hasn't lost.'

'I thought of freedom . . . '

This theme, of missing out on freedom, of being too young and not yet ready to settle down, was touched on by almost a quarter of both men and women who had doubts:

'I thought I might be too young to get married – I thought of freedom.'

'I had the fear of missing out on something.'

One man spoke even more strongly of his misgivings:

'I said I need my head examining, getting married at my age – I should be out enjoying myself.'

His wife also spoke of her doubts and fears about her readiness to leave her parental home and lose her family, a feeling, in her case, fostered or even induced by her parents' opposition to the marriage.

'This is for life . . . '

A handful of the newly-weds had had doubts about getting married because of the extent of the commitment they felt it involved: the 'enormity of the decision', or the feeling 'this is for life'. Others were apprehensive about the new and total experience of 'togetherness' which they felt awaited them. One woman spoke of her qualms before her marriage, which had been made much worse by the tiredness she felt as a result of trying to get the marital home together:

'Just all of a sudden there would be just us two together – do you know what I mean? – there's no going home at night on your different ways – you're suddenly together all the time. I must admit a few months before the·wedding I used to have little crying fits – not thinking "Am I doing the wrong thing?" – but I was worried . . . we'd be round here decorating – I think that got us down as well because we were coming here every night after work and decorating – staying here till about eleven – going home and falling into bed. We did talk it over and I got worried . . . I knew I was worrying him.'

'Are we right for each other?'

One final group of doubts was related to the wisdom of marrying that particular partner, either because of misgivings over personality traits or behaviour, or because of insufficient knowledge about him or her. One husband was worried by the prospect of his wife as a potential nagger:

'Oh yeah – I've *still* got doubts [laughs] well – I thought she might be a sort of nagging wife occasionally . . . even on the Saturday morning I went out to get the ring I was more or less having second thoughts.'

In contrast, another husband was concerned lest his future wife were to be too acquiescent and that he might be able to 'walk all over her'. In arguments during courtship he had always won; she had started agreeing with him over everything, and this compliance worried him: obviously, he wanted a 'sparring partner'.

One wife was aware of the very different backgrounds from which she and her spouse had come: she had had a warm and positive relationship with an affectionate family, whereas her husband's parents were divorced and he had never had a good or close relationship with them. She spoke of the discrepancies she had already observed in their responses to things and was worried because, "Simon is not one who shows his emotions . . . . ' And while she herself was very keen to marry, she felt he was 'dragging his feet':

'When we got the mortgage I was, "Ooh, ooh" you know and I said, "Aren't you pleased?" He said "Yes, I'm really pleased", but I like to *show* that I'm pleased and was the affectionate one of the two and I used to hate it really. When we used to go out with friends he would walk three feet in front . . . I just couldn't stand it.'

Another, and very young, wife spoke of the serious doubts she had had about her fiancé when he had struck her in a quarrel, 'But you know how you think everything *will* be all right'. She described the very first time he had hit her, when they were having an argument during their courtship:

'He really hit me hard and nearly put me in hospital. That was over sex . . . we were staying round his friend's house, looking after it for a weekend and he wanted a bit and I didn't want to know, and it started into a row and he starts picking on me – silly little things . . . he says, "I can see what sort of a wife *you're* going to be – once a week or once very three months".'

Other misgivings had arisen in those couples where lengthy periods of unavoidable separation in the courtship period had made them unsure about each other. Since it is this period when the couple are usually able to get to know each other in a variety of moods and situations, those who had been deprived of such an opportunity felt more uncertain about their partners.

One such couple experienced a year of separation. The woman was the daughter of an elderly mother (born when she was forty-eight) and had had no serious boyfriends before her fiancé. They had not lived together and, during the year prior to the wedding, they had met on spasmodic weekends only: 'phoning's not the same'. Both partners were uneasy about the situation, and the man even said:

> 'I was beginning to doubt my own mind – whether we could stand the strain having been apart for a year. Basically, we felt we didn't know each other . . . we didn't see much of each other for about a year.'

However, despite their apprehensiveness, this couple were obviously able to be open with each other and to communicate well, since their interviews revealed that they were the one couple in the study who not only had both expressed their pre-marriage doubts to each other, but were also, independently and accurately, fully aware of the misgivings experienced by the other person.

AFTER THE WEDDING – THE HONEYMOON

'Going away' after the wedding was an essential part of the wedding process for three quarters of the newly-weds. Honeymoon locations ranged from Miami to Clacton-on-Sea; several couples could not afford a 'proper' honeymoon so they took a 'token' one and spent their wedding night in a local hotel. The ideal honeymoon is reputed to be an intensely erotic experience, even though the honeymoon reminiscences of married couples sometimes suggest another side – the shock of intimate revelation. As we showed in the last chapter, the brides and grooms whom we interviewed appeared to avoid possible wedding-night traumas by anticipating them; several of the newly-weds gave this as a reason for pre-marital sexual intimacy.

Erotic discovery may no longer be the purpose of 'going away' yet the honeymoon has not become irrelevant to the marriage process. The contemporary significance of the honeymoon is as a mechanism of transition, a way in which the bride and groom can disappear and later reappear transformed into a newly-married couple. Incidentally, it also provides an opportunity for the couple to relax and recover from the stresses and strains of getting married.

So, the honeymoon, whether it consists of two weeks in a four-star hotel in the Canary Islands or just a long weekend in a caravan in Dorset, is actually the launch into the post-wedding phase of married life, a period when the new recruits to marriage are expected to hibernate, to be absorbed with each other and occupied with the business of setting up home together.

6 Setting Up Home

'It was a strange condition of things, the honeymoon being over, and the bridesmaids gone home, when I found myself sitting down in my own small house with Dora . . . I doubt whether two young birds could have known less about keeping house than I and my pretty Dora did.'

David Copperfield
Charles Dickens

A common portrayal of newly-weds is of them as homemakers. Advertisers, keenly aware of a new generation of consumers, frequently present the post-wedding pair as a smiling couple surrounded by the spoils of the wedding (the presents) amid a colourful chaos of wallpaper and paint pots. It is perhaps as a symbolic statement of the implicit power structure in marriage that *he* is usually shown as smiling *down* at her from his position on top of the stepladder while *she* smiles *up* at him. Nowadays, a wide range of institutions from the British Medical Association to the building societies are at hand with advice to the soon-to-be-married.[1] There are even specialist magazines catering for each season's batch of brides and grooms. Advertisers and marriage pundits alike seem to agree that starting off married life in a home of one's own is a crucial ingredient in the recipe for living happily-ever-after. According to a building society's advertisement, in a guide for those getting married:

> Cramped living conditions cause all sorts of extra hassles that you don't need when you're starting out together . . . of course, your own place is your own place, you can do what you like with it.[2]

This was a sentiment strongly echoed by the newly-weds.

Mr and Mrs Kirkham had put in an offer to buy a maisonette and were expecting to complete the purchase in time for their wedding. However, for a while, 'we thought we were going to lose this place and we knew we couldn't afford anything else'. The church had been booked and all the wedding plans made but nevertheless Mr Kirkham 'made it clear to all the parents that we were only getting married if we got this place'. Temporary accommodation was not an option for him:

> 'I think once you move into a council property or a one-bedroom flat or bed-sitter you can't successfully save as much as you do living at home [with parents] and although we both wanted to get married as quickly as possible, I felt it would have been a strain on our relation-

ship . . . because I've seen what it's done to my mum and dad, they had problems from doing that'.

The link between marriage and independence, symbolised by 'a place of one's own', has been discussed earlier (Chapter 3). Readiness for marriage may be inextricably bound up with a profound desire in young adults to exchange the world of parents for a 'life of one's own'. However, for newly-weds who leave their parents' home in order to marry, the pleasure of home-making can be marred by the fact that *my* home is also *our* home. The enforced togetherness of newly-wed life can at times be resented:

What things about being married do you dislike?
'Just that you can't get away from each other when you want that odd moment on your own. You can get away from each other but you have to tell the other person you want to be on your own – that's the only thing.'—*Mr Lawley*

The majority of the men and women had never lived anywhere but in their parents' home, so that having a place that was demonstrably their own, with decorations which reflected *their* tastes, rather than those of their parents, and which could be 'shown off', was a real pleasure:

'I like living here, just me and John – you can do what you want, you can go out and come in [your own place] and you can do it how you want to do it and have your friends in – show it off – it's nice, isn't it – I've never had my own flat before so it's nice.'—Mrs Cosgrove

The novelty of it all, a new home, new possessions, new routines, new responsibilities, was clearly one of the joys of homemaking, and wives in particular emphasised this. For them, washing up a new dinner service was not a chore (as it had been when they did it for their mothers); even basic routine housework could be exciting because there was the opportunity to use their own brand new household equipment. Setting up home was initially rather like playing in a Wendy House; everything was 'fresh' and 'shining' and indeed it symbolised the beginning of a new life:

'I know it sounds odd but when I've washed up and put away I like looking in the cupboard and seeing all the things, my plates and glasses, shining and new.'—*Mrs Brothers*

'Cleaning the lounge, for example, is my favourite – I love putting the cushions in place and arranging things . . . everything is so fresh . . . and I'll keep it that way.'—*Mrs Madge*

Creating a home not only focuses the future but it gives a sense of purpose to other aspects of life such as work. The newly-wed husbands, in particular, associated the acquisition of a home (and, of course, a spouse) with a new attitude to work – they had something (and someone) to work *for*:

What kind of things about being married do you like?

>'Coming home to *my own place*, to my own home . . . going out to buy things; I don't like shopping for food but if we're going to buy something *for the home* then we'll do it together . . . I like the idea of working *for something* instead of just wasting my life away.'

DETERMINING PRIORITIES

Guides to marriage present a clear set of goals for those contemplating matrimony: first, a 'proper' wedding with 'all the trimmings' followed by 'a honeymoon to remember' from which the happy pair return rested and suntanned to a well-equipped, freshly-decorated and newly-furnished home of their own. Of course, few couples have the necessary resources to achieve all three goals and so priorities need to be determined. For some of the newly-weds, for example, all their savings went into paying for a lavish wedding 'with the full works'. One bride sat on the bed in the bedroom she had slept in since childhood and which she now shared with her husband, surrounded by towering stacks of wedding presents, and proudly showed the photographs of the 'best day of my life'. These wedding photographs, expensively bound in an album bearing the words 'Our Special Day', showed her, princess-like in her full bridal regalia, being driven away with her new husband in a coach and pair. However, the debts arising from the cost of staging such a wedding forced a postponement of plans to get 'our own place' and so the fairytale trip had ended where it had begun – at her parents' home.

Mr and Mrs Cosgrove, on the other hand, had been planning a wedding equally as elaborate as the previous couple when the sudden availability of an unfurnished flat, together with a growing realisation that they would have no parental contribution towards the wedding costs, made them somewhat restrain their ambition:

>'We *were* going to have a horse and carriage but it turned out to be so much money that we had to have just a Rolls Royce.'

Having parents who were willing and able to foot the bill for the wedding allowed many couples to concentrate most of their resources on a proper honeymoon (at least a week of luxurious living) and setting up home. Mr and Mrs Maw had 'a lovely wedding – white Rolls Royce and all' which Mrs Maw's parents had paid for. They had booked to go abroad for their honeymoon but found that 'with the mortgage we couldn't afford both so we cancelled the honeymoon and stayed at home for the week'.

Mr and Mrs Harris had opted for a full white wedding with all the trimmings and spent 'an unreal' fortnight honeymooning in Bermuda. However, when they returned it was to live separately, each with their respective parents, having to content themselves with occasional weekend 'stays' with each other when other members of their families were away. Nevertheless, although this couple were without the accommodation to live together as a couple, even in someone else's household, they possessed more consumer durables than several couples who had bought their own homes. Indeed, one of the problems resulting from their present unusual arrangement was the 'aggravation' caused by the need to store the wedding presents:

> 'Its difficult all round plus the fact that my parents – they've got all the wedding presents in their lounge and upstairs . . . they've got the fridge-freezer in the lounge and the tumbledrier in the hall and boxes and boxes of things and, you know, my mum says she just can't clean.'

NEWLY-WED LIFESTYLES

Nest building is at the core of the newly-wed lifestyle. Not having a place that is theirs deprives a just-married pair of choice and control over their environment and results in a frustrating lack of privacy and autonomy. However, there is more to setting up home than simply having a 'place of one's own'. The key nest-building activities of homemaking and housekeeping assist the newly-married couple in assimilating into married life by providing them with the opportunity to play out the roles of husband and wife. Without a home of their own, the newly-weds have no setting in which to behave as proper married people and are unable to get very far with the serious business of 'being married'.

Mr and Mrs Owen had, like many newly-weds, started to look for a home while courting. They had planned to buy a flat around the time of their wedding but the sale fell through and they were forced to start married life sleeping in a spare bedroom of a friend's flat and visiting Mrs Owen's parents' for all their meals. A rise in property prices meant that this couple needed to save more money for a deposit for their own flat so three months after their wedding they had come to accept that this 'temporary' arrangement was likely to last well into their first year of marriage. Mr and Mrs Owen's frustrated nest-building had been confined to 'collecting' items for their future home – they were like a courting couple, building up their bottom drawer:

> 'We've been buying things like electric kettles and a toaster, we started saving up a bottom drawer – so when we do move in there's nothing we'll have to buy except the bed.'

And the delay in establishing their own household had affected Mr Owen's perception of the marriage: 'Well, it's not so much a marriage yet . . . because we haven't moved into our own place yet.'

It seems that in order to settle into married life, newly-weds require an independent setting which is adequate for their current needs and secure at least for the immediate future; somewhere worth settling into. Most (though not all) of the couples who were not sharing, were therefore settled. There were a few couples who, although living on their own, were in unsatisfactory and (they hoped) temporary conditions. Such transitory settings frustrated their attempts to settle down.

The settled couples

Just over half of the newly-weds (55 per cent) started their first year of marriage living on their own in accommodation which they had chosen and where they could expect to remain for at least a couple of years. Most of them were buying their own homes with a mortgage and for some the decision to take on the financial burden of a mortgage meant there was little money left over for buying things for the home. Mr and Mrs Evans had struggled to save the deposit for their new house and were finding that repaying the mortgage dominated their financial outgoings. Their only consumer durable was a refrigerator for, unlike other hard-up couples, they were not tempted to buy on hire purchase, having previously overspent with a credit card:

> 'We want to save up for things and not have them on HP . . . at one stage we just went berserk and spent on them [things for home] and wished we'd never done it and it's taking us a long time to pay if off now.'

The Sandfords were also finding it difficult to repay their large mortgage plus another high interest loan. Although their home was better equipped than that of the Evanses, they felt that they only had sufficient for survival:

'We've got enough to survive . . . enough to stay clear and be OK but we haven't got all the things that make life that much better . . . .'

It was more usual, however, for our young newly-weds to have a wide selection of household amenities; more of them owned washing machines, fridge-freezers and telephones than were owned by British households generally.[3] It was interesting to observe how many of these consumer durables had been received as wedding gifts:

'We was very lucky with wedding presents – we got everything we wanted – literally – the vacuum cleaner, fridge-freezer and electric knives, mixer, electric kettle, toaster, etc . . . there's nothing we've had to go and get, only silly things like a tin-opener.'—*Mrs Strong*

Opinions varied widely as to what was necessary to start married life in comfort. Mrs Strong, who considered she had 'everything she wanted', was nevertheless in the minority of wives without a washing machine. In common with most of the 1 in 5 newly-weds without this amenity, she took the washing round to her mother's house. Mr Emery and his wife had almost every amenity, plus two cars, yet felt that although they had received 'a good set of wedding presents' they had 'missed out on a dishwasher'. The Walters had nowhere to live just before their wedding but were fortunate to be offered a temporary flat by a wedding guest, and three months later they had just moved into their own home. Although they were without a washing machine, a fridge, central heating or a car, Mr Walter considered, 'We've been very lucky and we've been given much more than we needed – all the luxuries'.

Early married life, for the settled couples, centred on their homes. When not out at work, these husbands and wives spent most of their time in their homes, decorating and caring for them:

'My spare time is really only evenings in which case I am here in the house . . . if I'm not washing clothes I'm scrubbing boards [she and her husband were converting an old house] . . . that's about it. My spare time is mostly in the house or on a rare occasion we have popped out to see my parents.'—*Mrs Strong*

Since where they were living would be home for a while, they went about the business of settling down and began establishing a domestic routine. In some ways it was surprising just how clearly defined their domestic arrangements had become after so few months of living together as a couple. Many of these men and women had used the build-up to marriage as a time for careful preparation and so they started married life as they meant to go on. To have a routine and a clear sense of who did what offered security and confidence. However, the danger of routine boredom had already become apparent to one wife:

What do you dislike about marriage?

'It is quite a routine – I don't like that – I know life is a routine but I don't like the absolute pattern that you have to do so and so and let's do so and so and it's ready to do again and again . . . and again.'—*Mrs Inver*

Couples in transition

A fifth of the newly-weds had no 'first home' after the wedding, and they started married life boarding with one set of parents. Having to live in one or other partner's former home with mother, father, brothers and sisters was obviously a strain. Cramped conditions and a shortage of space meant little physical privacy, quite apart from the lack of emotional privacy. One bride, who shared her parents' small council home after the wedding, felt that the presence of her two younger sisters made the already crowded situation intolerable for her husband:

'He comes in in a bad mood and he wants to sit and watch the telly and be relaxed and me sister's got all her mates in playing the records . . . there's too much going on – there's too many of us – under each other's feet all trying to get into the sink at the same time.'—*Mrs Briggs*

It was clear that although most parents tolerated the situation, rarely did they welcome *not* losing a member of their household *and* gaining a new one, and sometimes additional stress was created where a parent who was lonely might be upset by the newly-weds' natural displays of affection:

'I like living here but we'd like more – not exactly privacy – but, say we're having a kiss and cuddle and mum comes in, you automatically break [apart]. She's on her own now and I don't know what it does to her – upsets her maybe.'—*Mr Gibson*

The couples who were boarding with parents were frustrated home-makers. They yearned for a setting in which to place their wedding presents, to be able to get on with decorating and furnishing rather than merely stockpiling colour charts, swatches of fabric and 'a bottom drawer'.

Mr and Mrs Norden were sharing the boxroom of Mr Norden's parents' three-bedroomed council house. The house also had to accommodate his two sisters, his younger brother and the lodger:

> 'The lodger and me used to share the room but now I'm married he's given his room up to us. We've managed to get a wide single mattress and we're managing like that – we have got a double bed but we've got nowhere to put it.'

They simply wanted to get on with 'those things that newly-weds do', things which the settled couples had gone a long way to achieving. On top of this frustration, the *boarding* wives in particular presented themselves as inhibited housekeepers; the domestic routine was usually in the hands of the senior wife (mother or mother-in-law) and these new wives were discouraged from preparing meals and doing their own laundry (although not from washing up). The boarding couples clearly benefited from the services of mothers and mothers-in- law, yet hardly ever was the lack of domestic responsibility regarded by them as a benefit. And it is true that they also had access to household amenities which the more established households of their parents provided: for example, every single couple who were sharing had access to a washing machine. Nevertheless, accounts of living within the domestic domain of a mother-in-law were at times reminiscent of a second wife describing married life within the shadow of the first wife. The life of these newly-weds was not, nor could it be, centred on the place in which they were living. Their only means of being together was when they went out – the reverse of the situation for the settled couples.

About a quarter of the newly-weds, although living on their own as couples, could be regarded as in transition, since they had unsatisfactory living arrangements, even though they knew, or hoped, these would not last for long. Since they hoped to move, there was no point in making improvements and getting involved in homemaking activities:

> 'Well, decorating – we haven't done much, hardly any – it's not really worth it 'cos we don't want to stay for more than a year or two.'

> 'There's no point in making it nice – good money after bad, as soon as we can manage to we'll buy our own place.'

What was regarded by these couples as unsuitable accommodation ranged from very limited facilities such as bedsitting rooms with no kitchens, to rented property which, though well appointed, was considered unsuitable in the long term because the couple wanted to buy a place of their own. The setting of their first home was not considered good enough to settle in. Some basic housekeeping was necessary but these couples *camped* rather than *settled* in their first home. The place they lived in was simply that, a place in which to live and not a home of their own:

> 'Well, we hardly ever have an evening meal – I eat at work . . . and we never eat at weekends either . . . we usually go round to the chippy because we don't use that kitchen [kitchen in a poor state and shared with others] . . . we have beans on toast if we have anything there.'—Mr Green

SHARING WORK IN THE HOME

According to one marriage handbook, it is in the early months that brides and grooms work out reciprocal patterns of husbandly and wifely behaviour as part of the organisation of the new family.[4] Traditionally, this has meant that the husband takes on the role of breadwinner and his wife that of housekeeper. It has been argued, and generally accepted, that the emergence of married women into the world of paid employment has been accompanied by the greater involvement of married men in domestic activities. For newly-wed couples in particular, the fact that both spouses are out of the home working and providing income for the household could create a pressure for more sharing of domestic responsibility. In Chapter 2 we referred to the study of the domestic division of labour in the marriage literature and argued that one of the weaknesses of earlier investigations into 'who does what' in the house has been that the questions asked have frequently been based on the assumption that there are specific roles for husbands and wives, and that these are allocated according to the traditional divisions of men's jobs and women's jobs in the home.

An alternative way to examine the organisation and execution of household chores is to consider the couple not as a husband and wife but simply as two members of the same household, and then to investigate how the basic jobs that are needed to service and maintain the household are allocated and carried out. If both partners are asked detailed questions about who did the specific task last time it was done, a picture of the domestic division of labour emerges which is relatively free of predetermination by the question. At the same time, however, it is important to establish the existence of any belief system which may be justifying and determining the domestic behaviour that is described (or, as in many cases, the belief system which obscures that behaviour).

Whatever the accommodation arrangements of the newly-wed couples, whether settled in their first home, boarding in the home of parents or camping in temporary accommodation, some basic domestic routine is a necessity. We therefore considered those tasks which have to be performed by someone in order to service a person or maintain his or her belongings and environment. Tasks were examined in three categories: daily, weekly and episodic. The daily tasks were: cooking the main meal of the day and washing up after that meal. Weekly tasks including tidying and cleaning the rooms lived in, and washing and ironing clothes worn by the couple. The simple maintenance and repair of household equipment used by the couple, decorating and car maintenance were regarded as episodic tasks. Each partner was asked who had performed each task (daily, weekly or episodic) *the last time it was done*, and whether this was typical. Questions about daily tasks were asked for each day of the preceding week. If the respondent exclusively performed the task two points were scored; if it was performed equally with another person, a score of one was given, and if the respondent simply assisted, the score was only a half. In theory, then, a couple who shared every task equally or who organised things so that each did half the tasks, would score a maximum of 24 (50 per cent each). For those couples where neither partner scored as high as 50 per cent, this was because another person was doing some of the work (with boarding couples this was nearly always 'mum').

In addition to questions about task performance, questions were also asked about the organisation of the domestic activities; who took the *decisions* about laundering, cleaning, meal preparation and shopping. After the total domestic routine had been described, respondents were asked if any discussion had taken place between them in order to establish the present routine: why they thought that particular routine was operating in their household, and what they felt about it. The financial arrangements of the couple were also examined, with detailed enquiries about each spouse's income and the handling of expenditure within the new household.

Newly-wed housekeeping: major and minor partners

The overall pattern of housekeeping which emerges is remarkably uniform: in most marriages one partner performs about three quarters of the tasks and the other the remaining quarter. Not surprisingly, partners with the *major* share of the chores also organise the execution of those chores, and partners with the *minor* house-keeping role perform mainly occasional tasks. In only a fifth of the marriages did both husband and wife make more or less equal contributions to keeping house: almost all newly-formed households the major housekeepers were the wives.

In most marriages, both partners were earning and contributing to household expenditure. Husbands were typically the higher earners and it was usual for them to pay the rent or mortgage and the major household bills, such as gas, electricity and telephone. The cost of housekeeping – that is, food, cleaning materials and other incidental expenses to do with the home, was the responsibility of wives. In the majority of newly-wed households, each partner's income was kept separate and so it was possible to trace the link between who earned what and who spent what. Curiously, in those marriages where income was pooled (usually into a joint bank account), both partners perceived that 'his' money paid for the mortgage and major bills and 'her' money went into the housekeeping. In the few households where the wife earned more than her husband, he still paid the mortgage and the major bills, with the wives 'chipping in' with extra help to cover the latter when necessary.

By the end of the first quarter of the first year of marriage, most newly-weds had established some routine for running their house-holds, one which normally meant that the major portion of domestic chores was performed by the wives. The origin of the current routines was not always easy to establish; they sometimes appeared simply to have evolved:

'It just happened.'
'It all fell into place.'
'I haven't thought about it really – its just how it started from the beginning.'

However, the majority of the men and women did offer explanations for the routines that had become established in their households:

'It was too much – after about a fortnight I thought, "I'm not going to manage with this" and my boss said "Well" – you know – "why don't you

cut your hours down?" – he didn't cut my pay so I was lucky – I have got
an exceptionally good boss so I managed OK'.—*Mrs Patmore*

This 22-year-old wife was a floor manageress for a high street shop, a
job with responsibility and good pay. Her husband was a management trainee in an insurance company. Although she earned more
than him, his job was deemed to be more important because it had 'a
future' and so, like many wives, her employment was altered to
accommodate her domestic role. Her spouse's relative lack of
domestic involvement (he dried the dishes and looked after the car,
put plugs on and helped her with the decorating) went unquestioned.

Some young husbands who clearly revealed their underinvolve-
ment in housekeeping, often expressed guilt (or over-justification)
about that arrangement. Their stream of negative replies about
housekeeping were followed by such comments as:

'It sounds as though I don't do much, doesn't it?'
'I'm glad you mentioned decorating, now that *is* down to me . . . keeps
me pretty busy, as busy as her with all the other.'

Indeed, for such husbands, simply to question the division of labour
was often interpreted as an implicit criticism of it.

Running a home: how things work out

It is not just sociologists and feminists who are concerned with the
division of labour in the home; there is a general awareness that who
does (or who does not) do the chores is a bone of contention in
modern marital relationships.

While the young husbands and wives were aware of the issue of
'who does what' in modern marriage, this did not result in a conscious
appraisal of who did what in *their* marriages, and few had ever
discussed the arrangements. Of course, explanations for the allocation of household chores may actually be *post hoc* justifications for
the way things happen to work out rather than clear reasons for
following a particular routine. Indeed, as we have already seen, a
fifth of the newly-weds could not offer any explanation for their
present division of labour; it had fallen into place naturally and there
had been no reason to question it.

Circumstances could make it more appropriate for one partner
rather than another to do particular chores, according to half of the
newly-weds. For example, the last person to leave in the morning
made the bed and the first home in the evening started to cook the
dinner:

'I usually get in first because I am only three minutes walk from work whereas he doesn't get in until 6.15 so I've virtually an hour before him, so I start the dinner – I usually have it ready for him.'

'I make the bed, he goes from the house at 8.15 and . . . I go later so I get up and get dressed and make the bed.'

In general, circumstances seemed to favour female domestic involvement – not surprisingly, perhaps, since many women made efforts to create circumstances where their jobs encroached as little as possible on their domestic life. Wives went out of their way to be at home more than their husbands and therefore to be available to do more (although, women were also expected to be less tired than their husbands because their jobs were 'less strenuous').

Competence of one spouse (and the reciprocal incompetence of the other) was another reason for the present sharing of household tasks. The experienced performer of a task was thought to be the natural candidate for that job. Such an approach was often, in fact, implicit support for the traditional roles, for men doing men's jobs and women doing women's jobs. Women were regarded as having had more experience and therefore to be more competent as cooks, cleaners, laundrymaids, shoppers, and so on. By the same reasoning men were expected to be better decorators and odd-job men. Since most of the newly-weds left home only when they got married, most of them – women as well as men – were equally inexperienced as housekeepers and homemakers.

Another aspect of competence is for one partner to stress the incompetence of the other:

'No particular reason [for household arrangements] it's just that I can cook and he likes cooking but he's – sometimes men aren't much good in the kitchen. I do cooking and ironing and bits and pieces but with electrical and car maintenance and things like that I don't know much about them so Ken always does those.'—*Mrs Milton*

'I do the cooking and washing – well, because he would get in such a state if he got out the washing machine [laugh] and it wouldn't be worth me clearing it up afterwards. He *could* do it but it's a lot easier for me to do it.'—*Mrs Trist*

These examples of female chauvinism could easily be matched with accounts from those husbands who guarded the decorating as their territory:

'The decorating is me and me and me always. She'd have a go but she only makes it worse.'

'Judy would like to do more decorating but I don't want to let her loose on a paint brush.'

Preference for a task was cited by about a fifth of the newly-weds as the basis for allocating tasks. It is, of course, true that being skilled at a task such as cooking often means that it is more enjoyable to perform. However, none of the four men who worked as chefs or cooks liked to cook at home and their wives excused them on the grounds that cooking at home would be for them 'a busman's holiday'. Interestingly, though, the women employed as caterers are expected to do the cooking at home just *because* they were skilled cooks. It was definitely a man's right to choose, as these husbands indicate:

'I would do the washing up normally. I mean she did it that Wednesday morning because we were both very tired after a busy day on Tuesday.'

'Well, I've never done any washing in my life so I don't see why I should now.'

'She does all I want her to do and I don't always do what she wants me to do.'

The chores which were most popular with husbands were shopping and washing up; around two thirds of men helped their wives in this way but very few took sole responsibility for either chore. About half of the men did some tidying up and hoovering, but doing the laundry was a really unpopular job; only a tenth of the men had ever done any ironing. Many husbands subscribed to the view that jobs that men do not like will automatically be done by their wives:

'I like cooking but I wouldn't like to cook every day. Cleaning – well I don't like that.'

What about Anna?
'Em, she's got to do it – so the best thing to do is to like it. I can't iron, I don't know how to do it – she doesn't like ironing but she's got to do it – that's about all I can say.'—*Mr Lawley*

'I hate ironing, so does she, but if I can do the washing – it just seems what seems fair. If she does the cooking I tend to do the washing up, that sort of thing.'

Do you or have you ever discussed the arrangement?
'They fall into place really. Apart from ironing and I wouldn't have anything to do with that. Because that is the one thing *neither of us can stand doing*.'

But she does it?
  'Yes but it wasn't the case of me showing this big arm and saying right [laugh].'—*Mr Martin*

Mr Martin, the husband just quoted, was, compared to Mr Lawley, a very domesticated husband. He performed about the same number of chores as his wife, whereas Mr Lawley's wife was doing four fifths of the chores. Nevertheless, when it came to the task that Mr Martin 'couldn't stand' (and neither could his wife), he expected his wife to do it. Husbands expected their wives to accept the unpopular jobs, because even though it seemed unfair, it was 'one of those things':

Why do you nearly always do certain things in the house and Lynne does others?
  'Well, I have an aversion, I hate doing certain things. There are other things that I don't enjoy but I feel I ought to help. I said right from the start that I never ever wanted to go shopping on a Saturday morning and follow her round a supermarket, never – that's not to say – I mean, I have done it, in fact and I hate it, I felt bad-tempered and I can't stand it.'
What does she think about it?
  'I think she accepts it.'—*Mr Walters*

Mr Walters was correct in assuming that his wife accepted the situation as determined by his preferences:

Why do you nearly always do certain things in the house and he does others?
  'Oh, because he can't bear doing them. I normally do the things he can't stand doing.'

Wives did demonstrate a very positive preference for any jobs to do with the kitchen. They frequently cited their husbands' incompetence as evidence for excluding them from this traditionally female territory, but, in fact, very few husbands were threatening to intrude. It is important to note that although women may present themselves (and be presented by their spouses) as the domestic managers, as the people in control of the home, directing their assistants (husbands), yet it is, in fact, the assistants who determine the nature and extent of that assistance. And this is almost always the case, despite some degree of assistance being regarded by the wives as a right and not a bonus. This became particularly clear in those homemaking activities which were regarded as joint:

Decorating?
  'That's James and me together.'

Do you do it together or do you do different things?
'He does the interesting bits and I do the boring bits.'—*Mrs Inver*

It seemed as if women usually made the decisions about when the cleaning was done, or when the laundry was done, because their husbands were 'not bothered'. (However, there was one domestic decision which was popular with most men and that was the selection of the evening menu!) One husband defended himself by saying that the world *may* be changing but it didn't change the way he was:

Have you talked about these arrangements – who does what . . . ?
'I mean, I don't regard myself as doing the domestic things [laugh]. Although we both work I don't really regard myself as doing the washing and the ironing and making the bed – but I do regard myself as doing the painting and decorating and these sort of things *so women's lib and all this sort of thing changes a lot* but that's the way I am.'

And how does Christine feel about that?
'Well, I mean sometimes she gets – "Why should I do this" – she's probably right but I can't change the way I feel, you know – making beds is not my scene.'—*Mr Strong*

Beliefs about marriage determined the division of household responsibilities, according to two in three husbands and two in five wives. The way in which domestic things got done in these households reflected deeper attitudes about the way the whole of married life should be lived. Most of these husbands and about half of these wives were following a traditional model of marriage; it was 'natural' for husbands to do 'men's work' and wives to do 'women's work':

Why do you do certain things and she does others?
'Don't think I'm a male chauvinist, but that's the woman's job and that's the man's job – it's not just like that but it's easy, I mean it's more convenient that way . . . the reason I do the garden . . . it's always flipping hard work so naturally I do it.'—*Mr Lawley*

Why do you do certain things and your husband others?
'I don't know – I think it's because I'm becoming a housewife.'—*Mrs Blond*

One husband thought that marriage should be all about spouses making equal but different contributions and was actually doing about half of the household chores. However, he thought that the present arrangements were due to his wife not working (she had become unemployed as a result of moving when she got married and was now seeking employment):

Why do you do certain things and Lucy does others?
'Oh, traditional – old-fashioned. I think there are roles we play – a good sociological word here, [he had taken O-level Sociology] segregated roles, yes. We have segregated roles simply because I think that is right and I think we have just slotted into them. I go out to work and I earn money, Lucy stays at home. If we both worked it would be totally different. Whoever got home first would cook but because she is at home I feel she should do most of the cooking and cleaning.'—*Mr Hill*

As this husband pointed out, the traditional roles are easily slotted into, and in terms of behaviour those who thought the present arrangements were due to circumstances or preference often had to admit that their arrangements turned out to be the same as those in households governed by the traditional allocation of domestic chores.

However, about a quarter of the newly-weds (more husbands than wives), thought that the division of household chores followed from a belief in egalitarian marriage and a consequential sharing of the domestic burden. It was usually stressed that this attitude was justified by the fact that both partners were holding down full-time jobs:

'We've always had an agreement between ourselves that we would both muck in together whatever each was doing so really it's 50–50 on everything apart from the washing, where perhaps you only need one person anyway.'—*Mr Kirkham*

'We both do our fair shares – quite equal – especially as we are both working full-time and that is how it should be – if I were at home all day, well, fair enough – I would be expected to do all the cleaning but as I'm working as many hours it's only fair that we both muck·in together.'— *Mrs Castle*

While both of these descriptions portray an image of sharing, Mr Kirkham was doing only one-third of the jobs and his wife the major part; he dried up while his wife washed the dishes, he sometimes vacuum-cleaned and helped her with the shopping. In contrast, Mrs Castle's husband did actually live up to her expectation of him; he did all the washing up every day and helped substantially with every chore except the cooking.

SETTING UP HOME: BEHAVING AS HUSBANDS AND WIVES

Most men and women 'knew' what was expected of married men and married women:

'I knew before I got married what I would have to do. I knew that by seeing other people being married – my sister has been married a long time before me.'—*Mrs Mead*

Adherence to the traditional roles of husbands and wives could help to reinforce individual identity. Being a husband actually helped some men to demonstrate their male identity:

'I think it gets back to my image, I follow my dad – it was always the wife who cooked the meals and did the ironing and did the vacuum cleaning and washed the kitchen floor and I do all the decorating because they're the more masculine jobs.'

Just as the marital relationship of parents could affect their children's attitudes to marriage, so the roles played by mothers and fathers often influenced the role performance of their sons and daughters as husbands and wives. And sometimes the novice wife did not compare very well with her husband's mother, as Mr Monkhouse explained:

'Do you think their marriage influenced your attitude to marriage at all?

'Well, in a way I suppose – because you expect your wife to be the same as your mother. Or to do the same sort of things. But you have a rude awakening.'

How do you mean – you expected your wife to be like your mother?

'I have to argue about the ironing – I say I've got no shirts left, whereas I would never have to with me mum – I'd go to the cupboard and there'd be a shirt there.'—*Mr Monkhouse*

Advice given to young couples accentuates the role of wives as carers for their husbands: 'How to look after your man', 'Keeping him happy', 'Keeping him healthy'[5] and the statistics do suggest that married men enjoy better physical and mental health than unmarried men.[6] Since in practice it is wives who do most of the housework, so it is they who are the chief carers of home and husband. One young wife conveyed the ambivalence this aroused in her; although she had come to accept that she could not expect her husband to do a lot, this 'got her down' at first. However, it was evident that she did not really want him to do more because 'then he wouldn't need me'. She had told him before their marriage that she would not be able to 'keep him like his mum had done', yet she still worried about the nights when she was too tired to cook; 'it's my fault that he has beans on toast'.

It was interesting that it was those husbands who had been cared for by their mothers who had to make the greatest adjustment after marriage:

'Well, I don't like it – it's getting used to something different. When I was living at home I used to get home from work and my meal was on the table, for instance, now it isn't. She's out working and we do it when we get in. It's just a different routine. It's not a case of not liking it, it's a question of adjusting.'—*Mr Martin*

Some women were confusing their role of wife with that of mother. Perhaps such a confusion was hardly surprising since they imitated their own mothers who were, after all, both wives *and* mothers. Most husbands, used to being looked after, seemed content with this kind of servicing, but a few men, most notably those who had lived on their own and were practised at catering for themselves, were critical of their wives for 'fussing' and 'going to too much bother'.

CREATING A DOMESTIC LIFESTYLE

It is said that 'you don't know someone until you live with them' and, of course, for the majority of couples (who had not cohabited), setting up home involved the merging of differing approaches to housekeeping and different standards about tidiness and cleanliness. Accounts of their or their partners' idiosyncratic ways of doing things (or failing to do things) were usually attributed to the effects of having grown up in different families. Understandably, these different styles of housekeeping and homemaking provoked some of the first 'tiffs' in these early days of marriage, as these respondents indicated:

Do you like housework?
   'No, I hate it.'

Does Brian like it?
   'He doesn't like it very much but his parents were very houseproud – their house is very spick and span whereas my mum's house is very well lived in. I think he's been brought up with the idea that . . . you fold in the corners of your bed – he thinks his mum carries things a bit too far but I think her ideas are in him a bit. If I'm not going to do something properly he'd rather do it – like, he cleans the oven – things like that – I can't be bothered with them. He says if I'm not going to do it properly he'll do it – although he doesn't enjoy it, he does it.'—*Mrs Trist*

'Would you like Matthew to do more, or less?
   'Not really – I think the only thing that annoys me is if I ask him to do something and probably he's had a bit of a tiring day at work as well – it sort of takes him that bit longer to get round to doing it – I get annoyed. I'm a bit like my mum in that way – if somebody doesn't do it when I ask

I'd rather do it myself. He'd rather not be pushed, whereas I suppose at home – because ours was a bigger family – you *did* jump when asked.'—*Mrs Mead*

Do you think you should do more?

'Well, she is – I shan't say she is a fanatic but she likes to keep the place clean. Although I like it clean, if I were on my own I would probably clean it when I felt like it but not *every* day.'—*Mr Butcher*

RUNNING A HOME: HOW THINGS SHOULD BE

The accounts of how things get done in newly-wed households clearly show young wives taking the major role in running the home at the same time as they are working full-time outside it. This picture of wives as the housekeepers with their husbands as the household aides reflects a neo-traditional view of the domestic roles of husbands and wives. It is not quite the traditional marriage of female housewife and male breadwinner (since the wife also is a breadwinner), but it is a long way from the egalitarian relationship which has been so often presented as the essence of modern marriage. When the views of the newly-weds on the way they consider things should be are examined, four distinct views emerge:

The egalitarian view

'As far as I'm concerned you've got to share the workload – a marriage these days isn't 10 per cent mine and 90 per cent the wife's workload – it's 50–50.'

This husband did actually practise what he preached, although he admitted, 'a lot of the time even if I stick my head round the kitchen door its "go away" '. However, only four men and three women (and among them only one couple) subscribed to this view that modern spouses should share everything equally. Not surprisingly, since they were breaking new ground, these men and women had discussed the matter and had come to an agreement about 'mucking in together' and at times expressed, with almost missionary zeal, the desire to escape from the traditional roles of husband and wife as practised by their parents:

'We thought about it and my view on marriage is make it like living together. When people get married, a lot of the time they just look back to what their parents have done and say, "Right – the *woman* has got to do the housework and the washing up and all the rest of it – sort of get me socks, get me slippers – and the man just goes out to work". Well, *I* said, "It's going to be different when we get married, we're going to do it all together and it's going to make it a lot better" – which it is.'— *Mr Ashworth*

The wife's economic role was usually given as the justification for the policy of 'mucking in':

'We both do our fair share – quite equal – especially as we are both working full-time and that is how it should be – if I were at home all day fair enough – it would be expected of me to do all the cleaning but as I'm working as many hours its only fair that we both muck in together.'— *Mrs Castle*

The equitable view

About a third of husbands and a similar number of wives thought that, although real equality was unrealistic, yet *the burden should be shared equitably*, by each doing different things and thus complementing each other. According to this view, the roles of husband and wife are counterpoised, and it is important that each does what they are best at so that the co-operative enterprise is efficient and successful. Mrs Dawson explained how things were managed in her home:

'I think it works out more conveniently because I think I'm a better cook than him – he makes more of a mess – and it's more convenient for me to do the cooking because I enjoy it and he can do the washing up. The washing I can do while I am getting a meal or something like that – Roger can be out of my way doing the hoovering or I'm out of his way – you know – whichever way you see it. The car maintenance *he* does because I'm useless on that and I wouldn't know where to begin or anything. And the decorating – when we were decorating, to begin with we both helped out – both of us painting and decorating but *he* done the majority of it by far.'

In practice, of course, this view tends to underline the traditional roles of husbands and wives since husbands usually do 'men's work' and wives 'women's work'. The question then is, are these contributions really counterpoised? Men's work usually comprised decorating, checking the car – jobs which are episodic and discretionary in comparison with, say, cooking and cleaning. Moreover, in the early phase of marriage, settled couples may be particularly preoccupied with homemaking activities so that decorating can genuinely complement the domestic chores. It is unlikely, however, that the intense homemaking of this phase will be sustained for long, although a particular pattern of responsibility having been set early on in a marriage may have longer-term consequences.

The neo-traditional view

'When we first got married I said, you know, "You will help me, sort of thing – you won't leave me to do it all" and he said of course he wouldn't because he's seen his own house where his mother did everything and he didn't want me to end up running around all the time like she was, so he does help out.'—*Mrs Inver*

The most popular view among the newly-weds, held by over half the men and women, was the idea that women should be mainly responsible for running the home, but with the right to regular help from their husbands. Opinions varied as to the amount of help which should be given by husbands; some people believed that husbands should take on a regular commitment, (for example to wash up after dinner) but in other marriages it was felt that husbands should play only an 'overflow' role and ease the wife's burden by taking on what was left over after she had covered the essentials.

The traditional view

Only a minority of the couples (a fifth of the husbands and a tenth of the wives) held the traditional belief that women should be responsible for the home, with help from their husbands solely as a bonus when they were sick or tired, as two husbands indicated:

'Well, I'll do it if I've got to – I mean, if she had to go into hospital or something like that.'

'I'm certainly happy with my lot, I don't think she does too much. I mean if she *couldn't* do it . . . when I was living with my brother and his wife I did my own things, they were washed by the machine but I brought them in and ironed them.'

Another husband stressed that it was important to appear incompetent at most chores so that his wife could not possibly take advantage of him:

'I could do it – I wouldn't tell my wife I could though otherwise she might take advantage – but I would do it, it doesn't bother me.'

Since most of the wives were working full-time, the expectation that they should be a 'proper' housewife as well as a full-time worker was a strain and this was sometimes acknowledged by the husbands:

'It's hard for her, really, she is always telling me how worked off her feet she is . . . I do accept she has a lot on her plate, not only has she got to work, she's got to keep the place reasonably clean and cook dinners.'

However, it is interesting that it is the full-time job which was perceived to be the cause of the strain and not the lack of the husband's involvement.

In fewer than half of the couples did the husband and wife share the same view of how things should be organised domestically. Women were more likely to expect only the minimum from their husbands, whereas men were more likely to assume that they were providing more assistance than their reported behaviour demonstrated. Overall, wives' views of the current situation seemed to correspond fairly accurately with how things actually were, the predominant style being that the running of the home is the responsibility of the wife with some (varying) contribution from the husband.

HOUSEKEEPING: THE WORKING WIFE'S BURDEN

Working wives shouldered a very heavy burden; over two-thirds of the young wives each performed at least three-quarters of the household chores. Those who did less were benefiting from sharing a home with a mother or mother-in-law. Nearly all the wives were in full-time employment so that all domestic jobs had to be done in the evenings and at weekends and housework was, therefore, a major leisure time pursuit for these married women. For the settled couples in particular, husbands spent most of their spare time decorating while their wives kept up with housework and occasionally gave their husbands a hand. It was hopefully assumed by the wives that once the bulk of decorating had been accomplished, the husbands would become more involved with the day-to-day running of the home:

> 'Hopefully, he will fend for himself a bit more but I find it quite a lot having to think of what to cook every night and to get to the butchers in time because I do such funny hours and to come home and cook every night and wash up . . . it would be nice if occasionally he would say, "Oh, I'll choose what we're going to have tomorrow, I can do it", but his answer usually is, "I've got the decorating to do so *you* do that".'—*Mrs Emery*

Although women were twice as likely as men to express any dissatisfaction with the present division of labour within the home, rarely was this levelled at husbands for their lack of participation.

Women seemed mainly dissatisfied with themselves for 'not coping' sufficiently well with the dual roles of employee and housewife:

'I've tried to get organised but I'm very, very disorganised in a lot of ways. Basically I try to keep the washing and ironing down. I do little bits every night by hand you know, smalls – get them out of the way and at the weekend maybe give it a good clean up – I get up on Saturdays – (I don't work Saturdays now) – I do the shopping say Saturday or Friday night and Jonathan comes with me and then I give it a quick clean round – I work pretty hard, then if I get all that done in the morning – if I *do* feel too tired before we go out, I have a little sleep in the afternoon. You see – it means mainly that you're working a lot at the weekends. It can get a bit boring – sometimes I feel just like throwing in the job . . . . '– Mrs Klein

The attempt to cram too much into the few hours after work was a worry for many women (and one their husbands acknowledged although usually without making any practical response). Several women spoke of their intention to change jobs or alter their working hours to accommodate the demands of housekeeping. One reason for this was that many women had moved further from their work or had had to change jobs as a result of getting married, with the result that the marital home was almost always more convenient for their husband's workplace than for theirs, so that wives spent more time travelling to and from work as well as having also to meet the demands of running a home.

SUPERWIFE: THE INVISIBLE SERVANT

Since most wives were full-time employees as well as housewives, their two greatest problems were overcoming of tiredness in order to to do housework and finding sufficient time in the week to accomplish it all. Weekends were sometimes the only opportunity they had for 'catching up with the chores'; it was also usually the time when husbands were busy with other things such as decorating, doing the car, playing football, working an extra shift, or 'down the pub'. If the husband was 'at leisure' the wives, rather surprisingly, did not resent it; they seemed glad of the oppportunity to have him 'out of the way', 'not under my feet', so that the housework could be completed unobtrusively. In general, if the husbands were not helping they were thought to be a hindrance. And some women perceived being able to make housework invisible to their husbands as a demonstration of their being good wives – women who could run the home without 'a hassle'.

A few women, disgruntled with their heavy burden of domestic responsibility, nagged their husbands and then felt guilty when their husbands did eventually help out – 'it seems like a defeat' was one wife's response. As we noted earlier, a few men withdrew domestically for fear of trespassing into their wives' territory, particularly from the kitchen, where it had been suggested to them that as inexperienced cooks they would create havoc. However, there was often more to it than that since, as some women admitted, at times they discouraged their husbands simply because they did not like to see men doing certain jobs; they felt it would either offend their notions of masculinity or might threaten their own identity as women and wives:

> 'Sometimes I feel I'm just an unpaid housemaid – you know, when I want him to do some more work for me and then when it comes round to it, I don't like seeing him do it.'

You don't like seeing him do it?

> 'No, sometimes I feel guilty – as if I should get up and help him.'

Do you think he should do more?

> 'No – not really – sometimes if I ask him to do something and he really won't do it, then I get mad and we have an argument and I end up doing it anyway. I wish he'd do some more things if I asked him, lay the table and that you know.'—*Mrs Allen*

> 'It works out like that really. I mean when we are both at work it's quite difficult to come home, sort of, I consider it a woman's job washing up anyway, I wouldn't like to see Jonathan doing it. But apart from that, when we get in in the evening, Jonathan will start decorating or you know, the fireplace – he'll start building that. Doing something or another to improve the house while I will continue with other household chores.'—*Mrs Klein*

THE DOMESTICATED HUSBANDS

If the typical newly-wed husband did relatively little in the home, who were the minority of men who chose to co-shoulder the domestic burden with their wives? In fourteen marriages husbands performed at least forty-one per cent of the chores and nine of them were doing half or more. On the whole, their behaviour reflected their attitude to the division of labour in the home but there was no clear explanation for why these men believed and behaved in the way that they did.

They were not particularly middle-class although the majority were non-manual workers, nor were their wives especially striving in their careers or paid better salaries. However, there were certain features which may have contributed to the way they shared the domestic division of labour. More of these domesticated husbands had some earlier experience of living in households where they had not been cared for. And in half of these marriages one partner was a shift worker, which meant that the husbands were at home without their wives at times when certain tasks might best be done (for example cooking and washing), and additionally, of course, being frequently alone in the home they were often forced to cater for themselves.

So it can be seen that in these marriages the circumstances of married life, together with the non-availability of the wife to be able to service the husband, may have inhibited any 'natural' slotting into traditional roles. It seemed to be the absence of the wife which was the principal reason why these husbands were not simply household 'aides' but were instead active housekeepers, taking many of the decisions and organising the housework.

COPING WITH THE DEMANDS OF HOME: THE UNDER-MINING OF THE WIFE WHO WORKS

The examination of 'who keeps house' took place at a time when the majority of husbands and wives were both working full-time outside the home, so that in this respect, there was equality between husband and wife. However, this symmetry in working roles was not mirrored in the home. Inequality between spouses in the home was only rarely recognised by the couples and few attempts were made to redress the balance of domestic responsibility. It seems that the first phase of marriage for these newly-weds was overshadowed by the event which would bring it to a close – the birth of the first child. The main impact of childbearing is usually perceived to be the loss of the wife's full-time employment and, in anticipation of this, these newly-wed spouses regard the first phase of married life as temporary. Thus both the current domestic role of the brides and their working role are already influenced by their future perception of themselves as mothers.

It is interesting that the wives saw themselves (and were so perceived by some of the husbands) as over-burdened *because of their working role and not because of their husband's lack of domestic involvement.* The full-time working role of the wife is not expected to last, and therefore the structure of the division of labour does not reflect a two-job household.

This is echoed in the newly-weds' perceptions of the funding of their homes. In the early months of marriage, both spouses were usually earning, both contributing to the economy of the new household. Although wives tended to earn less than their husbands,[7] the money they contributed was not merely an 'extra', it was usually needed to cover the expenditure of the newly-wed households. Yet it was husbands who were perceived, by both men and women, to be the providers, the funders of home life. Most couples kept their incomes separate and so they had to devise a system for who paid for what. There was invariably a gender division of expenditure which consisted of husbands paying the rent/mortgage and major bills, and wives taking care of the housekeeping expenses. Even in those marriages where the income was pooled, the cost of keeping 'a roof over our heads' was attributed, evidently symbolically, to the husbands' earnings. Both the wives (and their husbands) played down the importance of their financial contribution.

In a few marriages, the household budget had been worked out on the basis of the husband's earnings only; the wife's earnings were 'not that much' and 'not going to last'. The low pay of wives, coupled with the expectation that her long-term employment position was at best unreliable, and at worst terminable, reinforced the undervalued perception of her employment role.

These newly-married women were constantly in a state of tension: between wanting to run their homes to high standards and having to fulfil outside employment commitments; between wanting husbands who would help and thereby relieve the pressure, and wanting to prove they were good housewives and keep their own territory. As one husband explained, the state of the household still determines the reputation of a wife:

> 'Well, if she's at work and she comes home it's the – sort of – woman that is – sort of – relied on for everything – if there's a dirty house they never – sort of – think it's the *bloke*'s fault, because we went round one of me friend's houses and it's terrible and I always think, "Oh, she's a dirty girl" – you know.'

In order to cope with the unending tension between home and work, many wives were forced to minimise their employment role by adapting it to suit the domestic pressure, sometimes even having to abandon it altogether. Thus it is that the demands of the home, of setting it up and of keeping it going, undermine the work role of wives. Although in these early days of marriage both spouses are likely to be in full-time employment, yet the significance of the work role has already become very different for husbands and for wives.

7 Working Husbands and Wives Who Work

Friday November 13th 1981

Pandora and I had a frank talk about our relationship tonight. She doesn't want to marry me in two years' time! She wants to have a career instead! Naturally I am devastated by this blow. I told her I wouldn't mind her having a little job in a cake shop or something after our wedding, but she said she intended to go to university and that the only time she would enter a cake shop would be to buy a large crusty. Harsh words were exchanged between us. (Hers were harsher than mine.)

The Secret Diary of Adrian Mole
Sue Townsend

In their book, *The Symmetrical Family*, Young and Willmott outline three historical stages of family life. They argue that in the modern stage, two trends are discernible: first, the growing extent to which women work outside the home and second, the greater amount of work being done in the home by men. In their view, the inevitable conclusion of these trends is the symmetrical model of marriage:

> By the next century – with the pioneers of 1970 already at the front of the column – society will have moved from (a) one demanding job for the wife and one for the husband, through (b) two demanding jobs for the wife and one for the husband, to (c) two demanding jobs for the wife and two for the husband. The symmetry will be complete. Instead of two jobs there will be four.[1]

The post-war trend of the increasing participation of married women in the labour force[2] has provided clear evidence of wives assuming two work roles in marriage (one in the home and one in their place of work), although the corresponding participation of husbands in domestic work has yet to be proved (see Chapter 6). It seems that for the spouses of today, there are usually three roles, two for wives and one for husbands. But, of course, it is not as simple as that. The fact that married women currently form a significant part of the labour force is not the same as saying that married women assume a work role that is equivalent to that of their husbands. Although it may be statistically normal to be a wife in employment this statistic ignores the erratic work pattern of many married women, which is conditioned by childbearing and child-rearing.

In those marriages where both spouses are of working age and without children, wives as well as husbands are employed full-time, but they constitute only a minority of the total population of women who work outside the home. Just over a quarter of all employed married women work full-time, and this falls to 7 per cent for mothers whose youngest child is under five years of age.[3] In general, wives' work is part-time, largely because their work *outside* the home is acceptable only in so far as it can accommodate the requirements of their work *inside* the home. The real change that has taken place is not that symmetry has been achieved but that there is now a hierarchy of roles for the modern spouses, whereas earlier there was simply a division of labour by gender.

Married women are often regarded as forming a secondary workforce. Barron and Norris argue that in Britain such a dual labour market cuts across firms, industries and the manual/non-manual division.[4] The primary sector, predominantly occupied by men, consists of relatively well-paid, secure jobs with promotional ladders, fringe benefits and comparatively good working conditions, whereas the secondary market lacks all or most of these features. Women's employment in our society is regarded as essentially problematical, because sooner or later, most women become mothers. Although it has now been recognised that in general women workers are low paid, have little security of employment, and few prospects of advancement, these are perceived as the inevitable consequences of a woman's decision to marry, since by this act she has initiated the cycle which creates her 'unreliability' as an employee. However, it is also argued that since women workers usually marry workers in the primary sector, they will thereby have access to the standard of living of primary-sector workers.

The newly-wed couples, almost none of whom had children at the time they were interviewed, displayed the typical working pattern of married couples without children: in 85 per cent of their marriages, both partners were employed full-time and only 5 per cent of the young wives were working part-time. (The remaining 10 per cent of the wives were not working outside the home, either because they were pregnant, or because when they married they had to move away from their jobs and were having difficulties in finding alternative employment.)

In contrast to most married couples, these newly-married husbands and wives do appear to have symmetrical work roles, and since childbearing for most of them was to be delayed for a couple of years, they could be regarded as being in a phase of married life when both partners can share the economic responsibility of the household. However, such symmetry of responsibility was, in most couples, sharply confined to work outside the home; it rarely extended to the sphere of domestic chores. In this chapter we will show how this lack of equity in domestic responsibility can both justify and undermine the lack of equivalence between the paid work of husbands and the paid work of wives.

YOUNG PEOPLE AND EMPLOYMENT

Before we examine the employment experiences and attitudes to work of the sixty-five newly-wed couples, it is important to stress that these 130 men and women were all still young, having been under thirty on their wedding day, with the majority still in their early twenties. This meant that they had had only a short working life: two-thirds of the husbands and three-quarters of the wives had had no more than six years' working experience, while for those who had been in higher education, the work experience had been even shorter, typically three years. Studies of employment have pointed to certain features of work experience which are characteristic of young people: for example, they tend to change jobs more frequently than do older workers.[5]

Although this can sometimes take place without change of employer, since it may simply be a normal progression within a particular firm or organisation, this is not always the case; job mobility among young people can mean the abandonment of unsatisfactory jobs and a quest for more rewarding or better-paid employment. However, sometimes it can also reflect a 'pillar-to-post' approach to work; a job is simply a way of earning money, and, for women, may be a profitable way of marking time until they become mothers. It is, therefore, not surprising that young workers in general are more likely to express more dissatisfaction with their work than are older employees. Mrs Rudd was typical of the young wives in our study who had left school at sixteen and had tried out a variety of jobs:

'I've been a windowdresser – I've worked in shops – I've worked in a bakery shop and I was a traffic warden.'

Were you?

'Yes, for a couple of years and I worked in a factory for about six days.'

Do you intend to stay in your present job?

'Until such time as I have to leave, yes.'

How do you see the future in terms of work – do you have any plans or ambitions?

'No.'

Would you like to have a different job?

'No.'

Although her present job as a cashier in a café was 'a bit boring at times', she said she had no intention of changing jobs. She would stay in her present job 'until such time as I have to leave', a phrase which she and many other brides used to mean the time when they would have a baby. Mrs Rudd was able to 'settle with' her present job because she could see an end in sight: marriage would for her result in motherhood and a period away from paid work.

We have already shown the way in which getting married is a turning point for young people, a time of great significance when they can focus on the future and also reflect on the past. Not surprisingly, although it can be a time for hope it can also be one of regret: the single most frequent theme of remorse in the newly-weds, both husbands and wives, was their lament for the lost opportunities in their education:

'I wish I had studied longer.'
'Wish I hadn't wasted my time at school.'
'I wish I'd got some qualifications.'

It was clear that for many of them, their early entry into employment had been an escape in frustration from the tyranny of the classroom. However, by their early twenties these erstwhile reluctant students had discovered that the apparent freedom of the workplace could turn out to be just another kind of trap, in which they felt imprisoned by their lack of educational qualifications.

Although it is true that marriage offers a new beginning, and the opportunity to establish a new identity as a bona fide adult, there is a hidden twist. As we showed in Chapter 4, this new autonomy is inextricably linked with responsibility; indeed, marriage confers autonomy on the individual *because* it also confers responsibility. The act of getting married is, therefore, both liberating and restrictive. A job is no longer merely an activity which provides an income; it has become the means of sustaining a household, and of carrying out those responsibilities which define adulthood. For many men this gave paid work a new satisfaction and meaning, but for some it meant the sad realisation that the opportunities to change tracks and go back to square one, particularly in terms of education and training, had now been lost.

WIVES WHO WORK

In the twelve months before the interview, as many as two in every three wives had experienced some form of job change, with almost half of them having made this in the previous three months, that is, immediately following the wedding. A quarter had done so just before it and a further 10 per cent said they expected some change in their job situation in the near future. We have already indicated that job mobility is a feature of young workers in general, but the newly-wed brides were more than twice as likely as their husbands to have experienced a recent job change. And when we looked at the reasons they gave for having done so, there was often a clear link between the job changes and their newly-acquired marital status.

Moving homes and changing jobs

It is usually the case that when a worker moves to an area without having considered possible new job opportunities, the chance of getting a job equivalent to the previous one will be very slim. This had clearly been the experience of those wives who had had to try to find new jobs in areas where their husbands were employed; hence, there were many women who were either considerably under-employed or without any paid employment, after the move.

Although there was universal pleasure among the women in being married, nevertheless most of those who as a result had had to leave their jobs, regretted having had to do so. Some of them had thereby lost good promotion opportunities, and had taken their current job simply 'as a matter of expediency'. Mrs Bates had met her husband at university, where they had both studied mathematics. After gradua- tion they had both got good jobs, he a graduate trainee position in a computer firm, based near his home town in the north of England, and she a job in South Wales.

'He was a bit upset [about her job] because by going there I was even further away than at my parents' [Reading] . . . but I felt I had to get a job . . . and we weren't *that* serious at that time so I thought, "I can't let the relationship lead my life" . . . When I told him on the phone, I was enthusiastic, "Oh, I've got that job" [voice high]; he said, "That one in Newport?" [voice low]. I was a bit annoyed with him because I was really pleased at getting the job and he put a wet blanket on it.'

Mrs Bates stressed that as the relationship had not been *that* serious when she was seeking her first job, she could not let 'the relationship lead my life'. However, very shortly after taking up her new appointment, her future husband started to 'mention marriage generally' and after two months he proposed and was accepted. From then on the difficulties of continuing a relationship so many hundreds of miles apart began to dominate their lives and so the priorities were changed and she allowed the relationship to determine her new work situation:

'We decided that by December at the latest I would move whether I had a job or not because we were so fed up with all the travelling. I gave up my job in Newport to come here. He could have left his job but we decided to do it the other way because he's on a graduate scheme and if he left his job he'd have gone down on to the ordinary level and lost the special grade that he's on at the moment.'

How did you feel about leaving your job?
'I enjoyed it – I was happier there . . . but obviously I wanted to be with David so that was the main thing.'

However, although she is under-employed as a personnel assistant in a small firm, she in no way regretted having put the marriage first. She has resigned herself to a working future which will be determined by the demands of her husband's work and by her own responsibilities for bringing up their children. She felt that the ideal compromise in this situation would be for her to become a teacher, a view shared by other graduate wives: 'It would be an ideal job; once I've had a family, I'd be able to go back to the work and I'd also have the school holidays.'

Other wives also seemed ready to accept their fate with regard to their employment, and bore no resentment, although sometimes their replies were tinged with a certain amount of sadness:

Do you enjoy your work?
'Not really, no.'

What do you dislike about it?
  'It's too much . . . you have to sit down all day – you can't really – sort
  of – talk and work at the same time.'

Did you prefer your other job?
  'Definitely.'

So you're a bit sad that you had to leave it?
  'Yeah.'—*Mrs Sandford*

*How do you see the future in terms of work? Do you have any plans or
ambitions?*
  'No, not now, because – ambitions I had in my last job I haven't got now
  in the sort of job I'm doing now; there *are* promotional prospects but
  we're going to start wanting a family, probably in a couple of years' time.'

Is that a disappointment to you?
  'It is really, because every time I get to a point when I really think I've
  found something I like and I really want to get somewhere, I can't, and I
  had to leave. I find it a bit frustrating actually.'—*Mrs Walters*

Mrs Walters had resigned from being an advertising copywriter,
which had offered considerable potential for career development,
and after marriage had taken up a job as a secretary in a market town
in West Sussex. She expressed her frustration over this, but at the
same time it was evident that her attitudes to work in the future were
ambiguous. She was still ambitious, and she felt that there were some
limited prospects for promotion in her new job, yet she was aware of
the fact that to have children (which one day she wished to do) would
interfere with such prospects. And so, like most of the young,
newly-wed wives, she was reassessing her role as a worker, and
beginning to accept that as a married woman her working role would
be a limited one. It seemed that, for many women, having to change
jobs upon marriage had sharpened up the picture they had of their
futures, by clarifying the priorities accorded to work and home which
have to be established by both married partners.

Making the job accommodate to marriage

When a newly-wed couple move to an area in order to be near to the
husband's job, it is clear that the work of the husband has priority
over that of the wife. However, there are also other, albeit relatively
minor, changes made in their lives by wives who work, which reveal
the emerging order of priorities concerning work and home. For

many wives today, their acclimatisation to marriage involves a total reorientation of their lives, whereby everything (and especially their work) has to come second to looking after the household. The unspoken rule in most couples is that the work of the wife outside the home should not dominate her life to such an extent that the spouse or the house 'suffer'. In line with this, five of the newly-wed wives had altered their hours of work accordingly, and another five were expecting to make changes to their work-role in the immediate future.

When the wives found that their work impinged too greatly on their domestic life, the first adjustment they made was usually to negotiate a slightly shorter working week, or to seek exemption from working on a Saturday:

> 'Before I got married I used to work every other Saturday but we've got a few more staff now and I don't want to work so many Saturdays now because there's so much housework I can get done on a Saturday but it works out maybe one a month.'—*Mrs Tasker*

> 'Where I am now there is no Saturdays, which is quite important, you know, when you've got a house like this, you want to be in it most of the time because there is so much to do in here.'—*Mrs Strong*

Employers were expected to be sympathetic to the strain of being a working wife and generally appeared to be so. In the previous chapter we described how Mrs Patmore was allowed to leave work early without losing pay by an employer who obviously valued her highly. Another wife who was a hairdresser and had worked for many years at the same salon, had negotiated a shorter working day on the basis of her new married status:

> 'Working Tuesday to Saturday until 6 pm and sometimes a bit later is just too much and I told him; I said, "I'm a married woman now, I'm not like the girls, they just go home, and they are local, they go to their Mum's and their tea is cooked" – they don't have to have it ready for him, and then they are free to get ready to go out. When *I* go home I've 'got to start . . . I've got responsibilities.'

What did he [employer] say?
> 'Saw my point and lets me go earlier; an hour or half an hour makes all the difference.'

Those wives who had made such adjustments found that their overall situation improved; not only was life less pressured for them, but their relationship with their husbands was better too. Mrs Downing was one of the wives who had become unemployed after getting married. Now that she was at home all day, 'It's a lot easier for me because I used to have to do all the housework when I came home in the evening and I used to feel really tired', but she lamented 'I *do* find it boring'. In spite of the boredom however, she acknowledged that her husband 'prefers me not working' and that they had had fewer disagreements since she had ceased working outside the home:

> 'I think now I'm not working we don't quarrel as much as we used – we used to have quarrels but they weren't nothing really important, but . . . because I used to get – sort of – irritable – I used to come home and cook a dinner and start the housework, the ironing and that; it just used to get too much – if I didn't do it, it used to build up.'

'Home comes first'

Because so many of the wives altered their working roles at or around marriage, it is hard to distinguish between their general attitudes to work, and the specific effects that getting married may have produced. Certainly it was rare for a woman to express satisfaction with her current job, although she might be content with her overall working environment. Women tended to confine their favourable comments to such things as friendly work-mates or understanding employers.

Their responses were in sharp contrast to those of their husbands, who were often at their most articulate – surprisingly so – when describing their specific functions at work, as we see later. Those women who had started a new job after marriage, also tended to be at a disadvantage in that they were 'a new girl', a situation never easy but complicated by their status of being married, for they felt it was more difficult to become 'mates' with new fellow workers when married: 'When you're getting married you can't go out with them after work, so you don't get to know them so well.'

As we have already shown, when a change of job is necessary as a consequence of having moved house at marriage, and the choice of new jobs limited, finding a job merely becomes a means to an end — that of earning money. Additionally, since their jobs were not very attractive, the wives increasingly became caught up in the business of 'setting up home', and were often very happily involved with this, so that the new home seemed a very inviting place. At such a time, the thought of reducing the work commitment outside the home, or even of giving it up altogether in order to concentrate on housekeeping and home-making, could be very appealing, as one woman indicated:

'Women have the best of both worlds – work for so long and it's pretty well up to them, or a joint decision, to be at home (when children are quite young) for so many years and back to work later . . . at the moment it [giving up work] seems very appealing – to be at home all the time, and I think of all the things I would be able to do, gardening, sewing, cooking, and I'd enjoy it, but after being in the home for a couple of years I might want to go back . . . '—*Mrs Bates*

In one way, the accounts of this group of wives give a strong overall impression of them wanting to escape from the world of work into the home: however, it must not be forgotten that they had not yet started to have children, so that they were still to a certain extent free to choose their life activities. When we look at other research studies, in which the couples already have children, a very different picture emerges: wives tend to feel imprisoned in their homes, and are only too keen to be released from the four walls into the world of work, but by then they may not be able to make a choice.[6]

It is interesting that among the newly-weds it was those women who had already ceased to work who were most able to say what they had liked about working. Mrs Riley had given up work because of her pregnancy:

You said you worked as a sales administrator, did you enjoy your work?
    'I loved it.'

What did you like about it?
    'Meeting people and it was different every day – and knowing your job is exciting – when you know it – I used to train the other girls . . . and the responsibility was good to have. I think every woman likes to have a room which she can keep tidy and the office was my . . . well, I just loved that office, you know . . . it was my room . . . thinking back, I enjoyed my job, it upset me giving it up.'

Many young women, however, certain that they will one day marry, since almost everyone does, would consider any strong commitment to work as unnecessary or even incompatible with their desire to marry. Mrs Wolsey, who, relative to most of the other brides, was well educated, and who had married at a later age than most, described the way in which she had found marriage and a career to be opposing choices:

    'I thought I ought to be doing something. That's why I've always been a bit job conscious; I thought I ought to be doing either – if I wasn't going to get married, then I wanted to have an interesting job, or I wanted to go abroad. I was really wondering what I wanted to do, what I *ought* to do.'

After marriage she found 'my whole attitude to work changed'. But then her job had changed too. Getting married had involved a move from an exciting, well-paid job with a publisher to a secretarial job with a solicitor in Suffolk, which she had accepted 'as a matter of expediency'. It was a satisfactory job, though 'not challenging', but she doubted if she would have been able to hold down her previous job in addition to her newly-found role as housekeeper. When they first take a job, the prospect of marriage may influence some young women against choosing one which might one day compete with domestic responsibilities. By the time they do marry, most wives already perceive themselves, and are perceived by others, as part of the uncommitted work force. These women can never be, nor do they appear to want to be, part of any job structure which may take precedence over the domestic role of wife and mother. They may appear to have a great flexibility in employment, but at the same time they are the victims of that flexibility. Even before the arrival of children, which is more than likely to result in some break in employment, a wife will demonstrate that her availability for work is less than that of her husband since she wishes to support him in his role as worker. Mrs Monkhouse, a temporary secretary (the epitome of dispensable work), compared the different attitudes that she and her husband had to work:

> 'He's going to carry on working and I'm not. At the moment I might not get a job for a week or two weeks. Working doesn't worry me, I'd hate to think what would happen to *him* if he didn't work.'

According to Mrs Monkhouse, she and her husband wanted to have children in two or three years' time and she would then leave work. However, she was sure that she would leave work sooner than that 'if we found that he was working such awkward shifts that we just weren't seeing each other – we decided that before we got married'. Another wife, Mrs Pym, already faced with that problem, had actually given up her job as a shop assistant in a local supermarket, in order to spend more time with her husband, who was a shift worker:

> 'I was working at Superstore – full-time – Derek was doing day work then. Now he does night work – he goes off at 5 pm . . . so I found this morning job so that I could get home lunch time before he went to work.'

She explained her decision in terms of her type of work:

> 'My sort of career, that is nothing – shop work is something that anyone can do – I mean, you need no special qualifications for it.'

Most of the wives considered themselves to be 'not very career-minded' and, Mrs Milton, explained what being a 'career person' meant:

'Unless you know you want to be a career person, you don't put your work *before your home.*'

Do you think that you want to be a 'career person'?
'No!'

The issue of putting work before home was a clear one for women like Mrs Milton. However, there were others who enjoyed their work and wanted to do it well, and the critical factor for them was the attitude of their husbands. One such wife was a nurse, training in a specialist unit. Her working hours were erratic and often unpredictable, and, in addition, she was studying for an extra qualification. From the beginning of her marriage she found the job, coupled with housework, too much for her, but fortunately her husband was prepared to make a substantial contribution to the 'chores'. Nevertheless, she felt she was failing him:

'Initially, I felt very bad about it. I wanted to be a reasonable housewife and make myself available for him at all times. Anyway, he helps me [with the chores] and encourages me.'

Her husband was a medical student, so he had a real understanding of the pressure involved in work and studying. Not all husbands had his insight, nor could they all offer their wives the amount of practical help which he did. That a wife should be readily available to support and be with her husband was perceived and expected by many of the newly-wed husbands to be an essential part of her role. The attitude held by one husband towards his wife's work was typical: 'I'd like her to enjoy her work but I wouldn't want it to take up too much of our time together.' And one wife spoke of the 'bit of disturbance' which had been caused by her having once brought some work home with her:

'Steve didn't like it . . . I think what upset him was the fact that – you know – it was our spare time together and I was doing something else . . . I couldn't really focus my full attention on him.'

Wives who worked considered that they 'needed time' to run their homes, to be with their husbands, and to support them in their work roles. Mrs Owen felt it was very important for her husband to be 'really happy at his job' because *he* 'has to work for the rest of his life':

'If it came to the crunch his job would always come first in my eyes . . . he has to work for the rest of his life . . . so he has to be really happy at his job and that means more to me than my job.'

Even among those wives who did appear to have a relatively strong sense of career, there was a keen awareness of a future, albeit limited in scope. For example, Mrs Linden, who was a primary school teacher, thought that, as far as jobs went, hers was more important than her husband's:

'My job is more important in that what I *do* is probably more important, but his job is more important *to us* because his job is going to go on for a lot longer than mine – it's not going to have gaps in between.'

The foreshadowing of parenthood is therefore a crucial factor in the list of priorities about work and home which are often unconsciously drawn up in the early months of marriage. It is very unlikely that such issues will be considered by a couple only when the arrival of their first child is imminent; decisions about priorities would already have been made, either openly or tacitly, long even before a first child was conceived. Indeed, they would probably already have influenced the type of job that the wife had taken after getting married.

Even those few newly-wed wives who still appeared to be pursuing a career, were doing so within a very short time-span: one of these showed how she had tailored her ambition to accommodate to the time available to her before she became a mother: 'I know eventually I'm going to give up my job . . . so I'm going to get as high as I can in the time that's given me.'

In common with most of the other women with similar education, she was thinking of 'falling back on teaching', something which she felt could be successfully combined with having a family.

Women married to men who were absorbed with ascending a career ladder had to accept that to support their spouses' work could have a greater impact even than putting their own jobs second; the pre-eminence of the husband's work might mean that at times he would be completely unable to fulfil even those domestic responsibilities he had agreed to shoulder. Mrs Castle had been present when her husband, who was in the armed services, was discussing his work with some friends and she had been perturbed by his attitude:

'He said, "Look, the Army comes first and you come second", and that upset me a lot because I said, "I *don't* come second – I am your *wife*", and he realised straight away what he had said and he said he didn't mean it like that – "What I'm saying [is] that the Army, they don't care whether a chap is married or not, they are only concerned with the employee and they can sack you at any time – the wife comes second to them . . . " but I didn't really understand his point.'

THE WORLD OF WORK FOR MEN

In contrast to the women, fewer than a third (29 per cent) of the husbands had experienced a change of job in the twelve months prior to the interview. And, apart from the very few men whose job change was part of a history of personal work disruption, most of the changes in the employment could be regarded as career development, either of direct promotion within the same company or a move away to gain greater experience. Only rarely did their job changes have any direct link with the marriage, save for the few men who had decided to propose marriage when they were expecting promotion, because it would mean improved financial prospects.

Husbands, unlike their wives, did not have to relocate their work at marriage nor did they need to adjust their hours to suit their new, married status. However, their change of status was clearly reflected in their approach to work since for many, getting married meant that they had 'something to work for'. They now had the responsibility to have or seek a stable work pattern, and to 'keep going'; they valued a job which was steady and with good conditions. One husband demonstrated the way in which he saw his job as providing a basic security for his marriage: 'It's ideal for paying the mortgage and sick pay, so many advantages when you need money coming in constantly.'

Another husband described a quite different effect which his marriage had had upon his behaviour at work; he reflected upon the way in which he had become more responsible and subdued in the way he handled the apprentice under him:

'At work I approach things with a different attitude . . . we have an apprentice with us all the time – someone who has [recently] left school and they seem so mouthy. Before we were married I wouldn't think nothing of giving one a good swipe but when I got married I treated them different . . . I've quietened down quite a lot . . . I treat the job with a different attitude.'

The pressures that men were under were not only that they should keep in work, but also that they must do well at their job. Whenever an opportunity arose for advancement, greater responsibility or earning more money, these would be grasped; marriage seemed to provide a focus for striving.

For those husbands with a foot on the career ladder, it was important that they consolidate their positions by making sure they were free to respond to the demands made on them at work. Wives were expected to further this by going along with the company's plans. Mr Turner had recently moved to a new job within his company and he described this as a 'step in the right direction'. He would also shortly have an opportunity to take over a more senior job: 'to get myself into this new job – it's a few rungs up the ladder and it's quite responsible – so I've got to work hard at the moment'. He accepted that advancement in his career would mean moving around, and that this might involve job demotion for his wife in her job: 'though I think she would always get a job even if she had to drop down to, say, secretarial work'. Mrs Turner was an English graduate who was an assistant in the public relations department of a large public company close to her husband's work. She had originally considered teaching but decided to move into industry first and go into teaching later when she had a family. In the meantime, she intended to advance as far as she could in her present job. Like many of the wives, however, she showed pride in her husband's job and in his achievement in his career so far:

What do you think about Simon's job?
    'I'm proud to be an architect's wife.'

Why do you say that?
    'I'm probably a bit of a snob, if you like – I think to be an architect carries a bit of prestige and he's done remarkably well for his age and he enjoys it, which to me is very important.'

Women married to men who were in some kind of training which would provide a high status job in the future, talked with pride about their husbands' achievements. One such wife also spoke warmly of the importance of her own role, in which she provided the domestic support which would enable her husband to progress towards his goal, something which would ensure material and financial security and a 'good family life'.

Men and women gave strikingly different accounts of their lives at work. Although women said very little about what they currently liked or disliked in their jobs or what they wanted in the future, men talked easily about their jobs, particularly those men who had a skill or saw themselves progressing towards a goal at work. Overall, the men seemed more committed to their work, partly perhaps because they had already experienced, and could envisage, greater continuity in it. It was noticeable that even men who had otherwise found it difficult to talk about themselves were able to be very fluent when talking about their work and describing the functions of their jobs. One husband, who was a bus mechanic, graphically described the satisfaction he got from his job:

> 'Getting dirty [laugh]. It involves anything from changing an engine on a bus, gearbox or anything like that, right down to tightening up the smallest nut and bolt . . . '

Do you enjoy your work?
> 'Most of the time, yes. I couldn't do it if I didn't.'

What do you like?
> 'Don't know – have a laugh with the blokes, but really you do something. You can see that bus going out and carrying people and you think, "I fixed that all right" – it's just job satisfaction, isn't it?'

Another husband, who was a printer, likewise enjoyed the skill and responsibility in his work:

What do you enjoy about it?
> 'Don't know – people often ask me this – I've always enjoyed doing work – maybe because it's something that I'm good at – I enjoy it, it gives me immense pleasure to see a sheet of white paper going in one end and a full colour poster or magazine come out of the other – it's a lot of responsibility – you've got a train of 36,000 – 40,000 copies per hour so you've got to keep your mind on the job the whole time . . . you've got control panels with buttons and dials and things – I enjoy it, it's quite interesting.'

However, a few minutes later, he talked about his wife's job as an accounts clerk and he described that as 'very boring, she's sitting at her desk doing nothing, trying to make a little amount of work go a long way. *I* couldn't do that, I'm afraid.'

It was clear that the world of work was a vastly different experience for the men and for the women: nevertheless, the differences, marked as they were, appeared to be accepted by the majority of both the husbands and the wives as an inevitable concomitant of their having married.

HARMONISING WORK ROLES: KEY WORKERS AND SUPPORT WORKERS

A couple in the newly-wed phase of marriage and without children, might be perceived superficially as two independent, self-supporting workers who have set up home together. If this were the case, then there would have to be clearly defined strategies to enable each to be able to cope with the competing demands of each other's jobs and running the home would always be a major source of tension in the marital relationship. The fact that it is not, is because most couples automatically accept that the husband's work becomes the key job and the wife's of only secondary importance.

It is for this reason apparently that wives adopt the major housekeeping role, although at the same time continuing to work outside the home. This balance of roles in newly-wed marriage seems, after all, to be merely a variation on the traditional theme of the 'housewife marriage'. Indeed, it is firmly based on the assumption that wives will sooner or later become mothers, and mothers are primarily housewives, even though, at times, they may take on a 'little bit of part-time work' outside the home. But only rarely in their interviews did either men or women offer an explanation of this 'role segregation' in terms of the old-fashioned gender assignment of male breadwinner and female housewife. Nevertheless, when we examined the explanations which they gave for their combinations of domestic and working roles, we found that many of them were composed of a complex web of circular arguments which, when disentangled, turned out after all to be justifications of the traditional role segregation by gender.

'She'll have to finish when we have kids'

The work which wives did was viewed by both men and women as confined in scope, but there was also a constant awareness that it was limited in duration. Although husbands invariably talked of their future at work in terms of career advancement – moving up to be a foreman, starting their own business, or simply making more money – wives portrayed themselves as being generally content to 'keep going until the time comes for me to leave' which would, for most of them, be towards the end of the first pregnancy. And even those wives who, unlike the majority, had some potential for job development within their current employment, still worked towards a maternity deadline. Both men and women alike felt that the husband's job was the more important, and that the work of the wife was 'dispensable'.

Mrs Elder was a personal secretary and considered herself to be 'equal to my husband':

> 'I think his job is important to him and my job is important to me, but I mean, if one of us should give up work, then it would be me – *I'm more dispensable.*'

Her husband, a junior partner in a solicitor's firm, had prospects which exceeded anything she might ever achieve. So although, unlike most of the other wives, her job was not strictly dispensable, relative to her husband's it was not important enough to justify any alternative to the traditional division of responsibilities in marriage.

The jobs done by the majority of newly-wed wives were low paid and this lower earning power of wives was the most frequent justification offered by men for giving their own work first priority, although some women also put it in financial terms:

> 'My job is more important.'
>
> *'Why?'*
>
> 'Well, I earn more than she does and there will be a time when she'll have to finish – when we have kids.'—*Mr Cosgrove*

> 'His job is more important than mine – it's more basic, anyway – his will always be there because even with women's lib and all that, men still get paid more than women – in 99.9 per cent of the cases anyway. So his job is more important.'—*Mrs Klein*

As we showed earlier, the attitudes which wives had towards their work was compatible with the view that their working role was secondary to that of their husband. They considered that it was their work outside the home which was the heavy burden for them, rather than the extra domestic responsibility which they had to shoulder in addition to their jobs. Wherever they could, they made their jobs accommodate their housewifely duties and their husbands' needs and in every possible way demonstrated that their working role was dispensable. Husbands frequently corroborated this view by underestimating the value of their wives' jobs, both intrinsically and in financial terms, and argued that women were not really involved in their jobs:

> 'She can't wait to leave.'
> 'She's not so attached to it, she wouldn't mind moving.'
> 'She'd give up tomorrow if she could.'

'Her job is a bit of extra money.'
'Wouldn't miss her money, not *that* little bit.'

The constant underestimation of the financial advantages which resulted from the work the wives did was, in part, a strategy for coping with the time in the future when the wife would have to give up work in order to care for young children. This became very clear when we examined the financial arrangements of some couples, where the wife's income was handled in a way that excluded it from day-to-day expenses; in these marriages the running costs of the newly-wed household were borne exclusively by the husbands, and the wives' earnings were saved or used for 'extras'. Arrangements such as these were frustrating for wives, who complained of 'never seeing my own money' and 'not feeling that I contribute'. Mr Slater, unlike most husbands who favoured this arrangement, recognised that it made his wife 'a bit despondent':

> 'All her wages every month go into the bank . . . since we got married she hasn't spent any money . . . I think its a good thing. Eventually I will have to rely on her money one day . . . But she sometimes gets a bit despondent – how can I put it – that I don't ever say to her, "We need some of your money to pay this bill", do you know what I mean? She'd like to be put into the position of paying the bill.'

However, in spite of attempts to undervalue the earnings of the wife, most couples did in practice need two wage packets to manage their household costs, and some husbands were clearly already afraid of losing that extra income:

> 'My job should be more important and I would prefer it to be that way because, obviously, if I relied on her wages and she has to stay at home to look after kids, then it would put us in a state.'

LOOKING FORWARD: WORKING PARENTS AND PARENTS WHO WORK

After all the upheaval involved in getting married, the newly-weds expected their lives to go on, more or less without any major changes until the arrival of children. In general they expected that having children would make a difference – they would be less well off, more tired, have less opportunity to socialise – and these were all offered as reasons for delaying childbearing. But most importantly, the dawning of parenthood was perceived as the end of the era of the two-job household because somebody would have to look after the child (and eventually children), and that 'somebody' would 'naturally' be the wife:

'For generations it's been natural for the mother to be with the child and father to come home.'—*Mr Hill*

'A child needs a mother – it's a woman's job to look after the child.'— *Mrs Harris*

As far as the vast majority of the newly-weds was concerned there was no 'proper', 'suitable', or 'satisfactory' alternative to the traditional housewife marriage during the phase of family life when young children were being raised – at least, no alternative that 'made sense'. In Chapter 2 we stressed that it was important not to appear to offer definitions of 'proper' married life when interviewing.[7] We did not want our questioning of the newly-weds to suggest that women would, nor should, give up paid employment when they became mothers. So, we asked *all* the newly-weds, husbands and wives, about their working future: what plans did they have; could they imagine a time when they would change their present working patterns or stop working altogether?

The tradition of mothers at home and fathers at work was envisaged by most people, yet some men and women could imagine, and did favour, alternatives. We wanted to explore the reasons for choosing to follow tradition and rejecting possible new combinations of employment and domestic roles within the family. The problems in analysing the answers to these questions were similar to those raised in the discussion of household chores in Chapter 5 – it is difficult, if not impossible, to disentangle attitudes based on acceptance of the expedience of going along with the present order of things, from those which were part of a deeper gender identification with the breadwinner role.

The spirit of equality that most of the married men and women seemed to approve of, led some to believe that the only obstacle to their pursuing an alternative lifestyle was the inescapable disadvantage which they felt would arise from not following convention. For example, although some husbands said they would stay home to look after the children if their wives were the higher earners, they made this offer almost certain in the knowledge that it would never be put to the test. The way in which the labour market is presently constructed protects most husbands from acknowledging any other reasons for preferring the traditional housewife marriage in the child-raising years – reasons which some of the newly-wed husbands freely admitted:

'I couldn't give up work – I couldn't survive if I didn't work.'

'*Me* give up work? I just wouldn't.'

'I couldn't give up work to stay at home – it would drive me mad.'

One husband described this crucial gap between agreeing with role-swapping in principle and actually being able to disregard the influence of his upbringing. In this respect he spoke for many of the married men and women: 'I hear about men who do the dishes while the women go out to work – I can see nothing wrong with it but *I'd* probably find it difficult to do because I am so conditioned to going to work and the women being at home with the children.'

A handful of men described themselves convincingly as feeling drawn to home life and child care, but even in these cases it was usually on the basis of sharing these activities with their wives, rather than for a reversal of roles. Interestingly, wives were not in favour of their husbands 'mothering' although they were hopeful that their partners would 'do their bit', 'be really involved' and make it a 'joint effort'.

For the majority of the newly-weds, parenthood was not on the immediate horizon.[8] The fact, therefore, that so many of them 'knew' how this would affect their employment plans is testimony to the way in which traditional child care arrangements and the labour market are self-reinforcing. Four out of five of the newly-weds (husbands and wives alike) were certain that the wife would be the main carer for the children and that she would have to give up her job to do·so.

The impact of the change from full-time employee to housewife was rarely considered. Motherhood at a distance was idealised, and this strengthened the expectation that the work of newly-wed wives was temporary. So, quite apart from the justification that it was financially better for the family to be supported by the husband's job, and the notion that wives make better 'mothers', there was also the issue of who is going to look after the baby if it cannot be either of the parents. No alternative solution seemed popular:

'I wouldn't dump my kids in a nursery'

'There are child-minders I know – one of the girls I work with sends her child to one. But it's not ideal and I want the best for my baby when I have it. We both feel like that.'

'I could do a little job, evenings like, when he's home. Lots of mums do. But then when would we see each other? It would be all work, him out, me at home and then him in and me out. It's not what I like to see our family life as.'

A comparison was being made between the mundane reality of the present working role with the ideal of motherhood, as yet untasted, and motherhood always won. Women rarely expected to miss their job; motherhood would be so much more worthwhile, even though it might be boring, and their jobs were not particularly interesting anyway:

> 'I wouldn't miss it [her job] . . . after all, you would have the baby.'

> 'I suppose I might get a bit bored being indoors all day with the children, but that's part of having a family, isn't it?'

Several women looked forward to motherhood because it provided them with an excuse to leave work and, of course, as we have previously shown, a substantial number of wives had changed their jobs in some way as a result of marriage, so that work did not seem so very important:

> 'I'd love to give up work – if I have a family I will give up work. If we didn't have a family I would anyway, probably. It's just that I'm bored with the job.'

> 'I think I'd love it – not having to queue up for buses every morning – I'd be very happy.'

> 'I'm not a great lover of work really – I think I've been hairdressing for such a long time [5 years]. I'm getting fed up with it now and would quite like to get out of it . . . this [she had just become pregnant] is a good excuse.'

Rather unexpectedly, it was the husbands rather than the wives themselves who were far more likely to raise the possibility of the wives missing their work when they gave it up to have children. Sometimes this seemed to be so because men valued their own work and therefore assumed that their wives must feel the same, while at other times, although there was a more patronising air to the husbands' sympathy, they obviously felt their wives would need to get out of the house, and this would be the reason for their eventual return to paid employment:

> 'She'd be bound to miss it – she wouldn't be meeting so many people.'

> 'Ask her *now* and she'd say she wouldn't miss it – she'd be devoted to the children . . . but perhaps once the novelty wore off she might do.'

> 'She quite likes the ladies there . . . it gets her out of the house and into her own little circle, which is important.'

'I can't imagine coming home from work and seeing Tracy who has been pottering round the house all day long – she'd have no conversation, so a little job on the side would be a lot better.'

The fact that most first marriages begin with a period when both spouses are working full-time sustains the illusion that this is indeed the symmetrical phase of married life. But, as we have shown, wives who work (even wives without children) undertake the major share of domestic chores; their financial contribution to the household is usually underestimated and, perhaps most importantly, their employment role is perceived as only temporary and therefore unreliable. Work was certainly a major dimension of the lives of these newly-wed men and women, but whereas for the husbands, it was to be a continuous thread and accompanied their responsibility, for the wives it was a 'burden', a 'way of getting out of the house', 'something on the side'.

The distinction we have drawn between 'working husbands' and 'wives who work' illustrates the different worlds of husbands and wives and their dissimilar ways of perceiving home life and marriage. These are differences which lie at the heart of the paradox of modern marriage – the common expectation that the roles of modern spouses are symmetrical, whereas the reality demonstrates that it is the ability to integrate two widely contrasting worlds of experience which is the challenge of marriage today.

8 Becoming a Couple: Together . . .

A couple who are in love with each other form an organic unity; those who marry for the sake of a dowry or in order to have children form a union of component parts; and those who merely sleep in the same bed merely a connexion of separate individuals who would be described more correctly as sleeping together than as living together. Scientists tell us that when liquids are mixed together the mixture is total and entire. It should be the same with married people – a mutual blending of bodies, property, friends and relatives.

Moral Essays
Plutarch, Rex Warner (trans.)

'Coupleness' has become a by-word for modern marriage, although as the quotation from Plutarch shows, the notion that marriage is an amalgamation of personalities rather than an association of partners is by no means recent.

What exactly is 'coupleness' in the context of marriage? It has been accepted that over the centuries men and women have moved away from marriage as a legal bonding founded upon sound social and economic considerations, to 'the marital relationship', an emotional bonding founded exclusively on love and the pursuit of happiness.[1]

However, the notion that in the past the relationship between husband and wife was entirely focused and constrained by their publicly defined roles is as misleading as to assume that in the present, men and women conduct their married lives solely in terms of an intimate personal relationship. For, as we noted earlier, the concepts of marriage as an economic and social unit and as a union of personalities, are ever present; it is the emphasis in public rhetoric of one concept over the other which decides which is to be preferred and therefore taken as typical for a particular era. Thus the concept of marriage as primarily a social and economic unit is regarded as 'traditional marriage' and the concept of marriage as primarily a personal relationship has become a way of defining 'modern marriage'. The fact that the basis for getting out of a marriage contract in our society rests on the concept of the irretrievable breakdown of the marital relationship is evidence that we live in an age when marriage has come to be defined as a personal relationship.

What constitutes a personal relationship in marriage? For some husbands and wives today, although marriage is not just a legal association based on the carrying out of different but complementary roles, neither is it a very intense relationship; they lead separate, yet highly co-operative, lives. For other men and women, to be simply 'associated partners' in this way would seem to miss the point about marriage; in their view it should be a consummate union, a complete blending of individual personalities culminating in 'oneness'.

It is important, however, not to confuse this meaning of 'oneness' with the merging of husband and wife into a single legal identity which has long been an influential definition of the relationship between husband and wife. This legal 'coupling' is no mutual blending of identities, but the obliteration of the identity of a wife so that she becomes incorporated in her husband's identity. As a US Supreme Court justice observed as recently as the 1960s, 'this rule has worked out in reality to mean that though the husband and wife are one, the one is the husband'.[2]

Even before we interviewed the newly-weds, we were presented with the powerful image of marriage as oneness, since several men and women challenged our request to interview them and their spouses separately. For some, it seemed simply unnecessary – why put ourselves to the trouble of replicating material? For the rest there appeared a sinister side to our request – were we suggesting that they might have different things to say about 'their' marriage? Clearly our proposal to interview the spouses separately implied the existence of 'his' marriage and 'her' marriage apart from 'our' marriage. Our proposal only became more acceptable to these husbands and wives when we pointed out that since the first part of the interview consisted of questions about their individual pasts it would save time to do this separately; the fact that questions about the marriage followed was overlooked once interviewing got going! However, at certain points of the interview, most particularly the section concentrating on domestic activities, many respondents betrayed their curiosity, and anxiety, about the way their partner might be answering the same question – 'you'll get a different story from her', 'I'd love to hear what *his* answer is.'

For the newly-weds, 'being a couple' was clearly synonymous with being married although they were very unclear about what went into making a couple. They made references to 'being the same', 'sharing,' 'being equal' and 'being complementary to each other.' The only clear prescription was not to be different from each other, but they adhered to the ethic of jointness rather than equality.

However (and perhaps not surprisingly), these new spouses were more preoccupied with the new 'me' rather than the new 'us'. Their own words demonstrated that they were unaware of this: there were two new versions of 'me' masquerading as 'we'. The new 'me' seemed to be an extension of the old 'me'; 'me and my spouse' rather than a 'we' created out of two distinct and equally important personalities. The following remark from a young husband about the pleasure of being married illustrates a typical newly-wed unconscious confusion; his initial focus was on independence from his parents rather than interdependence with his wife:

> 'I'm on my own now – not answerable to anybody, me and Sheila [wife] aren't answerable to anybody.'

And a young bride described the issue, common to many of the newly-weds, of adjustment to a new identity, a new 'me':

> 'You get married and it's great – for the first few weeks – and then you are trying to sort out whether you've become a different person or whether you are the same. I want to be *me* first, as well as being married.'

THE COURTING EXPERIENCE: PREPARATION FOR MARRIAGE

The caricature of the courting couple is of lovers locked in an embrace, gazing into each others' eyes, oblivious of the world around them; a portrait of intimacy. We must take care not to mistake the intensely erotic pre-marriage relationship for an intimate relationship. Young lovers today are often the envy of their parents for the freedom they have to be alone together before committing themselves in marriage – and this was reflected in the way in which the pre-marital sexual activity of the newly-weds was accepted by their parents.

However, to regard pre-marital courtship as a foretaste of conjugal life is misleading; it is rarely a time for practising marriage because the focus of courtship is different from that of marriage. Prospective first-time spouses have an important purpose in common – to get married. They also share a common identity; they are both adults-in-waiting, ready to end their single days by settling down.

While most of the newly-weds were sexually intimate for a considerable time before marriage, the opportunities for getting to know each other were limited (apart from those who cohabited). 'Being together' is a synonym for contemporary courtship, with marriage as the goal of 'being together always'. Courtship is the process of coming together rather than an exercise in living together. Of course, there may be conflicts in courtship (see Chapter 5), but the opportunities for avoiding conflict are greater then than in marriage. When it comes to the matter of living as a couple, husbands and wives have to begin to cope with the differences which separate them. As we will show in this chapter, men and women have fundamentally different notions of togetherness and it is in the early months of living life as a married pair that these differences are revealed.

INTIMACY AND CLOSENESS

Physical intimacy: having sex and making love

We start by considering the sexual relationship, not because we regard this as the primary component of marital intimacy but because it was the first area of intimacy in which the couples became involved and, indeed, according to several men and women, their sexual relationship enhanced the development of closeness;

> 'I certainly felt that I had to have a sexual relationship with her before I could get to know her better.'—*Mr Walters*

> 'I think it helps to bring you closer together when you are courting.'— *Mrs Tasker*

In Chapter 4 we noted that only four of the newly-wed couples were sexually inexperienced on their wedding night; however, this did not mean that for the rest of the couples sex-after-marriage was simply a continuation of sex-before-marriage. The sexual relationship changed according to the context in which it occurred, particularly for wives: there is a transition from having sex to making love.

Throughout the courtship period, especially at the beginning, opportunities for sexual intercourse had been limited; as time passed and the wedding day approached, more couples had moved in together or were stopping over in each other's homes, and it seemed that many parents, confident that a wedding was going to take place, were more inclined to turn a blind eye. Nevertheless, apart from those who lived together, most of the couples had had sexual relations in awkward and unrelaxed circumstances:

> 'Our sex life then used to be tragic, terrible – I used to worry about it . . . We took our opportunities when we could get them because we weren't living together and you've obviously got to be in the mood to make love but when we *did* get an opportunity there was always something, someone at the door. It was only when we went on holiday together that we started to get to know each other sexually . . . we were just more relaxed.'—*Mr Evans*

Since marriage, this husband had observed a change in his attitude to the sexual relationship. Most unusually for a husband, he reflected a view held by many of the newly-wed wives:

> 'It's fantastic now, but the sex act isn't as important to either of us as the loving relationship, because we can go to bed and just cuddle up all night and get more out of that.'—*Mr Evans*

About half of the couples who had pre-marital sexual intercourse referred to difficulties. The problems most frequently mentioned were to do with contraception; over half the husbands and two in five wives mentioned contraceptive difficulties. Slightly more wives referred to problems with the Pill (men referred to their wife's problem with it) but where the couple were using the sheath (the next most popular contraceptive method) it was husbands who found it unsatisfactory from their own point of view. A husband was the more likely partner to report problems with contraception and it was usually he who reported his wife's difficulty with the Pill, such as fears about long-term effects, putting on weight, depression, loss of libido, headaches, tiredness and nausea. It sometimes seemed as if husbands were reporting contraceptive problems which had been offered as explanations for a wife's loss of interest in sex:

> 'She changed from using the Pill because it made her fat – she used to be thin. It worries her and I'd like her to be thinner so she switched to the coil but it hasn't worked even after a year.'

And this was corroborated by two of the wives:

> 'I was a little bit depressed at first and put on a bit of weight and I was a bit worried and he [her fiancé] said to me, "Well, if it's going to affect you, [not feeling like sex] you've got to come off". But other methods aren't 100 per cent effective so I said I'd see how I got on.'

> 'I was feeling off colour for quite a while – I mean I didn't fancy sex at all and I thought it was the Pill 'cos friends of mine have been on the Pill and had loss of libido as they say. I feel much better – I don't feel so tired. Maybe it was other reasons, I just don't know.'

Contraceptive difficulties apart, the most likely problem with sex in this pre-marriage phase centred on inexperience – disastrous first nights together, sexual initiation for virgins, shyness, or the inability to relax due to fear of someone walking in. Rather surprisingly, only one wife mentioned fear of pregnancy. There were only a few references to other problems such as performance, disputes over frequency or genital soreness.

Sexual difficulties continued after the wedding and in the early months of marriage; four out of five of the newly-weds reported difficulty in their sexual relationship but the nature of the difficulties changed, reflecting the changed context of the relationship. The couples who reported problems associated with inexperience were those who had refrained from sex until the honeymoon. The rest made far more frequent mention than in courtship of performance problems such as achieving orgasm, and genital soreness and infections. One of the greatest hindrances to frequent and satisfying sex after the wedding was simply tiredness; the demands of work and the relentless home decorating took their toll. This strain of adjusting to the demands of newly-wed life was another reason some couples gave for having started their sexual relationship before marriage:

> 'I'm sure having a sexual relationship before marriage makes it much better when you are married. Because when you get married it's a strain cooking and adjusting to a new way of life; I'm sure it must be far worse getting used to a sexual life as well – going to bed and thinking, "God, what's going to happen?" '—*Mrs Dawson*

Apart from those couples who were living with their families and who still lacked privacy, most couples were now in a situation where they could have sex whenever and wherever they chose. Disputes arose over who should be the initiator and how frequent sex should be. Men who had taken a lead in courtship (playing out the role of the wooer) were hoping that their wives would now show more initiative. Wives who had responded with enthusiasm to sexual advances in courtship were now less inclined when the request came every night. Several women also regretted the loss of that earlier restricted physical intimacy, of 'not going the whole way' that had often been necessary in courtship because of the constraints. Their fiancés had had to put up with it but they themselves had become accustomed to it (and some even grew to prefer it to the complete sexual act). Wives were also sad that, after marriage, their husbands were less likely to accompany any sexual overtures with loving words. In fact, the whole way in which they related to each other sexually seemed to have changed.

Bargaining over sex was different too. In courtship the lack of opportunity kept a check on ardour, so that it was always possible to avoid intercourse without either partner having to say 'no'. In marriage the only way to refuse was not to be interested and this could seem like rejection. As we have already mentioned, after marriage the Pill was often blamed, especially by husbands, for women 'going off sex', and it seemed that problems with contraception became the basis of explanation for not wanting sex – it avoided 'getting personal'. Another way of handling this situation was to develop a routine or etiquette for sexual intercourse which included signs of encouragement or deterrence, thus avoiding a direct refusal. One couple had worked out that it was better for the wife to make the approach for intercourse:

> 'It's easier for a man to get aroused – for a woman it really has to be within her. If he was aroused and the woman was not in the mood, then it would be a terrible let down for him. If I show my feelings then he knows it's alright.'

The sexual arena was one where men and women who were in favour of equality and breaking down traditional views of masculinity and feminity found themselves in confusion. Women wanted to please men, and wanted them to be 'dominating in a gentle way'; men wanted their wives to 'take the initiative more but not take over', as one wife realised:

> 'I don't like making the first move but if he doesn't when I feel like it then I have to . . . it's a bit silly really but I think I like to feel that the man is dominant, although I don't agree with that in life itself.'

The majority of men considered that they made the first approach; most women thought that it could be either or both of them together. Only three husbands and five wives thought that the wife made the first move and only one couple agreed that this happened. For some, the logical form of the expression of sexual equality was the mutual orgasm and there was concern if this wasn't achieved: 'Our difficulty is managing to have a climax simultaneously, it's something we are really trying to achieve.'

About two in five men and a third of women said that sex was very important to them, but there was really very little difference between the sexes over the importance, although slightly more women thought it was *not* important. About half the husbands and wives thought that their sexual needs were similar if not the same as their spouses. But well over a third of men and a quarter of the women thought that men had a greater need for sex.

In terms of sexual behaviour, women laid great emphasis on the expression of warmth and sharing. Foreplay, in particular being cuddled, complimented and talked to in a loving and gentle way, were as important to them as the sex act itself:

> 'Sex doesn't make me feel warm and secure, I'd rather he give me a cuddle, that makes me warm and secure more than anything else . . . I tell him I love him but *he* don't tell *me*.'

> 'I'd say one of the greatest pleasures is to lie down at the end of the day with him. When it comes to sex it's proving what marriage means to us. As I say, when you hit the pillow and you're both together it's one of the best times.'

Men also mentioned the importance of physical closeness and demonstrating their feelings through having sex. For some men, particularly those who were neither keen nor confident about expressing their feelings verbally, having sex was a means of showing their wives that they loved them; it was often the only context in which they felt able to say 'lovey dovey' things:

> 'I do say "I love you" and all this but only when we are in bed . . . not when we're watching telly or in the pub.'

It was important to the men that their wives had an orgasm (their own orgasm was regarded as inevitable); they wanted to feel able to arouse and please their wives. In fact, as far as women were concerned, their orgasms were more important to their husbands than they were to themselves. There was considerable uncertainty among women about what female orgasm was; descriptions ranged from 'I get satisfaction but I don't achieve what you read about in *Cosmopolitan*' to 'I know when I've had enough':

> 'He tries to work out how many times I come.'

And if you don't come?

> 'I wouldn't tell him, I'd make out I did.'

And from another wife:

> 'It's very important to him that I have a climax; men feel they are not doing their duty otherwise.'

And from another:

> 'It matters to him that I do [have an orgasm]: I explained to him that more
> often than not I don't but I still enjoy it . . . I think he accepts it now but
> he didn't to start with because he read what they say in the papers.'

Psychological intimacy: 'knowing each other inside out'

According to the thesis that marriage creates a crucial sense of reality
for modern people, modern marital relationships must include sufficient psychological intimacy for the partners to 'know' each other. In
this way the husband and wife become co-architects and co-
inhabitants of their unique private world – their marriage. In this
'haven in a heartless world' the partners achieve such closeness
(mainly through conversation) that they provide mutual confirmation
of their personal identities. The picture which emerged from
Komarovsky's study of working-class American marriage is considerably different; each spouse inhabits his or her own unique world:

> Men and women live in different psychological worlds whatever their class
> position. Much of the zest and the exasperation of the early years of
> marriage results from each partner's introduction into the mental world of
> the opposite sex. For many Glenton couples the confrontation brought
> more exasperation than delight.[3]

Komarovsky did point out, however, that this gulf may be wider in
the working classes than among the middle classes.

A similar observation was made in a study of adolescent boys and
girls; middle-class boys and girls tend 'to see one another as basically
the same sort of human beings', whereas their working-class peers see
men and women as 'essentially different'.[4] Several recent studies
have highlighted the importance to women of close confiding relationships[5] but in an account of marriages in trouble it was clear that
men regarded the matter of revealing feelings very differently from
women:

> Overall, the men's accounts of their attitudes and feelings about revealing
> private areas of the self to others suggest that, for many of them,
> non-disclosure constituted an unchanging, central, and even fervent part
> of their identities.[6]

A simple conclusion to all this might be that women are better at
expressing their feelings and value the disclosure of their feelings to
someone they are close to more than men, and that middle-class
women married to middle-class men are the most likely to achieve

such confiding relationships. This view of the intimacy within modern marriage has achieved wide currency of late. It suggests that from the first day of marriage many men (particularly those from working-class backgrounds) are unable or unwilling, or both, to establish an intimate rapport with their spouse.

It therefore seemed important to discover more about the background experiences of psychological intimacy for the newly-weds. So we sought evidence about the nature and extent of any confiding relationships the newly-weds had had before marriage, in their teenage years and in the pre-marriage courtship period.

Only two women, compared with a quarter of the men, said they had had no one to confide in when they were teenagers. Women had tended to choose a confidante who was a relative and the same sex, most usually their mother (almost half) but also sisters or a friend (a quarter). For some men (a fifth) their mothers were the most popular choice, followed by both parents or friends, but men also sometimes chose authority figures such as teachers or youth leaders, whereas women never went outside their family or circle of friends. This reflects the very different views men and women held about the purpose of confiding, which is explained in greater detail later on in this chapter.

It became clear that those people who had felt most supported emotionally in their teenage years were usually female. At marriage they expected to be able to transfer this supportive relationship to their spouses and were often disappointed when they found that their husbands were unable to fulfil this role:

'I like to talk about things on my mind – I used to talk to my parents because I was close to them, too close perhaps, being an only one.'

Too close?

'Because if you lose them it's a great loss but now I'm married I've grown a little away from them. But I miss having them to talk to. I don't talk to Alan as much as I'd like to because he doesn't respond, doesn't discuss.'

In some instances these wives confided in their husbands selectively, retaining their former confidantes for those areas in which their husbands seemed uninterested.

Almost one in four of the husbands said they had confided in no one when teenagers. Generally these young men had felt that it was not possible to do so; some remarked on the absence of appropriate people (fathers, brothers) while others described, often with difficulty, that the business of saying what you feel was awkward for them. Several husbands explained that they simply did not need to confide:

> 'Don't think I've ever been in that kind of situation [with a problem] – I wouldn't weigh myself down, and I wouldn't talk to the wife.'

> 'I don't usually have problems – I try not to . . . if I'm fed up I always go out. I don't talk to her, what's the point in worrying *two* people?'

> 'I don't think I really need to discuss anything with anybody – I only do it as a matter of courtesy because she is my wife and I think she'd want to know'.

While most of these non-confiding men continued through life to set little store by the expression of feelings, just a few remarked that living so closely with their wife (particularly if she was a good listener) had provided the right climate for self-expression and that as a result they had begun to open their hearts:

> 'When I was young, I lived with my gran and grandad – I didn't think of them as parents; they were something different. I didn't really confide in them and consequently it all bottled up inside, but now with Doreen I feel quite free to say what I want.'

For most people who had had former confidantes, courtship marked the beginning of the move from them to the future spouse. In courtship, the couple were still moving away from their families towards marriage and this process was reflected in their style of confiding. For example, girls might use both their mothers and their fiancés, selecting whoever was available at the time, or they might decide upon an appropriate division of issues between them. Everyday worries tended to be disclosed to mother and worries about the future to the future husband. Interestingly, on occasion, a mother who was perceived as being a good confidante was disclosed to by her future son or daughter in-law as well as her own child.

Once the couple were married it was clear that most brides and grooms expected to relinquish past confidantes and depend mainly, if not exclusively, on their marriage partners. Although mothers were the most enduring of the old confidantes, they were turned to only for specific things such as 'women's problems' or for other matters which seemed difficult to raise with the new husband. In some instances the continued use of a mother in this way hindered the development of intimacy within the marriage but in many more cases it was an outlet for women who found little interest or understanding from their husbands. According to the conventional wisdom, 'your son is yours on till he gets a wife but your daughter's your daughter for the rest of her life', and this was borne out by the greater tolerance for a woman to retain a confiding relationship (however limited in scope) with her mother than for her husband to do so with his:

> 'I used to be very close to my mother but it's inevitable once you get married you get closer to your wife. After all, I see her all the time and spend a lot more time talking to her.'

The fact that most husbands and wives regarded their spouses as their chief confidantes reveals little about the nature and relevance of psychological intimacy in marriage. It is only in their accounts of their own confiding behaviour and attitudes to disclosure that we begin to see their failure to understand their partner's behaviour and attitudes. These failures of comprehension are a fundamental source of incompatibility in contemporary marriage.

Two views of confiding: solving problems and airing feelings

According to the majority of wives, their need for self-disclosure was at least the same, if not greater, than that of their husbands. Two in five wives said that their need was the same as their husbands, but almost as many thought their own need was the greater. Although almost one in three husbands assumed that their need to confide was the same as that of their wives, many men found it impossible to judge – they found the whole business of expressing and discussing their feelings was mystifying (and certainly too difficult to discuss with interviewers!). However, just over a quarter of men thought they needed to confide more than their wives did; only five wives agreed that this was so. A mutual need to confide was expressed in as few as five marriages.

Several women who admitted that confiding in their spouses was a vital aspect of their marital relationship had been perplexed, and at times disappointed, when they realised that their husbands were not confiding in them. They assumed that their own needs for disclosure were the same as that of their spouses (evidence yet again of the pervasiveness of the newly-wed ethic of not-being-different) so they concluded that either they were not satisfying their husbands in this respect or that their husbands were confiding elsewhere. When the newly-weds' own accounts of how and why they did (or did not) disclose their feelings are closely examined, it becomes clear that men and women use the process of self-disclosure in very different ways.

'*Airing feelings*' was an important preoccupation of women and a vital aspect of self-disclosure for them. For some the feelings were aired in the course of general conversation. The following example of a detailed description of a trivial event in the day of one wife, in which references are made to personal feelings, was typical of one way in which wives ventilated their feelings:

> 'I'd been queueing for ages in Marks and Spencer and just as it got to my turn they shut the till down. I was mad; I could have *hit* the girl as she walked off. Anyway, then I had to start all over again.'—*Mrs Rudd*

Women did not expect the recounting of their frustrations of frustration and exasperation (emotions very commonly expressed by women – perhaps illustrative of feminine passivity) to be rewarded with anything more than a nod or grunt of solidarity; in other words (though words were not always necessary), 'I know how you feel'. Husbands quite often regarded this kind of disclosure as 'rabbiting on'. If they gave a hint of affirmation their wives felt listened to; if they demonstrated their lack of interest by reading the newspaper or walking out, their wives felt unsupported. Husbands who failed to see any point in these monologues of disclosure found them boring;

> 'She talks, it's boring; she goes right into the depths, tells me every single thing, every little detail. I say, "Shut up".'

Another aspect of wives' disclosure was expressing their mood, their feelings of sadness or depression, insecurity or uncertainty:

> 'A lot of the time he'll say, "What's the matter with you?" and I won't really know myself, perhaps going around with a long face or something and I have to delve around for a reason, but there rarely is one.'

> 'Sometimes when I'm moody I'd like to be able to explain how I'm feeling. I find it a bit difficult. I think he understands to some extent but as I can't put it into words, I don't really see how I can expect him to understand, but I wish that I could somehow. Like I say, I don't always understand it myself – there's no real reason behind it – it's just a feeling . . . it's the only thing he finds difficult about me, my moods, we've talked about. Otherwise he thinks I'm all right.'

Women expressing their feelings in this way were a threat for many men. Husbands could not understand what their wives meant, nor what they could do about it, or what it indicated about their marriage. It was a rare husband who could be confided in successfully; again, the helpful response from him was simply to listen, to take the mood seriously and then to encourage his wife to move on from it. To 'jolly her out of it' without acknowledging the strength of her feelings was perceived as being ignored. A few men tried to offer solutions and then withdrew on realising that these 'problems with no name' had no solutions.[7] Most men simply tuned off. 'Rabbiting on' might be boring and 'a pain in the neck' but to some extent it was 'what wives do'; it therefore had a place in marriage. 'The problems with no name' were disturbing because they could not be explained. Some men attributed them to 'the time of the month' or to the fact that women are 'more expressive', 'more sensitive', 'feel things more', 'more that way', but they were plainly baffled.

'Problem solving', in contrast, was for most men the main, if not the sole purpose of disclosing to another person. The point of any conversation or talking about feelings was in order to gain advice, information or a knowledgeable opinion. One husband recognised that he 'kept things to himself' and that his wife would like it if he approached her with things that bothered him, but 'though she would like it she can't do anything, she can't solve the problem'. If there were problems at work (and work was a very important part of men's lives), wives were rejected as confidantes because they 'wouldn't understand, they couldn't do anything':

> 'If it's a problem at work – she don't know what I'm on about half the time, so there's no point.'

Alongside this patronising attitude to disclosing to wives, there was, however, a protective element; some men would shield women from problems to do with work and money because they didn't want to worry them and also in order to protect their own image because it was not manly to admit to such feelings of inadequacy. Wives who challenged their husbands for more information or who probed and dug away were rarely rewarded for their perseverance. Several men were resentful of their wives' attempts to intrude into their world. One husband said he did not bother to disclose things to his wife because he felt his problems belonged to him alone, and he compared his wife's probing into his feelings to his mother's 'trying to get things out of me'. Both then and now, he did not wish to share his concerns: 'not that I had any disrespect, just that me problems are me own'. Like many men, he preferred to talk to 'mates down the pub':

> 'They tend to be a sounding board, you say it but they don't take in what you say, as you are standing round in a circle having a laugh.'

We have portrayed the different attitudes towards confiding as a gender difference, which, by and large, it is. However, in contrast to the behaviour of the majority, there were certain men who 'aired their feelings' and a few women who 'bottled up their feelings' and found disclosing difficult unless they had a specific problem to solve. About a quarter of the husbands and a fifth of the wives said they would disclose worries only after considerable probing from their spouses. If we include those who say they withhold their feelings and are reluctant to disclose, these proportions rise to almost two in five men and a third of the wives.

There is a strong desire in modern marriage to share as much as possible and, indeed, this is recommended as the key to a healthy marriage. Yet there are many obstacles to sharing confidences and letting out feelings. Confiding is not the same experience for men as it is for women; they have different ideas about the use and purpose of disclosure. It is interesting to note that the husbands whose wives most valued them as confidantes were almost all eldest sons (several from families where the absence of the father had forced them to be supportive to their mothers). In general, these fundamental differences in attitudes towards disclosure make the kind of empathy implied by the notion that marriage is 'oneness' impossible, and in some ways may undermine the more realistic opportunities for sympathy and support in marriage.

TOGETHERNESS: A 'LIFE IN COMMON' OR A 'COMMON LIFE'

For the newly-weds, the word 'togetherness' seemed to embrace their understanding of what marital relationships were all about; it was a word repeatedly used by them when they described what they found rewarding and satisfying about married life. With marriage comes a home of one's own, a home life, respect as a married person, and, above all else, security, since it offers a framework for the future. Of course most of these goals could have been achieved in other ways, although never so conveniently in one action. Marriage also has an added bonus – a partner with whom to create and share this new life. The marital relationship provides someone to share a home life with, a regular sexual partner, a confidante, someone who is 'on your side' and who cares for you and about you.

A home life

Settling down into marriage, as we have shown, typically centres on the home, which assumes a special significance as the status symbol of being fully adult. It is a place where newly-weds can be private and feel in control of their lives.

As we saw in Chapter 6, in the early months of marriage most of the couples were busy establishing organised patterns of routine and doing 'the things that married people do'. They expected their families and friends to regard them as 'home birds' and accept that they had temporarily retired from most social activities in order to concentrate their attention on their homes and on each other:

> 'The optician said I had healthy eyes – nothing to worry about. I thought that I might need glasses but he said, "Too much watching telly . . . because you've just got married and all this – that's a big step". And now that we are married we don't go out so much as when we were single and he said, "You're watching too much TV, you want less of that and more of the other!'—*Mrs Cosgrove*

> 'It is the early stages of marriage and people haven't encroached on our privacy for obvious reasons . . . entertaining is a bit of a strain because we are not used to it yet . . . We look forward to people coming but we are glad when they eventually go because we do like to be on our own quite a bit . . . We don't go out very much . . . we like being together, living together, just the things married people do I suppose.'—*Mr Hill*

> 'We don't go out very much at the moment because it's nice to have our own house and stay in.'—*Mrs Trist*

'Someone to come home to'

The newly-weds appeared to be overwhelmed by a sense of pride and satisfaction in being householders and having their own environment, but they were also beginning to appreciate the constant presence of another person. This was particularly true of the husbands:

> 'Having the home is lovely – and having Caroline in it is even better – marriage is terrific.'—*Mr Evans*

> 'I like the security of marriage – someone to love, who you'll see tonight – it is a very reassuring thing.'—*Mr Glass*

> 'It's the companionship – knowing she will be here when I come home.'—*Mr Ward*

> 'Having someone around all the time – someone to fall back on – someone to come home to.'—*Mr Coventry*

'You're together – you're one not two – you're not on your own.'—
Mr Riley

'Having someone to come home to', the presence of a wife in the
home, was central to men's concept of home life, and a wife
represented the very spirit of the home.

'Just being together'

For every four husbands who regarded marriage primarily in a
home-centred way, there was only one wife who held such a view.
Wives preferred to talk about the pleasures of married life in terms of
the *relationship* they had with their partners. Indeed, two out of three
wives referred to some aspect of this as giving them the greatest
satisfaction in marriage.

'Being together' was central to most wives' descriptions of the
togetherness and companionship of home life. They liked constant
companionship, talking to their spouses, telling them the minutiae of
the day's events and expressing their moods, both happy and sad.
From the moment of waking to the end of the day, they wanted to be
sharing their lives with their spouses:

> 'It's the company – being with the person you love . . . being able to
> share things.'—*Mrs Castle*

> 'I like sharing a bed with him every night . . . having constant com-
> pany – somebody you really love.'—*Mrs Gunter*

> 'Just being together and doing what we want to do.'—*Mrs Atkinson*

> 'Togetherness – doing things together – being able to talk to him about
> *anything*.'—*Mrs Bates*

> 'Sleeping together, not sex, sharing all our life together.'—*Mrs Lawley*

The importance of mutual suppport

'I like being looked after – well, I suppose I am a male chauvinist
pig', said Mr Oliver. Few husbands spoke so candidly about the
importance of being cared for by their wives, though it was implicit in
much of what men said they enjoyed and expected of married life.
When a husband spoke of the things he valued in his wife, or more
generally spoke about the 'ideal' wife, there were often comments
upon her physical attractiveness but equally there were references to
her skills as a housewife, and the way she looked after him:

'She's caring, she looks after me.'

'She'd do anything for anybody, especially *me*.'

'She looks after the place – always tidy and organised. I think she is going to run a good home when we get a place of our own.'

'I like the way she is – the things she does – she helps me – she keeps the house nice and tidy.'

'What attracted me to her was the way she was so incredibly neat and tidy.'

So, for husbands a supportive partner in marriage was someone who kept the home going, and who generally made their life run smoothly.

Wives who were demanding, and those who were 'moody', who sought attention and required expressions of affection (apart from sex), also posed problems for men:

'I never say I love her – I don't know why. Sometimes she asks, "Do you love me?" – I say, "I married you" – something like that. She knows she's not going to get a direct answer so she don't bother no more.'

Do you think she knows you love her?
'I suppose she does – she wouldn't have married me if she didn't would she? . . . She tells me she loves me, she is affectionate and cuddles up and says, "I love you" – you know that sort of stuff like you see on the telly – she's always moaning that I don't tell her I love her.'

The supportive element in marriage was highly valued by wives and two out of three wives talked about marriage in such a way. They wanted to share their feelings and to be 'understood'; to feel appreciated and cared about by their spouses. Generally, however, wives felt that *they* were the ones who reassured and were understanding and tender towards their husbands (and indeed their spouses recognised this), but they wanted reciprocity. Some wives did have supportive husbands and gladly acknowledged this:

'He's kind, considerate, very good to me – he's always there when you want advice and comfort and he's always willing to listen.'—*Mrs Vaughan*

'Basically, he loves me and cares for me and he is interested in me as a person.'—*Mrs Lockwood*

'It's his ability to cope with me – he doesn't take what I say in temper seriously . . . I can be myself and he understands me.'—*Mrs Wilson*

In their accounts of physical and psychological intimacy the newly-weds vividly reveal that as men and women they interpret togetherness very differently. Most (though not all) men seek a *life in common* with their wives, a home life, a physical and psychological base; somewhere and someone to set out from and return to.

But, for nearly all the wives, their desired marriage was *a common life* with an empathetic partner, who was to provide both material and emotional security. Women wanted a close exchange of intimacy which would make them feel valued as a person not just a wife.

Despite the promise of emotional fulfilment offered by modern marriage, the gender gap of expectation in many of these newly-wed marriages was wide and men seemed either to be unaware of this or unable to accept it. Wives, in contrast, acknowledged the existence of the gap and hoped to bridge it. There is, it seems, 'his' marriage and 'her' marriage existing apart from 'their' marriage. How then do modern spouses interpret and resolve the differences which separate them; the other side of becoming a couple?

9 Becoming a Couple: . . . Yet Separate

The Teviots reached the end of the second week of their honeymoon undisturbed, except by the visits of two or three neighbours. It was almost time that there should be some change, at least Mrs Tomkinson wished to goodness there might soon be what she called 'a little staying company' in the house, if only that my lady might wear some of her bettermost gowns; and she also thought my lady seemed rather moped somehow. Mr Phillips gave it as his humble opinion that 'our folks had had enough of their own company for a while'.

The Semi-attached Couple
Emily Eden, 1860

If the goals of modern marriage are togetherness and self-realisation then perhaps it is surprising that as many as two in three married couples remain together; as absolute marital goals these are incompatible. According to a study of identity and stability in marriage, the world of marriage is not ideal for nurturing the identity of the partners for 'in reality much has to be left unsaid; much has to be accepted without choice; many options are closed and people's lives run in predictable grooves when they become married'. A compromise is usually struck between constraining individual needs and restraining the dictates of coupleness and 'on the whole married people perform this balancing act very skilfully'.[1]

One way in which the potential for conflict in marriage can be reduced is for married men and women to avoid behaving in ways which would threaten their identity as husbands and wives, and follow some sort of ground rules. They usually already expect certain things from each other, because they assume that married people should behave in certain ways, but the rhetoric of modern marriage suggests a wider freedom than this. According to a guide for soon-to-be-marrieds, published by the British Medical Association, 'The adventure of marriage today is that you are quite free to work out together whatever sort of relationship you want'.[2] Many of the newly-weds had been drawn into marriage by the appeal of gaining personal and social identity as a married person. They sought 'Marriage', and 'my' marriage was interpreted as 'me' doing what married people do.

In Chapter 2 we commented that conflict has been regarded as endemic to marriage. It has been argued that marital conflict arises in two ways: the different ideas about marriage held by the partners will at times be incompatible; and, although resources are pooled in marriage, access to them will be uneven so that there will be competition. Conflict in marriage has generated a wide literature; there are studies of the management of conflict by husbands and wives, the way power in the relationship is distributed, and accounts of 'bargaining' between the partners.[3] It is a particularly complex area of research in newly-wed marriage, when romance is at a premium and there is a strong desire on the part of the couple to display harmony, so that differences will at the very least be muffled and at worst be smothered completely. The way in which modern marriage is regarded as egalitarian can create further distortions, and the newly-weds are eager to promote this image by the use of such phrases as were: 'fifty-fifty', 'split down the middle', 'joint', 'just the same', despite a wealth of evidence to the contrary.

In order to discover what had actually occurred as well as what could happen, we questioned each husband and wife about the *last* tiff/quarrel/difference of opinion they had had with their spouse. We had already been alerted during pilot work to the importance of discovering each newly-wed's terminology, in order to generate authentic discussion: whereas a 'quarrel' might be denied, a 'bit of heat', a 'rubbing up the wrong way' or a 'falling out' might be admitted to. We found that the different descriptions were often a form of classification: a quarrel usually implied an issue of some moment with a lingering effect, whereas a tiff was a momentary dispute commonly attributed to mood. The newly-weds wanted to be sure that the level of conflict was conveyed clearly:

'If it's a bad one we always talk about it . . . '

A bad one?

'A "being distant", put it that way. You know, something is not right and you are still doing it and you try to calm down, sort yourself out. You might be sitting in the same room but not *be* with each other . . . I wouldn't say we have rows, it's bad quarrels.'

We had originally hoped to examine each persons' account of the same quarrel, its context, the manner in which it was handled and whether it was satisfactorily resolved, and then compare the two versions. However, we were offered not only two different accounts, but usually two different *events*; only eight couples described the same quarrel, which presented us with problems of definition and of meaning. A wife might raise a dispute she and her husband had had over housework, something *she* saw as a fundamental issue in their marriage. Her husband may simply have regarded this as an instance of her moodiness, or her 'having a nag' and would not consider it a quarrel, so that he would therefore refer to a quite different dispute as the most recent one between them.

However, as we did not interview the spouses together it was never routinely possible to trace the interpretation of the same events for both partners. We could sometimes pick up the reactions of the second partner through a reference at another point in the interview, but more usually one had to accept the dispute described by one partner only.

When we analysed the content of each dispute, we discovered that it was often a key to a newly-wed's expectations of marriage and its ground rules, something we had not expected. In Chapter 7 we remarked how wives, although heavily burdened with domestic responsibilities, rarely voiced resentment or disatisfaction; they appeared to take a long-term view and accepted that their husbands suffered a counterbalancing pressure to remain in paid employment. It was the cardinal deal of married life.

However, although no wife expected her husband to share the domestic burden in equal measure, most wives wanted their husbands to help in some way, or at least to make gestures of response, such as occasionally offering to cook the dinner or clean the house, or show appreciation for a pile of ironed shirts. In other words, they wanted recognition and needed value given to the reality of their lives as wives. And at the very least, even if a husband could only offer the minimum practical and emotional support, he must not undermine what his wife was trying to do.

The content of disputes in these new marriages, where wives felt neglected and disparaged, were testimonies of disappointment, and these disappointments portrayed expectations that had not been fulfilled. The newly-weds were awkward and ambiguous about expressing what they had expected from marriage but their disputes showed that they had sometimes felt very let down by marriage and were disappointed with each other and with themselves.

NEWLY-WED CONFLICT: DIVERGENCE AND DISILLUSION

Divergence

The accent in newly-wed marriage is on harmony and there is a strong spirit of solidarity between the couple, who did not want to appear 'against each other'. This became particularly evident to us when we tried to question newly-weds about how and why they made decisions – all too often a frustrating and pointless exercise. When one husband and wife were asked about their last major decision, the husband said it concerned the purchase of a three-piece suite. According to him, they had agreed it was necessary to buy one, and had chosen it together: 'we have the same taste'.

Later in the interview, however, when reflecting on quarrels and tiffs, the husband returned to the purchase of the three-piece suite and admitted that his wife had been 'a bit unsure' about the price but, he hastily said, 'she was ratty anyway'. Because this particular suite was very expensive, they had discussed it further and 'by the time we'd had a chat, looked at all the cheaper stuff, we decided to buy the dear one'. His wife was apparently unhappy about the choice, and although she accepted his arguments that cheaper alternatives would be less hard-wearing, she still thought they could not afford the one he wanted. Quite clearly it was the opinion of the husband which swayed the 'joint' decision, though he did not see this, and perceived his wife as having 'been in a mood' rather than having had an opinion which differed from his.

The ways in which a divergence of opinion in marriage can be interpreted by the partners provides a fascinating glimpse of the undertow of power in marriages which are initially presented as having aspirations of jointness. It became clear that although some husbands 'let' their wives make decisions, in practice these often turned out to be ones they had not considered important:

> 'I would say Rosemary makes most of the decisions.'

Is that the way you like it?

> 'It doesn't really bother me – I mean if I felt it was something that I wanted rather than what she wanted, if I desperately wanted something, it would go my way . . . she might *say* "no" but she'd *do* what I wanted anyway. Otherwise I'm quite happy to leave it to her – unless, as I say, when it really affects me.'

Disillusion

In the early days of married life, the spouses have a lot to learn about each other. We have seen earlier (Chapter 6) how their different standards and different ways of doing things have to be combined in order to create a domestic routine. In the course of getting more used to each other the partners reveal themselves, and such revelations may not be welcome, so that tolerance has to be established along with the limits of acceptance. Deification of the loved one, so often achieved in courtship, can no longer be sustained, since a certain amount of disillusion inevitably accompanies the development of intimacy. Although in practice it can be comforting and reassuring for a partner to find that his ideal lover is, after all, as real as himself, it is none the less shattering to discover that you married an illusion. This fear, both of disillusioning and of being disillusioned, creates a tension for newly-weds, since it interferes with their wish to step off the pedestal and reveal themselves as they really are. In courtship, the lovers were fashioning their convergence into 'the couple' and even submerged their individual selves to achieve this more fully. But once married, the partners want to express *themselves*, and this movement towards divergence is difficult to handle.

Nagging and putting down

Even though in only eight marriages did both partners choose the same incident when asked to recall their last quarrel, the overall profile of marital conflict given by the husbands and wives is remarkably similar.

The overwhelming majority of accounts, from both men and women, suggest that it was wives who usually initiated or inspired the disputes. There was a similar pattern with regard to nagging. Two in three husbands accused their wives of nagging and three-quarters of the wives admitted they were naggers. A third of the husbands said they never nagged and about the same proportion of women agreed their husbands never nagged.

At first sight, this view of marital conflict appears to corroborate the 'trouble and strife' reputation of the wife, until one takes account of the different perspectives of the spouses. According to the Andy Capp theory of marriage[4] it is wives who are the great manipulators in marriage; they set the standards of a marriage and spend their time getting reluctant husbands to conform. If this is so, then the newly-wed husbands were willing victims, since only one dispute described by a wife involved a criticism of her husband. Wives were frequently identified as 'naggers', but husbands were equally often described as 'critics'; one in five husbands and almost the same proportion of wives reported disputes where the husband had personally criticised the wife.

The chief complaints made about wives were that they were poor housewives, or they failed to service their husbands adequately so that husbands felt it necessary to 'moan', 'remind' or 'have a go' to 'keep her up to scratch':

> 'I moan about her cooking – she doesn't salt the potatoes properly, not like my mum.'

> 'I have to remind her that the bin needs emptying, a little dig once a week keeps her awake.'

And from another husband:

> 'I have a bit of a go if I don't get my injection of coffee . . . she's untidy – not a good manager.'

And from another:

> 'She's naturally clumsy – leaves the rubbish bag dripping on the carpet . . . she never seems to learn by her mistakes.'

A few men admitted that they deliberately provoked their wives, finding it difficult to resist the temptation to tease them about such sensitive issues as their competence as wives or their personal appearance. As one husband admitted:

> 'I get her upset sometimes, I muck about with her now and then.'

How do you mean?
> 'I tease her, goin' on about her weight.'

How does she react?
> 'She gets uptight with me.'

So why do you do it?
> 'I don't know, it just happens, then she starts crying – and I just make up.'

At times it seemed that many of these critical husbands were trying to regulate the behaviour of their wives by putting them down, an effective method, since women were often only too ready to take any expression of divergent or negative feeling as personal criticism. We should emphasise that this interpretation of husbands' behaviour as 'teasing' emerged not only from the way the wives presented events but were also related by the husbands themselves in their accounts of their own behaviour.

Although most wives nagged their husbnds (and at least three-quarters said they did), only rarely was this in terms of personal criticism, and neither did any of the husbands interpret it in that way. It was as if wives were 'expected' to nag; husbands found it almost reassuring that their wives 'moaned' and 'carried on' about the house being untidy; it was, after all, 'what wives do'. And wives sometimes felt that recourse to nagging was the only way in which they could 'activate' their husbands:

> 'I've asked him to do something and he'll sit there watching telly – I'll say, "*Are* you going to do that?" and he says, "Stop nagging – you sound like my mum".'

However, nagging could also be counter-productive, as one husband rather patronisingly revealed:

> 'I was watching telly and we had someone coming round; she wanted me to hoover; I refused; she nagged, so I called her something and she lashed out. She shut herself in here and was upset because of what I said.'

What did you do then?

> 'I just carried on watching telly – I finished seeing what I wanted to see, then I came in and said I was sorry – not immediately – I gave *her* the chance to apologise first.'

If a husband took his wife's nagging seriously – and most suggested that they did not – it would usually be in such a way as to indicate that he had chosen to respond positively in order to do his wife a favour, rather than respond by action because he recognised he had been at fault in some way.

'Not so much a quarrel: more someone's mood'

Many marital disputes were attributed to one partner's mood, and, according to a quarter of the husbands and a third of wives, that partner was usually the wife. 'The time of the month', 'being on the turn' and 'a bit ratty' were all descriptions of triggers to marital disharmony. In other words, the actual issue, such as coming home to an untidy house, was less important than the need that the moody partner had to vent depression, tiredness or frustration. 'Taking things out on each other' was accepted as part of the 'give and take' of married life, as one wife explained:

'We have minor quarrels; I get a bit moody for no apparent reason; whether you can blame it on hormones I don't know. Silly things make me fed up.'

However, to assume that mood was the cause of a dispute was also a convenient way of handling divergence, a means of ignoring or diminishing the impact of the negative feeling being expressed by the spouse who is 'in a mood'.

We have already discussed in the previous chapter the way that wives, in particular, liked to 'air their feelings' and express their frustration and annoyance. To many husbands (though not all) these occasions indicated to them that their wives were 'simply looking for a fight'. Women also often commented on their own mood, 'I often get fed up when he's late home for dinner but I lost my temper because I was feeling down anyway'. Wives valued the expression and sharing of feelings with their spouses and may therefore have initiated conflict partly because they wanted to communicate these. Several women explained that 'they were the angry ones' in the marriage and were plainly disappointed that their spouses simply didn't retaliate; one wife lamented that:

'Usually when we quarrel it's very one-sided because he just sits and listens . . . he's very placid and I'm fiery, and it usually ends with me bawling my eyes out and him not saying anything.'

In the honeymoon phase of marriage, the temptation to avoid and ignore the manifestation of uncomfortable divergence is particularly strong, and one way of handling this is for couples to build up theories about their styles of conflict, so that they define each other as 'the one who argues', 'the one who sulks' or 'the one who gives in'. This 'routinisation' of difference meant that few women and even fewer men showed signs of having reflected on the meaning of divergence for the kind of marital relationship they were trying to create.

THE MARRIAGE YOKE

The accounts of those men and women who had reflected upon their quarrelling provided some ground rules for modern marriage. Although roles within marriage may no longer be distinct and incontrovertible (though in practice the traditional roles are still closely observed, even if adjusted in a novel fashion) there are none the less strong indications that these new spouses had definite views about the correct balance of roles within marriage and the balance between the individual spouse and the marriage. We have called this balance the marriage yoke. Getting the balance right in the tug of love called marriage is graphically described by Mrs Cosgrove:

And what was the quarrel about?

'I'm trying to think – ah – oh – I think it was something stupid but it started off a big row – I was in bed and he nicked the quilt off me. I was lying there and I was freezing cold and I'm pulling the quilt and as I'm pulling it one way he's pulling it the other way and that *gets* me and in the end – I slept on the camp bed – I didn't sleep on it all night, I got another quilt out and said, "I'm going to sleep on the *camp* bed" and I was going mad – big screaming row and, ah – I went and put the camp bed in the front room and he came and dragged it out – dragged me in the bedroom on it [laughing]. He wouldn't go to sleep so I got back into the camp bed and he said, "Come on – get back in *this* bed – don't be silly" and I said "No – that's *it*" – he does things – he really boils me up and then it's all – then he goes all different then, you know – he's all nice and everything.'

Balancing between 'you' and 'me'

About a fifth of the husbands and the same proportion of the wives saw in their most recent dispute implications for the way the marriage was working out; the quarrel was a symptom of the failure to balance the roles within marriage. It was not just a matter of disagreement over what to do or different ideas about how to do something; there was disappointment with the way things were working out. The balance in the marriage, the deal between 'me' and 'you', had not been achieved. Although both wives and husbands spoke in this way, the wives tended to express their own disappointment whereas husbands described the disappointment of their wives.

In general husbands gave no indication that they were disappointed. Most of the issues which triggered these accounts were centred on the division of labour in the home, and arose out of the heavy domestic burden of the wives. The few men who felt their wives were not 'playing fair' complained about being left to do too many of the domestic chores, or about their wife's monopoly of the money she earned. Essentially these disputes occurred because of breaches of the traditional roles: wives who were working full-time expected their husbands to help more round the house, especially if he was at home when she wasn't (as was the case with shift workers);

since both spouses worked, both were income earners and men often became suspicious about whether wives were paying their way.

Decisions about financial priorities in the new households illustrate the ambiguous feelings engendered by the attempt to create a balance between 'you' and 'me'.

The ideology of sharing was particularly strong in the marriage of Mr and Mrs Lawley; they were anxious to regard all their income as 'our' money, although they did not pool their respective incomes into a joint account:

> 'Anna has been paying the bills and she's trying to save for them when they come in and so she's not using her own money. She tends to use my money. We're trying not to call it "my" money and "her" money – we're trying to call it "our" money.'

However, Mrs Lawley's recent purchase of a grapefruit knife had aroused a vehement reaction in her husband because she had bought the knife with 'his' money. He was very aggrieved:

> 'She keeps using *my* cash card – she's saving her money for the bills, so she's not using *her* money. She came home with this grapefruit knife: "What do you want a grapefruit knife for?" I know it costs very little – it seems silly – but the point is I was saving *my* money for decorating and buying things for the garden.'

'Jointness' in marriage was strongly favoured by the newly-weds, although this was not necessarily interpreted as pooling income. Only a minority did this, usually putting both incomes into a joint bank account. Most couples retained their separate incomes and then worked out their own system for sharing the expenditure of their household.[5]

In these marriages it was, in theory, unnecessary for the spouses to consult each other about personal spending of money. However, it was also in these same marriages that the partners disagreed most about levels of spending or financial priorities. It was considered to be unfair to spend on oneself, unless this was part of a quid pro quo:

> 'We disagree about clothes – I always buy more than we can afford. I can't argue because I do spend a lot of money on clothes but then he has a hobby, photography, which he spends a lot of his money on.'—*Mrs Elder*

Spending on the home was justified since it was considered of mutual benefit, although some partners tried to extend this definition:

> 'When I said that he should "not spend so much on the car", he pointed out that it wasn't just for him, it was for us. But I can't drive and he don't take me out in it.'—*Mrs Sandford*

Balancing between 'you' and 'me' and 'us'

Apart from getting the balance right within the relationship, it is also necessary for a couple to achieve a balance between marriage and other competing demands of work, friends, family and one's own self. Almost two in five wives and a quarter of husbands described disputes of this kind. 'Coming home late' was a typical example of a quarrel which crystallised this issue. The reason for a partner being delayed could be working late, honouring a commitment to friends or family, or choosing to satisfy a personal wish to spend time away from home – all could be perceived as threatening to the couple and life together at home:

> 'Roger was working on a Sunday night sometimes so consequently as he was going to football on Saturday afternoon I felt it was *cutting down on our weekend* and I felt I had to say something – and Roger didn't really realise because once or twice he forgets he's married. It's not really one decision, my decision, it's *our* decision.'—Mrs *Dawson*

> 'I'm turning into a golfing widow already . . . I don't like it if he plays twice in one weekend, though – I don't think it's really fair – it takes up so much time.'—Mrs *Black*

We have already described the relatively isolated home life of the newly-wed couple. It is an isolation which is at times enjoyed, but at other times endured in the interests of coupleness. When one partner in the couple fails to return, the other partner feels abandoned. It was not surprising that it was wives who felt this more acutely; their social lives had been completely changed by marriage. One wife spent a lot of time alone as her husband worked night shifts. They had moved to a new housing estate which was fifteen miles away from her parents and the area where she had grown up; public transport was poor and she did not drive:

How often do you go out by yourself?

> 'Not very often – I went out with my sister once to our friend who had that clothes party – but very rarely do I go out on my own. Can't remember the last time I went out.

> I think it's nice to have a girls' night just to have a laugh; Francis doesn't like that, he doesn't think it's right. He's very old-fashioned in his ways, you know. He doesn't mind if we go out to the pictures but he doesn't like it if we go to a club or something like that. He doesn't like that.'

The Pearces were another couple who were trying to establish a satisfactory balance in their social lives. Mr Pearce had always enjoyed 'going dancing' and refused to give it up, even though he felt rebuked by his wife when he continued to go. He wished she herself would go out more, since that would counterbalance his dancing:

'I get the dig – "Oh, you're going dancing again". It's something I've always done and I always used to go out every night of the week – that's *me* and I've got no intention of changing. You compromise to a certain extent but I enjoy going out. I feel if you are tied to the home it's a waste of a life . . . in fact, I wish *she* would go out a bit more – she goes out very seldom.'

It was interesting to compare his views with those of his wife. Mrs Pearce appeared to accept that her husband goes dancing on Friday nights and said she did the washing while he was out:

'I tease him about always going out but I don't really mind – I think it would be wrong for him to give up things he's always done – I don't say *every* night but it's good to have an interest.'

There was another aspect of life together in which the newly-wed couples had to find a balance. Many wives who led a restricted social life expected their husbands to be close, attentive companions who returned to them every night to share a common life. However, husbands, as we have already indicated, often had very different ideas; they wanted wives who would create a home, look after it and them, and, most important of all, who would be there when they chose to return. It was rare for husbands to experience 'aloneness' and when they did, their reactions were extreme; their wives were not behaving as 'proper wives'. Wives were becoming resigned to the fact that husbands did behave that way, but they felt it was unfair. They had hoped that in marriage they would find close friendship, and that their husbands would not *want* to be away from them and so they simply felt let down when their husbands were repeatedly late home.

'Feeling let down'

It became noticeable that in many descriptions of the most recent quarrel, the emotional loading of the issue was often far greater than the apparently trivial trigger. Again it was more frequently wives who felt that way, both according to their own narratives and from their husbands' accounts also (a third of wives and just over a third of husbands). Only two husbands and one wife referred to a husband having felt this way. According to husbands, women were 'more sensitive' and 'take things to heart', but when wives were describing their own feelings it was clear they expected much more of their husbands emotionally than these men were prepared, or felt able, to give. In some cases it was clear that women simply felt unsupported, that their husbands were not 'backing them up', were neglecting them and even ignoring them. We realised that to some extent wives had expectations that their husbands would automatically do all these things and felt peeved when they did not.

It was a much more serious matter, however, when wives felt they had been promised specific support which did not materialise, or when their belief that their husband was supportive was destroyed by an incident which demonstrated otherwise. Wives most likely to say they were 'feeling let down' were those who were highly dependent on their husbands. For some wives the isolation they experienced in marriage was acute; they had moved away from their own family and friends, or changed their job and lost their work-mates. Certain wives had done both of these things and had also ended up unemployed because they had been pre-maritally pregnant. These were the ones in greatest need of a supportive husband; they were the most vulnerable wives.

'Nothing in particular, but everything basically'

Even wives who were not the most vulnerable, however, were keenly aware of the strains which marriage could impose. Mrs Butcher had moved to a new area when she married, convenient for her husband's job, and was seeking a new job when we interviewed her. She had reluctantly given up her job becauses she found the travelling too much. While she had been working, her husband had helped her in the house, but he now did little in the home, although she felt that was fair since she was at home all day. She felt isolated because her widowed mother lived over the other side of London and all her friends were there too and, anyway, they were part of 'a singles set'. She described herself as 'bored' and 'lonely', and felt that moving away and leaving her job had 'shifted things' between her husband and herself. The most recent quarrel for both spouses had been an incident the previous week. Mrs Butcher had asked her husband to buy something and bring it back with him on his way home from work, and he had forgotten.

This quarrel encapsulates all the features of divergence, disappointment and disillusion that we have already catalogued. According to Mr Butcher:

'It was over nothing in particular but everything basically – she's been at home a bit frustrated – I think she was due for her period so she was a bit scratchy. I'd been particularly untidy round the house which annoyed her and she'd asked me to get something and I had forgotten. I forget quite a lot of things and I'd come in from work tired and wanted to sit down and relax and she said had I remembered this and I just snapped back.'

Mrs Butcher's reaction was to go quiet: 'she just wouldn't speak to me'. Half an hour later he tried to make it up to her but 'she still wouldn't speak to me':

'I got really annoyed and if ever I'm going to hit her it would have been then; I didn't but I felt like it. I walked out and slammed the door, got in the car, went for a drive. When I got back I was determined to speak first – usual thing, I thought *she* was wrong, she thought *I* was wrong, so we went for two days without speaking . . . she was thinking of leaving and getting a flat on her own. I think everything built up and she couldn't take any more.'

Mrs Butcher also accepted that it was a 'build up of things' and that she had been 'a bit depressed' staying home and that she was 'snappy 'cos of the time of the month'. The couple had discussed the incident later and their accounts of it were similar. What Mr Butcher had not mentioned, perhaps because he had not realised it, was that his wife's reaction centred on being 'let down' and disregarded, feelings that for her were of crucial importance:

'It was a very little thing but it happens so often; I ask him to do something, some very little thing, and things crop up at work and he doesn't do them. If anyone else asks him, it's done straight away. It is like I don't *matter* as much. It wasn't like that when we were going out – he couldn't do enough.'

Many of those who lament the increasing breakdown of marriage attribute this to unrealistic expectations of it held by modern spouses. On the other hand, there are those who consider that the extent of divorce and remarriage today indicates how much marriage matters.[6] When asked what they expected from marriage, most newly-weds were unable to say. Yet, as this chapter has shown, they readily (though indirectly) expressed their disappointment and disillusion with married life, which suggests that they had, in fact, held marked expectations about it.

'A life together, a life apart'

This chapter brings to a conclusion the portrait of contemporary marriage which forms the second part of this book. Throughout this part we have recounted the story of newly-married life. It is a life founded upon notions of coupleness, togetherness and equality. Yet, at each point in the story it becomes clear that the worlds of husband and wife are separate and asymmetrical.

Despite the superficial appearance of symmetry in the first phase of marriage, it is, in fact, 'a life together; a life apart'. Both spouses may be out all day working, returning at night to share a home life, yet, as we have shown, the worlds of work and home hold very different meanings for them. Husbands and wives cannot avoid moving further apart when they become mothers and fathers, because fathers are expected to be *primarily* breadwinners and mothers are expected to be *primarily* housekeepers. The power of this future reality inevitably shapes the present, so that from the very beginning of marriage, brides and grooms follow this implied structure. Furthermore, as Chapter 8 showed, an additional barrier to a life together lies in the fact that these men and women also inhabit different psychological worlds; even when they are alone together, 'just the two of us', the perception of that experience is different for each of them.

To allow oneself to be seduced by the notion of the couple as a symbiotic union, and regard them as an undifferentiated pair, is to miss the essential difference in marriage – the heterogeneity of the spouses: men and women *are* different. Modern marriage is a paradox. The language of marital relationships denies difference; the reality of married life defies sameness.

Part III

An Approach to the Future

10 A Sense of the Future

Looking back on the last six months, Margaret realised the chaotic nature of
our daily life, and its difference from the orderly sequence that has been
fabricated by historians. Actual life is full of false clues and sign-posts that
lead nowhere. With infinite effort we nerve ourselves for a crisis that never
comes. The most successful career must show a waste of strength that might
have removed mountains, and the most unsuccessful is not that of the man
who is taken unprepared but of him who has prepared and is never taken.

Howards End
E. M. Forster

The portrayal of any aspect of human experience is essentially an
exercise in understanding human behaviour. Researchers have
tended to segment human experience into separate worlds, to focus
on people in employment or at home. As a result, the complex
network of experiences and relationships which make up the *total*
course of each of our lives is often disregarded. Such approaches can
provide us with only a very partial view. Additionally, such seg-
mented scrutiny can impose an artificial stasis which can be very
misleading, since human experience never does stand still, but is
constantly shifting and responding to the world around:

'Experience is a stream, a flow; social structures are seamless webs of
criss- crossing negotiations; biographies are in a constant state of becoming and as they evolve so their subject accounts of themselves evolve.'[1]

Although it is true that our present study of marriage can offer only
a partial view of the total lives of the men and women, nevertheless,
because marriage is an integral part of those 'seamless webs', these
accounts of married life offer glimpses into individual interpretations
of that total network. In describing their present experience of being
married, the newly-wed husbands and wives have revealed their
sense of where they have come from, where they think they are at the
moment, and where they hope they will be going.

Our study of sixty-five marriages is, therefore, not simply a study
of the 'just married': we believe it can also provide a valuable insight
into the whole experience of young men and women who were born
mainly in the 1950s, educated in the 1960s and early 1970s, who
entered employment in the 1970s and who were all experiencing a
critical transition in their lives – that of getting married – on the eve
of the 1980s.

A theme which has run throughout this book has been the importance of the personal and social context of any transition in life; the way in which the past has not only conveyed the individual to the present, but has also helped to constitute it. A sense of the future was influential in shaping what happened next, but it was also revealed as having been of crucial importance in fashioning the present, both in terms of attitudes and of behaviour. And the orientation held towards the future by an individual, as we shall show later, was likely to have been either reinforced or deliberately opened to the possibility of change by the transition of marriage.

TRANSITIONS: MOMENTS OF REFLECTION AND CREATION

Although change is the very essence of living, we are probably only aware of the myriad changes which constitute our individual lives at the times when they make direct impact on us and provoke or promote a discernible shift of direction in our lives. The impact will, of course, be modified by many factors, such as whether or not we foresaw the changes and whether we consider their effects to be beneficial or harmful.

Marriage is a prime example of such a change and transition – one of particular significance, since most people do marry at some time in their lives; it is a common expectation, and part of a cultural sequence which has probably been impressed on most of us from childhood. The persistence of courtship and wedding rituals in contemporary Britain demonstrates how ingrained this sequence is.

We set out to understand more about the experience of getting married, and of being married, through the exploration of the motives, goals, choices and plans of the men and women whose marriages we are studying. In practice, this turned out to be rather easier than we had expected, since we found that the newly-weds were at a point in their lives when they were particularly reflective about the choices they had made in the past, those they were currently making, and the possible future directions their lives might take. Many of them commented that being interviewed 'at a time like this', a time of heightened awareness, when they were poised between the experience of their pasts and the prospects for their future, meant that both perspectives were particularly 'available' to them.

When the couples had made their commitment to marriage, they had recognised that they were beginning their adult lives; they were aware of the past that had brought them to that point, and, although sometimes regretful of opportunities they felt they had lost (as in education), nevertheless almost all of them were brimming over with a sense of 'becoming', and were imbued with hope for the future. This was encapsulated in a remark by one of the husbands (from which we have taken the title of this book):

> 'Getting married is where it all starts. You're not a kid any more, you're branching out on your own – it's the beginning of the rest of your life.'

Despite the general portrayal in our culture of romantic love as a motive for marriage, we have already seen how the decisions to marry made by the newly-weds appeared as part of their logic for living.[2] Marriage made good sense to them because it offered a means to independence and freedom, and released them from the ephemeral period of being in between the world of their parents and their own adult life; it symbolised for them the opportunity to settle their own future. Marriage would enable them to sort out their own sense of who they were, by providing them with new and socially approval identities – those of married men and women. They felt ready to be regarded as *adults* and this was translated by them into being ready for *marriage*. Although they did have notions of what marriage would be like, and how they should behave as husbands and wives, these ideas were overshadowed by the far stronger sense which they had of creating their future. The biographer Phyllis Rose has poignantly evoked the meaning of the moment of getting married:

> I believe, first of all, that living is an act of creativity and that, at certain moments of our lives, our creative imaginations are more conspicuously demanded than at others. At certain moments, the need to decide upon the story of our own lives becomes particularly pressing – when we choose a mate, for example . . . Decisions like that make sense, retroactively, of the past and project a meaning onto the future, knit past and future together, and create, suspended between the two, the present. Questions we have all asked of ourselves such as "Why am I doing this?" or the even more basic "What am I doing?" suggest the way in which living forces us to look for and forces us to find a design within the primal stew of data which is our daily experience.[3]

The fact that marriage crystallises a sense of the future in this way is bound up with its definition as a commitment for life, the crucial characteristic which distinguishes it from cohabitation:

> Even a cohabitation 'formalized' by declaration appears to operate on a
> different level to marriage, for it can be no more than a declaration of an
> existing state of affairs with no implications about future conduct, which
> still remains the essence of marriage.[4]

The wedding service articulates this vision of the future which
marriage captures; in this case a future limited only by death: ' 'til
death do us part'. Therefore, when a marriage breaks down, a sense
of the future is lost. The same theme emerges from a study of people
whose visions of the future were shattered when their marriages
ended in divorce, as Nicky Hart poignantly describes:

> Almost everyone in my sample thought of the end of marriage as the end
> of an era in their lives. 'Beginning all over again', 'starting one's life
> again', 'making a new life for oneself' was the way they spoke . . . it
> suggested that the marital status lies at the very core of the individual's
> social existence; so much so, its termination was almost the end of life
> itself.[5]

IDENTITY: A SENSE OF DIRECTION

We have said that marriage has come to symbolise the start of adult
life, surely a powerful key to its enduring attraction. Although there
are other ways to achieve adulthood, none is so convenient or clearly
arranged. The process of getting married is ceremonially choreo-
graphed; boyfriend and girlfriend become fiancés, they then move
towards the wedding to become bride and groom, and finally they
emerge as husband and wife. The whole process can provide continuity through a period of great personal flux and can considerably ease
the evolution of a new identity.

Social identity has been portrayed as a constellation of roles: a
woman may be, in turn or simultaneously, daughter, wife, employee,
mother. Over the course of our lives we take on new roles, which can
be incorporated into our continually developing social identity, and
some of these become of greater importance, while others simply
fade out.

After marriage, the individual's personal hierarchy of roles will be
rearranged, with the role of husband or wife assuming particular
importance. Although identity considered in this way is helpful in
enabling us to understand how individuals handle and interpret their
social existence, it fails to provide any answer to the question of how
an individual creates his (or her) unique sense of self – 'me', the very
core of personal identity.

Personal identity has been descibed in a variety of ways, but for our purposes it seems most useful to regard it as something which is fashioned from the meanings and experience of past actions, and used in order to choose and guide actions in the future. To define it in this way introduces a directional dimension over time, one which enables an individual to 'make meaning out of past events' and to 'delineate a certain character for himself which will guide his behaviour in future interaction'.[6] Marriage can, therefore, greatly sharpen and stabilise personal identity, not merely in the conventional understanding that it can provide the socially scripted roles of husband and wife but more importantly, because it creates a sense of the future.

Marriage is a transition, and transitions have often been regarded as problematic because any change requires that the individual restructures his ways of looking at the world, and his plans for living in it:

> Whether we construe the change as a gain or a loss it is likely to require effort. Old patterns of thought and activity must be given up and fresh ones developed. It is not only losses which are commonly believed to carry a risk of maladjustment, gains too can be hazardous.[7]

There are some ways in which marriage can be regarded as a loss, or at least, as a restriction. Present-day emphasis upon the importance for the individual of being able to make completely free choices has an initial in congruity with the concept of marriage and commitment. Yet this is exactly what many people seek; the limiting of personal choice and the binding of commitment is one of the attractions of marriage.

The newly-wed couples revealed their need for on outline to their lives, a starting point and a signpost for the future. Marriage can, for many, provide the framework upon which to create the rest of an individual's life. The very 'narrowing of future projections of each partner' referred to by Berger and Kellner, can help many adults-in-waiting to gain a firm sense of personal identity.

> Before marriage the individual typically plays with quite discrepant daydreams in which the future self is projected. Having now considerably stabilized his self image, the married individual will have to project the future in accordance with this maritally defined identity.[8]

We have shown how marriage can both codify and sharpen assumptions about the future, and how the past and present are interwoven in it, through the creation by the individual of his 'assumptive worlds', which both derive from his past experience and shape his purposes in the present:

> The assumptive world is the only world we know and it includes everything we know or think we know. It includes our interpretation of the past and our expectations of the future, our plans and our prejudices . . . [9]

Our own past experiences will influence our assumptions about the range of options, such as marriage, which life has to offer. And our understanding of ourselves, based on our perceptions of how we have acted in the past, will suggest to us how we are likely to respond and react. In addition, our knowledge generally of what happens to people like us, and what has actually happened to people we know, further influences these assumptions.

The present: informed by interpretations of the past

What took place in the past is a critical key to understanding what is happening in the present. At the beginning of their interviews, the questions asked of the newly-weds about recent events in their lives and those of people close to them, enabled them to reflect in some detail upon occurrences in their immediate (and sometimes more distant) past, and upon the implications these may have had for the present.[10] Of course, individuals are not always able to make such links themselves; in Chapter 3 we noted some of the 'coincidences' which we had observed in the pre-marriage lives of some of the newly-weds which could well have influenced their decisions to marry, although they appeared to have been unconscious of them.

The present: shaped by perceptions of the future

Despite having been aware of the way in which the past acts upon the present, we were surprised to discover the extent of the influence which perceptions of the *future* can exert upon present life, in terms of both expectations and behaviour. We repeatedly found that choices in the present had been guided by assumptions about the future, and a strong thread of the awareness of a 'future reality' ran throughout the narratives of the newly-weds.

Settling the future had been a significant motive for marriage. We have already shown how the newly-weds set up homes, mainly as couples without children, yet with the idea of children very much in mind. The asymmetrical division of labour in the home was bound up with the assumption that the employment role of the wives was temporary, and would always come second to that of the husbands, because in the future wives would become mothers. The support of the family was, therefore, the responsibility of the husband, even though most newly-wed households consisted at that time of just the two spouses, both of whom were earning. It was as if the inequalities and asymmetries of married life were regarded as justified if viewed in terms of a 'swings and roundabouts' formula for equity, extended over the whole lifetime of the marriage.

WAYS OF LOOKING AT LIFE

In Chapter 2 we outlined the influences which initially shaped this exploratory study and this outline forms the first part of the diary of the research. But our research was further shaped by the material in the interviews. Although in any study there will always be areas which do not yield as much as had been hoped, fortunately the converse may also be true: exploratory research can sometimes bear unexpected fruit. Revelations can emerge from the data which challenge existing understanding, and sometimes a thread is discovered running through the accumulations of these new meanings which generates a fresh perspective. However, because much of human experience is ambiguous, such challenges cannot always be answered.

Although our initial focus had been the transition to marriage, we realised that another way of regarding the newly-weds was to view them as a cohort of people, all of whom were negotiating the same transition at the same moment of historical time. We therefore needed to understand more about that particular transition, and we were especially drawn to those perspectives which include a time-dimension.

The 'natural' sequence of a life has been most famously and elegantly catalogued by Shakespeare in his seven ages of man, which range from infancy through to the second childhood of 'mere oblivion'.[11] As a typology of stages in an individual lifetime it includes several features of the life cycle approaches which were to gain such popularity with social scientists some four hundred years later.[12]

At a time when the static functional images of the family still held sway, it was an advance to have the new emphasis which was offered by the *life cycle* perspective, with its focus on temporal change. Nevertheless, this approach has been widely criticised for its emphasis upon stages in life and neglect of the transitions between them; its assumption of one single stereotyped progression through which all must pass; and for its failure to acknowledge that a life follows a linear rather than a cyclical sequence.[13]

By the time we had begun our research, historical studies of the family started to demonstrate the impact of the historical setting and historical change, both upon families and upon individual family members. This new perspective, known as the *life course* approach, revealed the way in which the concept of the life cycle had failed to take account of the social and economic context.[14]

We realised that this socio-historical approach fitted in very well with our own wish to consider marriage and the family as a process. Life course studies managed to capture the way in which experience in the present both incorporated the past experience of the individual and located it in a context of historical change, promoting reflective considerations of how 'then' becomes 'now'.

We were also attracted by the emphasis which the life course approach gave to the resourceful and varied strategies used by people to deal with their individual environments at a given historical moment: this was individual biography within an historical process. Transitions and their timing were also central features of these biographies which accorded with our own view of marriage as one such major transition.

Transcending the present: perspectives on the future

Although the life course perspectives emphasised experience over a given period, the direction this took was usually from the past to the present, whereas the material from the newly-weds showed us that their present choices and actions had been shaped as much by their sense of the *future* as by their past experience. We were, therefore, alerted to the importance of the future as an influence.

To clarify our own thinking, we considered further some of the ways in which others have presented the concept of the 'rest of one's life', and we hoped to find some which resonated with our own findings. Among the views we came across was one which suggested that the rest of one's life can be perceived as a 'designed project', with decisions seen 'as a means to an end in terms of the overall life-plan':

> This design includes identity. In other words, in long-range life planning the individual not only plans what he will do but also plans who he will be. In the case of the individuals who are of great personal importance to each other, these projects overlap, both in terms of planned careers and planned identities. One individual is part of another's projects and vice versa.[15]

Marriage can, therefore, become the way in which the project of becoming a particular kind of person with a chosen style of living can be achieved.

Another way to consider marriage is as a project, with the focus on the relationship between the spouses, and the way in which each has to rely on the co-operation of the other in order to realise his own future plans.[16] David Morgan cites several well-known family studies to illustrate this: although a middle-class man in a Canadian suburb in the 1950s may well have chosen his wife in order to enhance his own project (his career), *her* project may also have been defined in the same terms, that is, of her husband and his career.[17] In contrast, in working-class households in downtown America in the 1960s, the main project was more often the home and family than the career of the husband, so that in these families both partners realised their projects through each other.[18]

Another perspective on the future emphasised the importance of choice, the reason why one path rather than another is taken. Alfred Schutz categorises choices into 'because' and 'in order to', and shows how the 'because' motives relate to the past experiences of an individual and account for what he did, whereas the 'in order to' motives express the intention to bring about a desired state of affairs in the future, a preconceived goal.[19] It seems to us that the transition of marriage includes both types of motive: an individual can look back upon his motives for getting married and reflect forward to his desired life within marriage.

By this time we realised that the sense of the future and the shaping of choices in the present, so strongly conveyed to us by the newly-weds, was something about which many others had speculated and theorised. The notion of transcending the present, which seemed to run through many of the perspectives, was one which accorded with our own view that the present can only make any real sense when considered in the light of assumptions and aspirations about what will happen next. And in an individual this orientation towards the future, whether strong or weak, is bound to be intensified at times of critical transition, especially a transition as socially and culturally constructed as marriage.

The future orientation: a typological key to the present

The influence of the future orientation upon present action first became apparent to us when we were examining the accounts the newly-weds gave of their courtship: these revealed the symbolic and practical significance of marriage as a way of settling the *future*, through actions in the present. In particular we noticed that there were intriguing differences in the ways they planned and organised their life before marriage and the timing of the wedding. For one group of newly-weds, courtship was a period during which particular goals, such as 'getting a home of our own' had to be achieved before marriage. The date of the wedding entirely depended on the success-ful achievement of these objectives, considered essential precondi-tions of a successful and happy marriage.

But we soon became aware that this preoccupation with planning reached far beyond the wedding; this group of newly-weds were getting ready for the launch into complete married life – and even their whole future. We realised they had a strong sense of direction and very clear ideas and when they described these they tended to use strikingly similar words and phrases, such as: 'you know where you are going'; 'being careful'; 'a "proper" wedding'; 'needing to make sure'; 'exactly the way we planned it'; 'saving'; 'responsibility'; 'being prepared'; 'having to watch both sides'; 'just what I had in mind', and so on.

The men and women who were planning their lives stood out from the other newly-weds: not only were they deciding what to do (and what *not* to do) but they seemed to be planning *who they would be*. Getting married had assisted them in the project of 'becoming a certain kind of person and successfully maintaining a certain style of life'.[20] They had definable characteristics in common, particularly in their planning orientation to the future, and we began to refer to this group as the **planners**.

We then realised that even though all the planners shared this predilection for planning, yet there were differences among them. Some of them chose to design their future with prudence and simply made wise provision against the vagaries of life. But other planners needed to do more than this; they seemed beset with anxiety and planned a secure future defensively as protection against disaster. Nevertheless, despite these differences of emphasis, we were reasonably sure that all planners shared a common perspective and could, therefore, constitute a 'type'.

We then turned our attention to the rest of the newly-weds, the **non-planners**, and discovered that they could be divided into two distinct groups. Although the first group had no detailed framework for future action, they certainly could not be called unprepared. For them marriage seemed, like other choices in their lives, to be more a venture than a plan, and they viewed the future in terms of broad strategies and general schemes rather than in terms of the detailed requirements of the planners. After members of this group had decided to marry (and they usually made up their minds about this very quickly) their courtship was simply the length of time it took to arrange a wedding.

Unlike the planners, this group had a speculative approach to the rest of their lives. Such an attitude could be explained in the light of their past: it was likely that they started out from a well-founded and well-funded home base, so that from their previous experience they could afford to be confident and optimistic about the future. These newly-weds tended to strike out towards future goals they considered desirable or exciting, and took chances which could involve a certain amount of risk. Like the planners, this group also drew upon a common vocabulary of orientation, and spoke of: 'risk';' 'gamble'; 'taking a chance'; 'being lucky'; 'we discuss a lot'; 'great fun'; 'a big step'; 'tough but OK'; 'good opportunity'; 'knew what I wanted'; 'matter of choice'; 'good experience'; 'no set ways', and so on. Since we considered that their orientation to the future had an uncertain, venturing quality, we decided to name this group the **venturers**.

The other group of non-planners were characterised by a relatively weak sense of the future. For them the future seemed to be quite simply what happened next, and they had neither plans nor strategies – they appeared to 'take life as it comes'. Some of them had simply roamed into marriage as they had into many other things, simply because it was on offer at that time and was convenient. Their general movement through life was unsystematic and lacked any specific aim, although it could be said to have a general flow. Their vocabulary reflected their happy-go-lucky approach: 'just as it comes'; 'do the next thing'; 'easy-going'; 'it just sort of happened'; 'I don't worry'; 'drift along'; 'happy either way'; 'I'm easy about things'; 'we buy what we fancy', and so on. We felt that the essential orientation of these newly-weds was a roaming one, and so we called them the **roamers**.

Among these roamers, however, we observed some whose lives were similar in general orientation, yet who exhibited a certain quality of drift. They tended to be preoccupied with overwhelming experiences from the past, legacies which often seemed to relate to predicaments in their present. We realised that these **drifting roamers** were too caught up with the demands of the present (and past) to be able to have any strong sense of the future. They appeared to have drifted into marriage, partly as an alternative to unpleasant circumstances in their lives at that time, and partly because they seemed never to have had any free sense of choice in the present, let alone the future. However, we did not feel they constituted a separate group – we still considered them roamers, even though they tended to drift with the prevailing wind.

We therefore ended up with a working model of a typology in three parts: profiles for **planners, venturers and roamers**.

Since the whole concept had arisen from the data, we could not define these categories with any great precision, nor were we entirely certain about their constituent items. Nevertheless, we felt the typology contained the basis for an unusual and even exciting way of grouping our newly-weds. We were unable to disentangle the effects of social class and educational opportunity upon the categories, but we had sufficient evidence to rebut the possibility that they might simply be artefacts of such influences. It was true that venturers seemed to be the most favoured in terms of social opportunity and the roamer/drifters the least likely to have experienced support. Nevertheless, this was not necessarily so; the wife whose portrait later in this chapter represents the roamers was a university student, albeit only for a short time.

Planners, venturers and roamers: the application of the typology

We have already described our construction of the typology of the newly-weds, and how this was based primarily on the accounts of their pathways to marriage.

When we set out to assign individuals to one of the categories, this was done by reference not only to courtship but also to other material, such as their views about their future behaviour as parents, their attitudes to change and their hopes and fears about the future. We therefore had a contrast of focus: in their courtships they had spoken of their past, and in their approach to parenthood they portrayed the future.

Although it was possible to be reasonably certain about the assignment of the majority of the newly-weds, some could not be put into any of the three categories because they had expressed contradictory attitudes to the future at different points in the interview, thus making it difficult for us to decide which orientation to select.

At first we were concerned that this revealed deficiencies in our typology which might even invalidate it. However, we reminded ourselves that since the three categories had developed from the study of the data and had not been part of the original research design, problems of assignment due to insufficient material were to be expected.

Moreover (and perhaps more importantly), despite our already being well aware of the need to allow for some ambiguity in any actions that people take, particularly in personal relationships, it took a while of vexation for us to recognise that we were failing to acknowledge inevitable ambiguity and seeming contradiction when it faced us in practice. We accordingly accepted contradictory orientations as a valid paradox and later in the chapter we consider these 'shifts' as positions in their own right.

We want here to examine the three categories in the typology in more detail and illustrate each orientation, first in general terms, and then with a detailed portrait of three newly-weds, each of whom is a typical planner, venturer or roamer.

The planners

As might be expected, these were the easiest to identify, since their orientation was so explicit and well-defined. Although our starting point had been with their courtships, which were noticeably longer than the average for the newly-weds, we had to be careful not to be misled by this evidence, since the typology was assigned to individuals and not couples.

In order to identify the planners, we needed to establish who was the influential partner in the courtship decisions. If, for example, one of the partners was a marriage 'seeker'[21] this would have had a major effect on the timing of the decision to marry, on the engagement and the wedding. Strong reasons given by an individual for hastening or delaying a wedding; mention being made of such courtship goals as getting a house; saving a specific sum of money; emphasis being placed on a distinct sequence of pre-marriage events; all were taken as evidence of a planning orientation.

Planners also tended to reveal themselves by their attitude to their work. They were concerned to have a secure job with a sustained income, and if they were contemplating a change of employment they wanted to avoid taking undue risks:

> 'I'd like to move into something different, there isn't much of a future in this work now. But I don't want to make a hasty decision, I think you have got to work it out to the last letter what you are going to do before you make a change. One of my mates has just left, he took a job that came out of the blue. No way would I do that, take a risk, especially now with being married, even if that means losing an opportunity.'

It was not surprising that the attitude towards parenthood held by planners was similar to the way they had approached marriage. In general, although they did not want to start a family in the immediate future, parenthood was already on the agenda, since for them marriage was principally a nest-building activity. However, they could not contemplate having a child until the 'right moment', when everything would be ready.

They were able to describe the conditions for parenthood they were aiming for: a suitable home (a house, not a flat and three bedrooms if they only had two at present); enough money to offset the loss of the wife's earnings (achieved either by waiting until the husband's income increased or by hard saving); and an adequate accumulation of material assets to buffer the inevitable decline in their standard of living which children would bring.

They wanted to make the most of their limited period of childlessness by having well-planned holidays and a good social life, thus building up a store of happy memories for the future when the demands of child-rearing would preclude such activities.

We were surprised at the extent of some of the planning; one husband's projected future ranged over the whole of his life:

> 'I want to have my own house – have three kids – be happy – I want us to have a good life together – share responsibilities over the children – and retire to the seaside.'

As we indicated earlier, some planners were uneasy about future events which might lie outside their control, and against which they could not fully insure. When they spoke of their fears about the future they referred to the vagaries of the economic climate which might bring redundancy; the possibility of sudden illness (or even death) for themselves or their partners; and their concern lest their yet-to-be born children might be ill or handicapped in some way.

They expressed hopes that 'when we start a family the kiddies are all right' and worried 'if we had a deformed child I couldn't bear it'.

The venturers

In contrast to the notes of caution and insecurity which characterised the planners, the venturers spoke purposively and confidently about their 'trail' to marriage and their future projects and proposals. They had made up their minds about marriage quickly and decisively, so that the period of courtship from initial meeting to the decision to marry was short, relative to the other newly-weds. Venturers had no need to rush into marriage but neither had they any reason to wait: a venturer simply wanted to be with his or her chosen partner.

The sense of assurance which characterised many venturing men sometimes revealed itself in their aspirations:

'If you have a good job you can take it to infinity.'

'The overall thing to remember is when I'm gone I'm gone – that's the whole point of existence – if I haven't done something to be remembered by then I haven't existed . . . I want to do as many things as I possibly can – I often think if you are ambitious you are never really satisfied.'

Venturers were somewhat vague about their readiness for parenthood. Some were already open to the possibility of becoming mothers or fathers, although they tended to be avoiding steps to prevent a baby rather than actively trying for one. Other venturers did not want to start a family in the near future, since they felt it would limit their freedom to be spontaneous, to enjoy themselves. One wife spoke of her present unwillingness to become pregnant:

'I want to have my life with Jonathan to begin with – I want to learn about living with him and being together, just the two of us, and I think it would be an intrusion on my life.'

Another wife worried about the effect children would have on their relationship: 'I hope we don't grow apart with children because we are *so close* at the moment.'

There were still other venturers who, although uncertain when they would have children, were confident that whenever they did it would feel 'just right', which was similar to the intuitive way in which they had decided upon marriage. As a wife explained:

'Put it this way – I don't think I want a family, but I'm sure I will when I'm about thirty – I'm sure when I'm ready I will *know*.'

Although the sense of the future which the venturers had was characterised by uncertainty, this was something they willingly accepted, even when it might involve their marriage. One wife who agreed with divorce, was very open about her views:

> 'Marriage is always a gamble – it's what you make of it. If there are circumstances that change your life you may not always be responsible for those, and *people* can change. I mean, we have taken our marriage vows and we intend them to be for life, but should anything happen. . . .'

Perhaps the two words which most epitomise the venturers as a group are 'options' and 'optimism'. Their air of discovery meant they wanted to keep all options open, and their basic assurance enabled them to face most future uncertainties without anxiety.

The roamers

Since one of the marked characteristics of the accounts which the roamers gave was a lack of purpose, it was perhaps surprising that they had been married in church, an event which requires at least a modicum of forward planning. In fact, several of the husbands who were opposed to the ceremony involved in a church wedding were roamers, and the newly-wed brides who had experienced parental opposition to the actual marriage were drifting roamers.

Roaming courtships had little sense of direction: there was no observable pattern about them and they ranged in total length from being very short (a few weeks or months) to being extremely long. Although we must not forget that the length of the courtship reflects the influence of both partners, nevertheless since roamers (especially drifting roamers) often married roamers, the very short courtships suggested being almost swept into marriage, while the prolonged ones implied the couple's inability to make up their minds.

The roamers are the most difficult to characterise, since they often appeared to do something *as a reaction* to external pressures rather than setting anything in motion themselves. Factors almost of chance, such as a death in the family, an accident, or simply having met up with the person they eventually married, affected the direction of their lives, so that they could not avoid giving an impression of aimlessness.

This is not to suggest that roamers were colourless people; the impression we gained was that they were happy to accept the way life unfolded, and often revealed a sense of ease and adaptability which their partners clearly found appealing. One roamer wife conveyed this when she said all she wished for was: 'Just to have a happy

marriage – children – good health – I don't really ask for too much.'
The air of uncertainty which so characterised roamers, lay at the
heart of their reluctance to plan:

> 'I think it's a pretty uncertain world we live in – I think we should live
> from day to day – really it's a mistake to think fifty years ahead.'

Although many of the roamers wanted children they were very
uncertain how many to have and when to have them. At the time they
were interviewed, three months into the marriage, several of the
women were not using any contraception and could, therefore,
become pregnant at any time, the implications of which they appeared not to have considered seriously. Other roamers said they
themselves were uncertain about the timing of children, but implied
that this was not a problem, since the matter would be 'decided'
simply by their partner being certain.

It was perhaps to be expected that in all five of the newly-wed
couples where the bride had been pregnant before marriage, the wife
was a roamer, in three instances with a marked 'drifting' quality.
Indeed, for these three brides the pre-marital pregnancy appeared to
be yet one more predicament in a constellation of incidents.

Although we want to avoid portraying the roaming/drifting newly-
weds as victims of their circumstances, nevertheless they did appear
to have experienced an unusually high incidence of physical and
environmental mishap, either in their own lives or those of their
immediate family. One such wife not only regretted most of what
happened to her in her life but also felt unsure about her marriage:

> 'Ain't ever really been happy – always been so – every time I try and do
> something something bad happens – I'd like to start all over again . . .
> We argue a lot – the marriage certificate's been torn up already and we've
> not been married that long – and I've been in hospital and he gets a bit
> violent and sometimes I wish I hadn't married him – and yet other times
> when he's nice I'm glad I did.'

THE TYPOLOGY: THREE PORTRAITS

A planning husband (married to a roaming wife)

> 'I thought a lot about married life before we got married and really it's
> how I thought about it – how I planned it, really. . . . '

'We've got a plan kind of thing – wait a few years to start a family – we've thought about our plans for the future.'—Mr Browning

Nigel Browning met his future wife, Sheila, one Saturday night at a friend's party. He was eighteen and she was sixteen. Sheila had just left school and he was doing an apprenticeship at the local technical college and neither of them had been 'serious' with anyone else. They started 'going out' immediately and very soon they were seeing each other regularly 'three or four times a week'. The relationship continued in this way for a couple of years:

'It just comes natural to phone each other and say "Are you going out tonight?" It just went on like that, liking each other, seeing things in the same sort of way so that obviously after a year you know there is something.'

The couple started to talk about marriage in the summer, three years after meeting. Nigel had just finished his apprenticeship and was in a position to 'plan to get married': 'we started talking about it in the summer and planned to get engaged in the December on Christmas Day'.

The plan involved saving hard to 'be in a position to marry'. It did not include wedding arrangements as such, since he felt these could only begin when the right conditions for marriage had been achieved. Nigel therefore went on night work for a period to earn more money and the couple 'put up with always staying in' in order to save money. Buying a house was an essential part of the plan: he felt it was 'the right thing to do'. He said his parents had done things in the wrong way – they had got married without finding a home first, had spent their early married life living with one or other set of parents and then within the first year of marriage they became parents themselves 'which was not a good idea'. He was firm about parenthood for him and his wife being organised in a similar fashion to their courtship:

'Well, we've got a plan – wait a few years to start a family – well – we've thought about our plans for the future.'

The Browning's wedding was a moderate one, but with 'most of the trimmings': it was 'what Sheila and her family wanted'. Although Nigel declared that he was not religious in any way he had no objection to a church wedding and, indeed, he appreciated the slow build up to the 'pomp and ceremony':

'The pomp and ceremony . . . the general atmosphere . . . I think it makes people a lot more happy . . . it's the build up to it, buying the dress, getting people ready . . . the surroundings of it, of a church wedding.'

The actual wedding arrangements were not decided upon until the 'ideal house' had been bought: 'It was an ideal house – a bit shabby but we knew we had enough time over a year to get it right.'

'Enough time' had to be left before the wedding in order to accomplish the carefully-planned sequence of restructuring and redecoration so that it would be ready to move into. Once the plans for the house were under way the wedding was booked and that too proved to justify all the planning. Nigel was enthusiastic: 'I can't put a fault on the wedding – it was a *perfect* day.'

Sheila came from a close family where she was the youngest, the only daughter. She said she knew she always wanted 'to marry and have a house' but not too young (under twenty) and she was twenty on her wedding day. So far, she had had 'a good life – I've always had what I wanted and there's nothing I've ever wanted changed'. She described herself as 'easy going' and 'I like to please people'. Her husband said he particularly appreciated these aspects of her personality as an antidote to his own preoccupation with planning and he stressed her 'cheerful, happy-go-lucky personality'. But most of all he said he liked the fact that: 'problems don't get her down – she *never* worries and that's what I like'.

He recognised that just as she had valued guidance from her parents, so now she 'looked to him', and he was pleased that she 'relies on my opinion', and also thought that she 'likes my responsible attitude'.

The influence he had on her way of looking at the future, their future, was particularly evident when their separate accounts of parenthood are compared. It was 'important to be ready for children', according to Nigel and, unlike his parents, he was going to wait long enough to be able to 'better himself', to move to a larger house and to achieve 'a proper standard of living' before he would contemplate parenthood. All this would take four to five years and he therefore expected to wait that long before starting a family. He described his wife as 'a great lover of children' and acknowledged her desire to become a mother sooner rather than later. Nevertheless, *his* plans for parenthood had become *their* plan, as Sheila explained:

'It's Nigel that wants to wait longer. *I* would have a baby next year because I love children, and that was my first feeling, but as Nigel says, when you get your own home you realise the bills and the money you have to pay out . . . so we will wait and get the house the way we want it and do the things we want to do, get some money behind us, like Nigel says. And that's what *I'd* like to do now.'

Sheila was on the Pill because her husband felt it was the safest way of preventing an unwanted child, although he was concerned about 'the dodgy aspect . . . I made a point of finding out about it, reading all the literature on the pill before deciding'.

The detailed planning and preparation of the courtship appeared to have eased the couple into married life, so much so that, according to Nigel, 'my timetable hasn't changed really'. Married life was all that he expected it would be; it had given him a sense of autonomy and authority and when he was asked what he liked about marriage he said it was the fact that 'I'm not answerable to anyone . . . and I like being a houseowner'.

Although the marriage was still in its infancy, yet his vocabulary was peppered with 'usually' and 'normally' and, indeed, he admitted that 'we've got into a set pattern'; for example, when the couple did their weekly shopping they knew exactly what they needed for the week. Nigel regarded domestic routines as 'half and half', though by that he did not mean equal shares, but rather that both he and his wife fulfilled what they felt were their roles: 'we both do what we expect of each other'.

Both of them seemed to feel clear about what married life involved and they simply got on with the plans. 'We hardly ever disagree,' Nigel said, 'we've got the same tastes', and since he was sure his wife relied on his opinion, he was reasonably certain that there would be common goals in their married life:

'She likes my responsible attitude . . . she respects me – in that sense going for what she likes – if she likes a certain thing and she knows I probably like it, I'll work my way towards it as well – we work towards a goal together.'

Nigel could not contemplate divorce 'we'd *never* consider being apart' he said.

A venturing husband (married to a roaming wife)

'We realised that we loved each other and we got on very well and really enjoyed each other's company and marriage seemed to be the logical conclusion – so we got married.'

'Not that we are particularly worried about her getting pregnant, but we weren't aiming for her to get pregnant now.'—Mr Roberts

When Steve Roberts met his future wife at a social function organised through their work, he was in his mid-twenties, and had lived away from home for almost a third of his life. Nine months later they were married. His wife was also in her mid-twenties, and she, like him, had lived away from her family while training for her eventual career. Steve had not thought twice about going on to higher education after leaving school, but he did change his degree course because he discovered that 'working with things was not as much fun as working with people'.

His upbringing had been in a comfortable middle-class home, but he did not feel close to either of his parents, and he was determined not to turn out like his father, whom he regarded as a workaholic. He had fallen out with his parents in his late teens and had been forced to support himself, which was 'a bit tough' but something with which he could cope.

Both he and his wife had been previously 'involved' with other people. A serious relationship he had had broke up after a year because 'we grew up, changed in different ways and drifted apart'. He had never considered marriage until meeting his wife, and he decided he wanted to marry her within two months of their meeting. 'It was,' he said, 'the biggest step in my life', but one which he was certain about once he'd decided to take it.

His wife Suzy was not so sure. She had left school ten years earlier, 'I was a rebel, I wanted to get out and earn some money', and she then went through a string of jobs both in Britain and abroad. During this time she had several serious relationships, and considered marrying each of the men with whom she became involved, but somehow 'avoided it'. After each relationship finished she went off to another job. She said she hadn't expected to marry until she was thirty 'because there were so many things I wanted to try'.

As soon as the Roberts met they dated almost every night, 'we used to go out a lot, for meals – it was very expensive'. When Steve proposed after only two months, Suzy was:

> 'Very reluctant for a while . . . I knew I wanted to marry him but I didn't know if I wanted to so quickly. He got very impatient – if he wants to do something he can't wait. He's such a sure and confident person. I wish *I* was like that.'

Four months after their first meeting the couple got engaged and the wedding was set for August because, according to Steve, 'having decided to get married and having decided to get somewhere to live, we thought it was better to marry sooner than later'. Although a professed atheist he agreed to a church wedding in deference to the wishes of his future in-laws. It was a small white wedding with no bridesmaids and just close friends and relations 'who meant something to us'. The date of the wedding was determined by the vicar, and as Steve ruefully said, 'It seems that unless you plan these things way in advance you can't just have the day you want'.

The couple had been 'lucky to get this place' which was a rented flat, tatty but spacious. Their joint income was very low compared to most of the newly-weds yet they 'manage quite well'. However, their present circumstances were only temporary since they expected that their training would provide the opportunity for a good standard of living in the immediate future. Although they were not yet home owners they 'knew' they would buy a house within the next year or so, and already had money from parents to go towards it.

Their present domestic life style was determined by their respective work schedules which were irregular and demanding. They needed to take things as they came and their present division of labour 'just evolved like that'. Each valued the other's work and supported any career decisions that had to be made. Not long after the wedding, Suzy found that her job was too much and thought of changing it, but her husband said, 'We discussed it and came to the conclusion that she should stick it out'.

Most aspects of their lives were discussed: 'We discuss everything that crops up – there are no set ways of doing things so everything has to be decided'. Major items of expenditure would be decided by him, 'He's much more sensible than I am', but otherwise, 'We both do our own sort of thing . . . we are both sort of quite different'. Both spouses viewed the future optimistically; Steve said, 'I don't think I shall have too many problems' but his wife said, 'I suppose the only worry – well it's not *really* worrying me, but you know one hears about so many divorces I sometimes think, "Will we still be together in twenty years?" '

Neither of them was certain of their plans for the next few years, since much depended on the development of his career, and where they moved to when they did have a baby. Both of them wanted children and were greatly looking forward to parenthood, but said they would prefer to delay childbearing until they had a suitable home. Suzy had come off the Pill and they had opted for the sheath, which her husband felt was reasonably safe – 'not that we are particularly worried about her getting pregnant but we weren't aiming for her to get pregnant *now*'.

A belief in persevering and confidence in taking on a challenge were central to the approach to life Steve had. He felt that 'most goals in life are achievable if you stick it out' and if you could not there was no point in continuing – you just moved on to something else. His views on divorce echoed this:

> 'I don't see any point in living together if you are not happy, just for the sake of a thing called marriage.'

His wife valued his assurance and, indeed, was grateful to him for helping her to stick at things, yet she was sometimes infuriated by his confidence, which she described as arrogance 'He's very dogmatic and he can be arrogant at times and stubborn and that annoys me – I'm not saying he always *thinks* he's right, he *is* right and that's the problem'

A roamer wife (married to a venturing husband)

> 'We didn't really plan – no definite date set for the wedding . . . just see how it goes . . . drifted along I suppose. Andy got fed up on his own . . . so we decided to marry.'

> 'If I started a family tomorrow it wouldn't worry me – I'm not fussy either way.'—Mrs Slater

Pauline Slater had got to know her husband through her brother; 'He was my brother's best friend . . . my brother got three tickets for a concert so he asked me and he asked Andy. We went out together from then on.' She was seventeen and he was her first boyfriend 'my one and only'. They got on well together, her mum liked him and they just 'drifted along', which suited her.

Andy had his own small business and was advised by an accountant to buy a house, which he did. He did not like living on his own, so Pauline and her mother used to come and cook for him and after a while he raised the idea of marriage, 'so we decided to marry'. Pauline had left school at sixteen just after the sudden death of her father, which had unsettled her considerably. She had taken a job and then left to go to college to study for her A Levels. After that she 'had a job lined up as a dental nurse but didn't fancy it at the last minute'. She then accepted a university place at short notice but left after only one term because 'it was boring'. However, she thought she would try 'some other course' at a future date. Since leaving her university course she had taken an office job, which she found dull and 'if anything better came along I'd leave tomorrow'.

She got engaged to her husband about a year after their first date and married him two years later. He organised and paid for the wedding: 'he wanted to get married'. Although a register office wedding would have been cheaper, Andy agreed to a church wedding because it was what Sheila and her mother wanted. She said, 'I would have been a bit disappointed if it had been in a register of-fice . . . and I suppose you feel more married in church'. The house they lived in after marriage needed a lot of work done on it, so she said they would probably remain in it and get things done 'unless anything came up – then we might go earlier'.

The Slaters' household routine was vague; she did most of the work, though her husband would help: 'If it [the house] looks really dirty or something then we will both get going on that – you know – do it as it comes up.' She was similarly rather haphazard about shopping for food: 'I just wander round and pick up odd things and say "Oh, that will do".'

Andy's working day began early and ended late, so that his wife was often left alone but she did not mind: 'It's good really, we don't spend a lot of time together, else we would run out of things to say.'

Sheila liked her husband because he was able to fit in to her rather happy-go-lucky approach:

> 'He's easy going, if he comes home and there's no tea he'll go out and get something – or wash a shirt for himself. He's generous, would give you anything, always in the same mood, never miserable. I don't think he ever worries.'

Her only worry was over her husband's health: 'My dad died and I see my mum as a widow . . . I wouldn't like to be left on my own.' She thought that her husband liked her because 'I am fairly easy-going – we just get along together really, never really argue about anything, just ramble from day to day'.

Sheila thought the best thing about marriage was, 'It gives you some *purpose* – I feel more secure – and I've got a purpose – getting the home together. Before, I suppose you just kind of drift along from week to week.' She added that she had never been a liker of great romance: 'I'm quite down to earth.'

She was hoping to restart her studies at some vague time in the future, but whether before or after children, she wasn't sure. On the one hand she didn't want to be tied down by children, but 'if I started a family tomorrow it wouldn't worry me – I'm not fussy either way'. If ever her marriage was no longer a source of satisfaction for her, she was sure she would divorce: 'I definitely believe in divorce . . . if you are living together and you are unhappy then there is no point, is there?'

SHIFTS IN ORIENTATION

We have already referred to the problem we faced when we could not assign a newly-wed to one category because of evidence indicating contradictory orientations, and to our decision to accept this paradox as a position in its own right – that of shifts in orientation.

In one such instance, we had a woman who had definitely been a 'roamer' during her courtship, but after marriage she spoke in the language of a 'planner', and, indeed, appeared to have become one. We gradually realised that her shift of orientation reflected her own developmental process, and was entirely consistent with having undergone the transition of marriage. There was ambiguity, but this was because it was not entirely clear whether she had married her husband (a planner) in order to facilitate or effect this shift, or whether she had simply been influenced by him.

Women who were 'roamers' at the time of their courtship but who changed after marriage are by definition those most likely to be influenced by a partner with a stronger sense of direction. There were several of these young wives from a relatively sheltered upbringing whose orientation was nascent in courtship. After leaving school they had got a job but continued to live with their parents. Since they had been protected, their experience of life was limited, and they appeared to have no purpose in their approach to the future other than to get married.

The world beyond their parents' home appeared enticing but confusing, and they found it hard to make decisions about it, so it is not surprising that several of them were attracted to 'planning' husbands who 'knew where they were going', since this enabled them to gain a sense of direction for their own lives.

Nevertheless, despite an emerging 'sense of the future' which could be detected after marriage in the accounts of these erstwhile 'roamers', paradoxically they had not entirely shed their earlier orientation, so that they oscillated between the two. We therefore decided to regard them and others in ambiguous positions as 'on the cusp' of two orientations. In the following portrait we describe a wife who was a venturer/roamer.

A nascent orientation (a roaming/venturing wife married to a planning husband)

Harriet Moncrieff was an only daughter of 'loving and protective parents'. They had encouraged her to stay on at school; she did well at O Level and remained to sit her A Levels. However, her A Level results were disappointing and she ended up taking a 'boring' office job. At the time of the interview she had moved to another office job, one which she hoped would be more interesting. When she met her future husband Ian she was sixteen, and three years later they got married.

She regarded her parents as being 'far too over-protective' and she expected to be different with her own children: 'I hope I won't be the same, I don't think I will because I am aware of it . . . and I'm definitely not going to have just one child'.

She said that when she was younger she had thought that she would leave marriage until she was 'about fifty and then marry for company. It was something within me to have lots of adventures', but she married in the last year of her teens because, 'I've admitted the fact that I need security because I've always had it and I couldn't do without it'. She was optimistic about still having adventures (her husband was in a job with travel concessions): 'You can still have adventures when you are married. I don't feel tied down . . . I've always had a bit of a travel bug and we can travel whenever we want'.

Her husband's job was well paid and secure and he was well liked by her parents: 'He's just like a son to them.' Her parents were highly involved in her marriage, and she said her new home was decided upon by her husband and her parents. She was happy to leave much of the domestic decision-making to Ian:

'Ian makes the decisions because he is more down to earth. If it was left to me I'd just drift along. I wouldn't really get much done . . . I would muddle along but not as well as we are doing now. I'm very satisfied with Ian's realistic outlook.'

She said that she admired his precise and careful approach to running their marriage: 'his realistic outlook' acted as a 'good counterbalance for me in a way because he brings me back down to earth'. However, she was beginning to find there was another, less attractive, side to it:

'Everything has to be just so . . . he irritates me when everything has to be exact, although a lot of the time it does turn out for the best that he takes so much time and trouble . . . For example – he's very particular about his food, whereas I like exotic things and I like to mess around. I feel occasionally – I know I'm careless and I tend to be clumsy but I don't think I am *that* bad – I feel sometime he's a bit intolerant.'

In general, though, Harriet was pleased with marriage, 'so far it has worked out well – it has given me many of the things I want':

What things about marriage do you like?
'The independence. A nice home and – ah – being with Ian I think is nice, being on our own.'

Her only reservation about marriage was 'missing out on other relationships: I'm a bit of a flirt, I must admit, and occasionally, you know, to have to admit that you're married to somebody cuts off other possibilities'.

Her hopes for the future included 'a house out of London with a garden in a quiet area, though,' she added, 'yet I want a lively life with plenty of things to do. I get bored very easily and need a lot of variety'. The exact future was rather uncertain: 'With Ian and me you can never really tell what's going to happen in the future':

'I think we'll probably grow closer together and work out our various problems in the future. I think we probably would be able to but it's a slight worry that we won't.'

In what way is it a worry?
'At times, Ian's irritability – his exactness – drives me up the wall. I know one day I will probably lose my temper and go mad.'

What do you think you will do?
'I don't know, to be honest, I very rarely lose my temper and I am hoping that it won't pull us apart.'

A PARTNER FOR THE REST OF YOUR LIFE?

A planning orientation is, as we have seen, founded upon the notions of preparation and insurance, so that while the conditions have to be 'right', and the 'ideal' aspired to, yet preparations have to be made against adversity. It is, therefore, unlikely that a 'planner' would knowingly marry the 'wrong' spouse, someone whose plans did not seem to coincide with his; planners referred to their partners as entirely fitting their expectations:

'I like everything about her – she's a natural – she was everything I was looking for.'

'She's my *ideal* woman . . . an extension of me.'

But equally often a planner chose someone who was 'easy-going' and willing to fall in with his plans, someone with a roaming orientation.

The planner invests in his plan, a plan which includes predictable change, as with parenthood, but change must be able to be foreseen, and thus prepared for:

> 'No, nothing will change in the future, I hope not anyway – except for the family . . . Children do affect your life and that will change me – I'll be far more a family man.'

However, these events and circumstances which cannot be anticipated are perceived suspiciously by planners. The emergence of a strong orientation in the spouse can become a threat if it results in the creation of a rival plan for the marriage. The 'ideal partner' may no longer be the 'easy-going' person but may be perceived as 'not the person I married'.

The gender gap in communication, which was illustrated in Chapter 8, can easily foster misunderstandings about the assumptions that partners hold about the rest of their lives. Thus two planners might have married each other on the basis of sharing the same horizon, only to discover later that while the goals remain the same, the detailed stages of achieving them (which are so critical to planners) cannot be harmonised.

Spouses with a roaming orientation may also prove to be risky mates for planners. After becoming married they may gradually discover that they have their own plans and choose to reject those on which the relationship was founded. Such renegotiations in marriage are likely to be perceived by planners as threats to the relationship, although their commitment to the original plan (and by implication to the marriage) will still be strong: 'Divorce is the last thing I would think of – it's ever so easy to get out of marriage – much better to stick to it.'

Venturers married to venturers start married life with a flexibility and an openness to the variety of situations and circumstances which they expect to encounter. As far as marriage is concerned, this openness is both their greatest strength and their greatest weakness. A marriage between two venturers is one in which companionship is highly prized, and, indeed, that was often one of the principal reasons for marrying. The lifestyle of these venturer pairs reflected the value they placed on sharing and the freedom to be spontaneous. For them the prospect of parenthood engendered mixed feelings – they liked the idea of a new experience but were uncertain about the intrusion of a third party in their close relationship.

Roamers may be attracted to venturers in the same way that they are to planners – attracted by their strong sense of direction. But a roamer who depends on his or her partner to set the parameters of the future will probably find a planner sustaining and reassuring, whereas a venturer might turn out to be far less predictable, since venturers can be distracted from their initial goals by external enticements, and their future life can change direction completely.

Although some of these roamers are influenced by their partners and can develop into planners or venturers, others still continue to 'take life as it comes' and such acceptance could lead even to divorce, 'if he didn't want me any more I'd divorce'.

Roamers with a drifting element are unlikely to associate themselves with planners, because planners will avoid them. Although they could form relationships with venturers it is most likely that they will drift into relationships with other drifters or with roamers. The instability of such relationships is heightened because of the inherent vulnerability of the circumstances in which the relationship is usually formed and in which it continues. For example, a young bride who marries her boyfriend primarily in order to escape from parental problems has already mortgaged her sense of the future. The lack of preparation for such a marriage, both materially and emotionally, compounds the problems of a young life already dogged by varying difficulties and disadvantages.

Such people – they were usually women – were the most likely to have experienced doubts about marriage, for example that they were too young. Frequently they were also the people where there had been the greatest opposition to the marriage from both sets of parents. These drifting roamers seemed the least optimistic of all the newly-weds; they simply hoped that the rest of life would turn out to be better than what had gone before but were afraid that it might not. One such wife feared for the future of her marriage, and felt herself being drawn into the same current of disaster as had her mother:

'I worry that we will get divorced. I just don't want that – I think that was one of the reasons why I didn't want to get married so young – because I thought that it wouldn't work and that we'd be wasting our time. I don't want to be like my mum.'

What next?

The discovery of our typology of future orientation among the newly-weds adds an additional dimension to the profile of contemporary marriage, for it offers hints about what might happen next.

To regard marriage as a strategy for handling 'the rest of your life' enables us to begin to appreciate the basis upon which a marriage may be contracted. Certain strategies are essentially short-term, and perhaps that is a reason why some marriages turn out to be short-lived ones. In such circumstances a marriage can become redundant, once it has achieved all that one partner (at least) has required of it. The most obvious example of this is the marriage which provides an escape route for a young woman fleeing a troubled family life for security in the haven of marriage (see Chapter 3). And those people with a weak sense of direction, or who simply lack confidence about pursuing their own future (we found these were usually women), may see marriage as an opportunity to form a close association with a partner who knows where he is going. If, at some time in the future, such a wife were to discover her previously latent sense of direction, it would be questionable whether the marriage would remain attractive to her.

The stability of a marriage is not simply a question of the attitudes of the two spouses; situations and events alter and these changes have to be incorporated into the relationship. The knowledge of a person's future orientation could yield clues to probable future choices, allowing speculation upon the impact of such changes. The birth of the first child is a good example; it is a common transition in early married life, one often regarded as disruptive, if not traumatic. Planners (and those whose marriage is directed by a partner with such an orientation), will guard against this, since they are likely to wait until their strategy for becoming parents is realisable; only then will they be ready to have children. The arrival of their first child will, if everything goes according to plan, provide an opportunity for them to enjoy their carefully worked out programme for becoming mothers and fathers. However, their dependence on forecasting and achieving ideal conditions may well make it difficult for them to cope should something go wrong (a handicapped child, or the father losing his job, for example).

Venturers may well find becoming parents a disruptive experience because of the emphasis they place upon companionship in marriage.

The arrival of a third party (the child) intrudes upon that intimacy, and can alter the texture of their marital relationship.

Our exploration of the typology has necessarily been limited; we could not pursue many of our hunches. Nevertheless, we were able to detect some intriguing patterns. Since strategies develop from experiences in the past, they constitute the major part of individual repertoires for handling the rest of one's life. We found that planning husbands were more likely to have been first born sons – had they had to develop their sense of personal responsibility and self-direction at an early age? And did the predominance of women with a developing sense of the future (nascent orientation), among the roamers, reflect the lack of personal and social opportunities for young women in our society to generate and develop their own strategies for life? The answers to these and many other questions were not immediately available from our material, yet there are hints which resonate with other studies of contemporary relationships between men and women.

What we have discovered in this study, and what we have been able to portray, at least in outline, are some differing attitudes towards the future and their relevance to, and incorporation into, strategies for life. These attitudes appear sometimes as legacies from the past, and sometimes as signposts for the future, but they are constantly shaping the present.

Although glimpses of these strategies were evident at particular moments throughout the interviews, it was the words and phrases used by the newly-weds when talking to us which most vividly revealed their own 'sense of the future'. These men and women were not simply recounting the stories of their lives; they were also presenting who they were at that moment, and rehearsing in their minds the people they wished to be for the rest of their lives.

Afterword

On the face of it, marriage has changed a great deal in recent decades. For one thing, there are acceptable alternatives; increasingly men and women are opting for less formal relationships, including partnerships of the same sex. Marriage is no longer the only way for women to obtain lifelong social and economic security; nowadays many can and do stand on their own feet. Those women who do marry ought to be able to expect to be treated as equal partners by their husbands; they are no longer obliged to pledge obedience in the marriage service. In addition, divorce is relatively easy to obtain, so that few people can claim they have to remain shackled to their spouses for the sake of an institution called marriage.

These are just some of the ways in which it is argued that marriage has altered. The new ideology of marriage lays stress upon its evolution; it is maintained that the layers of oppression have gradually been peeled away from the traditional institution to reveal its 'true' essence – the relationship of the couple. This unique personal relationship between a particular man and a particular woman is now regarded as the core of a marriage. Idealised, exalted, and regarded as almost mystical, this relationship is held to be the source of the emotional security and fulfilment which are today considered essential for a satisfactory life.

Because of the emphasis currently placed on the relationship, it seems to be generally accepted that the *institution* of marriage is no longer potent enough to oblige a couple to remain together once they have decided that the *relationship* has ceased to make them happy. Also, for many couples who are not married, the institution of marriage is an irrelevance; they claim they have no need of the buttress of a public commitment: the relationship alone binds them together. Since the institution of marriage is thus subjected to censure both from within and from without can it any longer be said to matter?

If frequency of occurrence is any guide, statistical evidence indicates that marriage still matters. Forecasts from present trends suggest that the vast majority of men and women marry at some time in their lives, and, with increasing probability, more than once. Why is this so? Since our newly-weds gave us their reasons for having

228

chosen to marry, we can put forward the ways in which marriage appears to matter to one group of contemporary men and women.

First they regarded marriage as a 'natural' thing to do. They were following as 'expected' tradition: getting married symbolised the powerful tradition of both family life and their own individual families.

Second marriage was an important signifier of the seriousness of their commitment to each other. It was the specific occasion of their 'troth' and a public recognition of the moment of their transition to the married state.

Third, getting married marked out boundaries within their lives: it reduced an open range of options and possible involvements to a range within limits, which offered containment, security and a measure of certainty.

Fourth, marriage held the promise of a 'home' and a 'place of one's own' in both a physical and emotional sense. The marriage contract offered a more stable financial future, the prospect of fulfilling material aspirations, and an accepted context for having children. But 'getting married', for the newly-weds, was more than simply settling down with a partner for life; they recognised that they were committing themselves to the direction of their whole future – *beginning the rest of their lives*. Above all, marriage for them held the key to life as adults: it provided a point of departure from the past, and of embarcation for the future; and it defined the shape of things to come.

It was striking that when the newly-weds recounted how they came to get married, they described rites of initiation which led to the state of marriage rather than stories of falling in love. Yet when they defined their images of married life, they spoke almost exclusively about 'the relationship' and not of the roles of husband and wife. Although they might have entered marriage because it made good sense to them, it seemed they would only remain married if it continued to make them happy. Indeed, at the end of the interview, when they were asked for their views about marriages breaking up, almost everyone spoke in terms of the failure of the relationship.

This, then, is the central paradox of marriage today: the relationship is thought to be all-important, yet people still continue to seek the institution. In getting married they are making a public commitment to the institution while at the same time idealising the relationship. And there is yet a further paradox: although the consequence of a failed relationship is usually divorce, which undermines the institution, divorce, in turn, can provide the opportunity of pursuing another relationship, and may well result in a second marriage.

The model of marriage as the relationship of intimate friends is very appealing, but how realisable is it? It implies little notion of gender difference, but the portrait of marriage provided by our newly-weds poignantly revealed the wide gulf that still exists between men and women, not only in their past experience, but also in present expectations and assumptions about the future. The lives of husbands were invariably dominated by their jobs; their view of domestic life was of a place to come home to, a comfortable base where they could expect to be well cared for. They were reluctant to become more fully involved in the domestic arena because they regarded it as female territory, both uninteresting and bewildering. Wives, in contrast, were primarily home-centred; although they too worked outside the home, their jobs were almost always accommodated to their household responsibilities.

Although the positions of both men and women appeared to be fixed, with neither expressing any strong desire to breach the conventional divisions of territory, there were, nevertheless, signs that the *ideal* of an equal and sharing relationship appealed to many of them. Wives, in particular, hankered after this because they believed it could offer a bridge between the separate worlds.

Despite the current rhetoric of sexual equality, it seems that husbands and wives frequently experience each other as 'intimate strangers'. In the past it was accepted that men and women inhabited different worlds and that married partners led parallel lives. If spouses happened also to be good friends, that was a bonus, since in those days fulfilling the roles of husband and wife was considered all that was necessary to have a satisfactory marriage.

It is a very different situation today, when it is assumed that men and women will have a common outlook and purpose in life, and that this will inform all their behaviour. Such an assumption is sharply challenged by the fact that in practice most men and women experience considerable inequalities. What happens in a marriage is bound to reflect the relationship between the sexes in society as a whole.

The cult of 'the relationship' allows no room for division, however; the oneness of the couple is all that matters. In some measure the concept of 'being as one' has been translated into a notional spirit of equality by disregard of the differences between the sexes. It is true that women have now invaded traditional male provinces and are coming to be accepted in them, but a mistaken inference often drawn from this is that a woman can be exactly like a man. A reciprocal invasion of female territories by men has yet to take place; it seems that few men want to be exactly like a woman. To some extent this simply reflects the fact that society is still male-dominated: who would want to venture into the world of the 'female', a world regarded as relatively unimportant and where the material rewards (that is, social recognition) are so meagre?

Men and women *are* different. They may appear united in marriage because they have a purpose in common but they are forever finding themselves divided by the reality of trying to achieve that purpose. The traditional *institution* of marriage was oppressive for wives because its 'oneness' entailed the absorption of the female by the male. In the current emphasis upon the *relationship*, both partners are oppressed by an ideology which fails to understand and appreciate the vitality and complexity of their differences. Thus the story of marriage (and each and every marriage) is still the continuing struggle of men and women to come to terms with each others' foreignness.

Glossary: The Newly-Wed Couples

This list of pseudonyms, with information about education, age at marriage and current occupation, is intended to augment the quotations throughout the book from the newly-weds. In order to preserve confidentiality many of the occupations have been disguised.

Duncan Ashworth left school at 16, married at 22: an insurance clerk.
Jenni Ashworth left school at 17 with some qualifications, married at 22: a building society cashier.

Chris Allen went on to further education, married at 22: a senior shipping clerk.
Heather Allen went on to further education, married at 21 a housing management officer.

Mark Atkinson left school at 16 with some qualifications, married at 22: a draughtsman.
Sylvia Atkinson left school at 16 with some qualifications, married at 19: an assistant supervisor in an accounts section.

David Bates went to university married at 23: a graduate trainee in a computer firm.
Jennifer Bates went to university, married at 19: a science technician.

Peter Bell left school at 16, married at 26: a barman.
Maureen Bell left school at 16 with some qualifications: a secretary.

Tim Black left school at 17, married at 20: a printer.
Angela Black left school at 18 with some qualifications and also married at 18: a secretary.

Howard Blond left school at 15, married at 25: an engraver.
Marie Blond left school at 17 with some qualifications, married at 23: an accounts clerk.

George Brothers left school at 15, married at 22: a roofer.
Myra Brothers left school at 17 with some qualifications, a telephonist.

Richard Briggs left school at 15 and married at 18. Currently unemployed, he was a tyre-fitter.
Laura Briggs left school at 16 and married at 20. Currently unemployed, she used to work in a draper's shop.

Nigel Browning left school at 16 with some qualifications, married at 21: a self-employed metal worker.
Sheila Browning left school at 16 with some qualifications, married at 20: manager of an electrical shop.

Robin Butcher left school at 18 with some qualifications, married at 21: a parks supervisor.
Ann Butcher left school at 15 and married at 20: currently unemployed, she was a sports assistant at a leisure centre.

Tony Castle left school at 18 with some qualifications, married at 27: a railway traffic officer in the army.
Mary Castle went on to further education, married at 21: acting deputy officer-in-charge of a nursing home.

Robert Cooper left school at 16 with some qualifications, married at 21: a shipping clerk.
Judith Cooper left school at 16 with some qualifications, married at 19: a dress-maker.

John Cosgrove left school at 16, married at 21: a plasterer.
Jane Cosgrove left school at 15, married at 22: a sales kiosk attendant.

Mike Coventry left school at 15, married at 22: a postman.
Liz Coventry left school at 17 with some qualifications and married at 19: currently pregnant and not in employment, she was an export sales clerk.

Roger Dawson left school at 16 with some qualifications, married at 26: a tax inspector.
Julie Dawson left school at 16 with some qualifications, married at 26: and a personnel clerk.

Robin Downing left school at 15, married at 27: a delivery van driver.
Johanna Downing left school at 15 and married at 17. Currently unemployed, she was a telephonist.

Colin Elder went to university, married at 23: a junior partner in a firm of solicitors.
Rachel Elder went to university, married at 22: a secretary.

Alan Emery went to university, married at 26: aeronautical engineer.
Shirley Emery left school at 16 with some qualifications, married at 20: a travel courier.

Derek Evans left school at 17 with some qualifications, married at 22: a catering accountant in the navy.
Caroline Evans left school at 16 with some qualifications, married at 20: a cashier in a bank.

Paul Gibson left school at 16, married at 22: an insurance salesman.
Julia Gibson left school at 16, married at 20: a filing clerk.

Patrick Glass left school at 16 with some qualifications, married at 24: systems analyst.
Phoebe Glass went on to further education, married at 22: a teacher.

Malcolm Green left school at 16 with some qualifications, married at 20: a delivery driver.
Ruth Green left school at 16 with some qualifications: a bank clerk.

Neil Gunter left school at 16 with some qualifications, married at 24: manager of an amusement centre.
Christine Gunter left school at 16, married at 20: a clerical officer.

Bob Harris left school at 16 with some qualifications, married at 26: an insurance clerk.
Debbie Harris left school at 15, married at 24: a customer service clerk.

Geoffrey Hatch left school at 15, married at 20: a telephone engineer.
Doreen Hatch left school at 16 with some qualifications: married at 19: a telephonist.

Andrew Hill went on to further education, married at 23: an insurance office manager.
Lucy Hill left school at 18 with some qualifications and married at 21: currently unemployed, she was a dental nurse.

James Inver left school at 18 with some qualifications, married at 22: a trainee accountant.
Maggie Inver left school at 15, married at 23: a beautician.

Godfrey Kirkham left school at 17 with some qualifications, married at 23: an import clerk.
Monica Kirkham left school at 17 with some qualifications, married at 21: a trainee cook.

Jonathan Klein left school at 15, married at 21: a heating fitter.
Sally Klein left school at 16, married at 21: a wages clerk.

Ivan Lawley left school at 16 with some qualifications, married at 22: a kitchen equipment salesman.
Anna Lawley left school at 18 with some qualifications, married at 20: a secretary.

Stephen Leeming left school at 16, married at 21: a bus mechanic.
Emma Leeming left school at 16 with some qualifications, married at 20: a book-keeper.

Frank Linden left school at 16 with some qualifications, married at 20: a cashier in a hotel club.
Sandra Linden went on to further education, married at 21: a primary school teacher.

Dennis Lockwood went to university, married at 22: a schoolmaster.
Gwen Lockwood went on to further education, married at 20: a student teacher.

Jeremy Madge left school at 15 with some qualifications, married at 20: an engineer on the trains.
Gillian Madge left school at 16 with some qualifications and married at 18: currently pregnant and not in employment, she was a trainee accounts clerk.

Nicholas Martin went to university, married at 26: manager of a structural organisation.
Helen Martin left school at 18 with some qualifications, married at 21: a secretary.

Francis Maw left school at 15, married at 21: a milkman.
Penny Maw left school at 16, some qualifications, married at 20: a copy-typist.

Matthew Mead left school at 16 with some qualifications, married at 21: a plumber.
Tracy Mead left school at 16 with some qualifications, married at 20: a secretary.

Ken Milton left school at 16 with some qualifications, married at 23: a camera operator.
Frances Milton left school at 16 with some qualifications, married at 23: a secretary.

Ian Moncrieff left school at 16 with some qualifications, married at 23: a surveyor.
Harriet Moncrieff left school at 18 with some qualifications, married at 18: a clerk/typist.

Dave Monkhouse left school at 16 with some qualifications, married at 23: a coach driver.
Sue Monkhouse left school at 16 with some qualifications, married at 19: a temporary secretary.

Kevin Muckle went to university, married at 23: a biochemist.
Margaret Muckle left school at 16 with some qualifications, and married at 19: they have a child and she is not currently in employment but was a dental nurse.

Graham Neath left school at 15, married at 22: an assistant compositor.
Linda Neath left school at 15, married at 23: an accounts clerk.

Jimmy Norden left school at 16, married at 20: a maintenance worker for British Rail.
Kate Norden left school at 17 with some qualifications, married at 18: a senior administrator.

Julia Oliver left school at 16 with some qualifications, married at 25: a draughtsman.
Rosemary Oliver left school at 15, married at 27: a waitress, her child lives with them.

Martin Owen left school at 16, married at 20: assistant manager of a milk depot.
Wynne Owen left school at 16 with some qualifications, married at 19: a clerk.

Keith Patmore left school at 19 with some qualifications, married at 22: a management trainee in an insurance company.
Nora Patmore left school at 16 with some qualifications, married at 22: floor manager in a shop.

Eddie Pearce went on to further education, married at 26: manager of an estate agency.
Kathy Pearce left school at 16 with some qualifications, married at 21: a secretary.

Jonathan Pitt left school at 17 with some qualifications, married at 23: a head chef.
Kathleen Pitt left school at 16, married at 19: a nursery nurse.

Derek Pym left school at 15, married at 18: a night freight manager for the Post Office.
Susan Pym left school at 15, married at 26: a sales assistant in a supermarket.

Gordon Riley left school at 16 with some qualifications, married at 17: a kitchen assistant.
Sheila Riley left school at 16 with some qualifications, married at 19: currently pregnant and not in employment, she was a sales administrator.

Steve Roberts went to university and married at 25: a medical student.
Suzy Roberts went on to further education, married at 25: a staff nurse.

Malcolm Robertson left school at 16 with some qualifications, married at 23: a mini-cab driver.
Diane Robertson left school at 15, married at 28: a bank clerk.

Terence Rudd left school at 16, with some qualifications, married at 28: a self-employed blacksmith.
Clara Rudd left school at 15 married at 25: a cashier in café.

Philip Sandford left school at 16 with some qualifications, married at 21: an engineer for British Rail.
Elaine Sandford left school at 16 with some qualifications, married at 21: a punch-card operator.

Andy Slater left school at 15, married at 21: a baker.
Pauline Slater went on to further education, married at 21: a bank cashier.

Kenneth Strong left school at 16 with some qualifications, married at 27: a tailor.
Christine Strong left school at 17 with some qualifications, married at 28: a curtain sewer in a department store.

Mick Tasker left school at 18 with some qualifications, married at 24: a systems analyst.
Sarah Tasker left school at 18 with some qualifications, married at 21: a negotiator in an estate agency.

Brian Trist left school at 16 with some qualifications, married at 26: a printer.
Shirley Trist left school at 16 with some qualifications, married at 29: an accounts clerk.

Simon Turner went to university, married at 24: an architect.
Judy Turner went to university, married at 23: an assistant in a public relations firm.

Barry Vaughan left school at 15, married at 22: a fireman.
Sandra Vaughan left school at 16, married at 19: a wages clerk.

Nick Walters went on to further education, married at 25: a librarian.
Lynn Walters left school at 17 with some qualifications, married at 23: a secretary.

Michael Ward left school at 16, married at 23: director of a coal yard.
Jacqui Ward left school at 15 married at 22: a hairdresser; she has just discovered she is pregnant.

Gregory Wilson left school at 18 with some qualifications, married at 27: a self-employed entertainer.
Phillipa Wilson left school at 17 with some qualifications, married at 26: a cook in a restaurant.

Trevor Wolsey left school at 18 with some qualifications, married at 29: a relief transport manager.
Nicky Wolsey left school at 18 with some qualifications, married at 26: secretary to a solicitor.

Notes and References

1 Images of Marriage

1. See, for example, P. Macdonald and G. Mars in Butterworth and Weir (eds) (1984); B. Lewin (1982); J. Burgoyne (1985).
2. Harris (1983) p. 207.
3. See Chapter 2 for a detailed account of the selection of the group of newlyweds and for a discussion of the research objectives and methods.
4. O. R. McGregor quoted at the beginning of Fletcher (1966) p. 10.
5. Ibid., p. 239.
6. For example, 'A key strategy, then, must be to change all the State policies that currently privilege "the family" at the expense of other ways of living' (Barrett and McIntosh, 1982).
7. The General Household Survey shows that premarital cohabitation is increasing. The proportions of women aged 16 to 34 at the time of marriage in 1980–83 who had cohabited with their husbands before marriage, were 26 per cent where the marriage was the first for both partners, and 73 per cent where one or both partners had been married before. These proportions are much higher than the corresponding proportions for women whose current or most recent marriage took place in 1970–74, where the proportions are 7 and 42 per cent, respectively. *General Household Survey, 1984* (London: HMSO, 1986) Table 4.13, p. 33.
8. *The Sunday Times*, 9 October 1983.
9. *The Mail on Sunday*, 9 January 1983.
10. *The Observer*, 1 May 1983.
11. Lemert (1972).
12. Rose (1984) p. 9.
13. Morgan (1985).
14. In 1985 in England and Wales, 151 803 marriages were solemnised with a religious ceremony where both partners were marrying for the first time. Of these, 116 378 marriages were within the Church of England (including the Church in Wales): OPCS *Marriage and Divorce Statistics 1985*, Series FM2 No. 12 (London: HMSO, 1987).
15. Report of the Commission on the Christian Doctrine of Marriage, appointed by the Archbishop of Canterbury, *Marriage, Divorce and the Church*, (London: SPCK, 1971) ch. 2.
16. *Convocation of Canterbury*, 1938.
17. Report of *Proceedings*, General Synod, vol. 12, no. 2, 7 July 1981.
18. Report by the General Synod Marriage Commission (CIO Publishing, 1978), often known as the Lichfield Report.
19. Terms of reference, the General Synod Marriage Commission, 1975, reproduced in *Marriage and the Doctrine of the Church of England*, House of Bishops' Marriage Education Panel, 1985.

20. Lord Hardwicke's Marriage Act, 1753. Prior to this, under Church law two forms of valid marriage were recognised: the exchange of consents to marry followed by intercourse, and the promise to marry in the future followed by intercourse.

21. *The Gentleman's Magazine*, September 1753.

22. A. Bottomley *et al.* (1981).

23. For example, the Legitimation Act (1926) reintroduced the old doctrine of legitimation upon subsequent marriage. The Family Law Reform Act (1969) allowed an illegitimate child to inherit on the intestacy of either parent. And as a result of the Family Law Reform Act (1987) the only rights now denied to an illegitimate child are the rights of succession to the Crown and to titles of honour.

24. *Bromley's Family Law*, 1976.

25. J. M. Eekelaar, in Eekelaar and Katz (eds) (1980) p. 450.

26. The most recent Green Paper on this issue, Cmnd 9756, was published on Budget Day, 1987. In his statement to the House of Commons on the reform of personal taxation, Mr Norman Lamont, speaking for the Government, said that tax penalties on marriage should be removed. However, it was felt there was insufficient support for far-reaching reforms. (*Hansard*, 18 March 1987: pp. 10 and 12.)

27. See, for example, a discussion of the changed economic role of women in the discussion paper contributed by the Law Commission on the financial consequences of divorce: *The Financial Consequences of Divorce: The Basic Policy*, Law Com. no. 103, 1980.

28. *Marriage Matters*, a consultative document by the Working Party on Marriage Guidance set up by the Home Office in consultation with the Department of Health and Social Security (London: HMSO, 1979) p. 23.

29. England and Wales has one of the highest divorce rates in Europe. In 1983, 147 000 divorce decrees were made absolute, two and a half times the number in 1970. However, the majority of all children, four out of every five, live with both their natural parents. See *The Family Today: continuity and change*, Fact Sheet 1, Family Policies Centre, September 1985.

30. The cuttings from newspapers, magazines and periodicals published within the first six months of 1983 were provided by Romeike and Curtice, the Press Clipping Bureau.

31. *The Matrimonial and Family Proceedings Act 1984*, enacted October 1984.

32. *Monitors*, giving summary statistics of divorces, marriages and births, were first published by the Office of Population and Census Surveys (OPCS) in 1976.

33. *The Mail on Sunday*, 9 January 1983.

34. *Options* magazine, January 1983. This report of findings from questionnaires about marriage, completed by readers, was widely reported and commented on in the Press generally.

2 Exploring Marriage

1. Morgan (1975).
2. *The Times*, 17 August 1976.
3. Dunnell (1979).
4. OPCS, *General Household Survey, 1979* (London: HMSO, 1981) p. 126.
5. Morgan (1985) p. 4.
6. Helpful discussion of theoretical perspectives on marriage can be found in: Askham (1984) and Burgoyne and Clark, (1984). Robert Chester also has provided a concise but comprehensive review of the current scene in his chapter 'Marriage in Britain: an overview of research' in Dryden (ed.) (1985).
7. Thornes and Collard (1979).
8. Our attention was drawn to this by Dr Jack Dominian and other colleagues at the Marriage Research Centre.
9. The second round of interviewing took place in 1984–85.
10. An excellent discussion of the functionalist perspective can be found in Morgan (1975) pp. 17–59.
11. Turner (1970) pp. 187–97.
12. J. Bernard in Christensen (ed.) (1964); L. Safilios-Rothschild (1976); Scanzoni and Scanzoni (1976); and J. Sprey in W. R. Burr *et al.* (eds) (1979).
13. Blumer (1969); Rock (1979).
14. Natanson (ed.) (1962).
15. Morgan (1985) p. 202.
16. Mills (1970) p. 10.
17. P. L. Berger and H. Kellner in Dreitzel (ed.) (1970) p. 5.
18. See, for example, Askham (1984); Backett (1982); and N. Hart (1976).
19. A useful reference to illustrate the family life cycle approach is: Rapoport and Rapoport with Strelitz (1975).
20. P. L. Berger and H. Kellner in Dreitzel (ed.) (1970).
21. The theme of the 'captive wife' was established by Gavron (1966) and it has been echoed in later studies: Oakley (1974a); Oakley (1979); Edgell (1980); and Boulton (1983).
22. Askham (1984).
23. Komarovsky (1962).
24. For example, Bernard (1972).
25. Winch (1958); also Kerkoff and Davis (1962). For a full review of the literature see T. L. Huston, C. A. Surra, N. M. Fitzgerald and R. M. Cate, 'From Courtship to Marriage: mate selection as an interpersonal process' in Duck and Gilmour (eds) (1981).
26. Rapoport (1964).
27. Ibid.
28. Young and Willmott (1975) Ch. 10.
29. Oakley (1974b) Ch. 8.
30. Young and Willmott (1975).
31. The interviews were undertaken by Penny Mansfield, Margaret Stoneman and Margaret O'Brien during 1979. Jean Collard joined the study

in 1981, after Margaret Stoneman and Margaret O'Brien had left. Penny Mansfield and Jean Collard, the authors of the present book, were responsible for the analysis of all the material.

32. In his preface to the second edition of Bott (1957) Max Gluckman describes it as a 'path-breaking study'. It did indeed lead to a whole canon of research: for example, Askham (1984); Backett (1982); Hart (1976); and Leonard (1980).

33. Since 1950 there have been major changes in marriage patterns. K. E. Kiernan and S. M. Eldridge have demonstrated the different marriage patterns of three cohorts of women (Kiernan and Eldridge, 1985).

34. All newly-weds were British or Irish born: (129 born in Britain, one in the Republic of Ireland).

35. Bott (1957); Oakley (1974); Young and Willmott (1962).

36. See chapters by C. Delphy and A. Oakley in Roberts (ed.) (1981); and Murgatroyd (1982).

37. Permission to obtain the names of couples through the Marriage Notices was not granted by the Registrar General, on the grounds that to do so was not in accordance with the Marriage Acts. The Marriage Research Centre appealed against this decision through the then Secretary of State for Social Services, but without success.

38. We kept in touch with nearly all the couples by postal questionnaire, and in 1984–85 a second interview was obtained with 47 couples from the original group. By this time six of the marriages had broken down.

39. Whenever an interview was refused we were usually able to ask a brief list of questions on the doorstep (place of birth, education and occupation), and in most cases we were thus able to record details of those who declined the full interview.

40. Richardson, Dohrenwend and Klein (1965). See also Brown and Rutter (1966); and Rutter and Brown (1966).

41. The interviewer leads the respondent through the areas to be covered according to the interview schedule, but in the course of the interview the respondent may raise topics in a different sequence. Throughout the interview, the interviewer has, therefore, to balance the importance of keeping to the schedule order to ensure standardisation, against the need to allow the respondent to be spontaneous.

42. The life events schedule was loosely based on one used by George W. Brown and Tirril Harris (Brown and Harris, 1978).

43. These different orientations to the future are fully described in Chapter 10.

3 Ready for Marriage

1. Sarsby (1983) pp. 59–60.
2. *General Household Survey, 1979* (London: HMSO, 1981) p. 127.
3. For a discussion of the different contexts of cohabitation see Brown and Kiernan (1981).
4. See Mansfield (1985).

5. Busfield and Paddon (1977) p. 118.
6. Blackstone, the renowned legal scholar, described marriage under the Common Law as the merger of husband and wife into a single legal identity; 'the very being or legal existence of the woman is suspended during marriage', William Blackstone, *Commentaries on the Laws of England*, vol. 1 (1765) p. 442.
7. Jacqueline Burgoyne argues that 'having a place of one's own', the ideal of home ownership, has gradually come to represent a basic building block of family life. See Burgoyne (1987) pp. 12–14.
8. 1981 Census, unpublished tables.
9. 'Measures of central tendency, such as mean and median ages at marriage for first time brides and grooms, also increased throughout the period 1972–1980. These period measures taken together show that there has been a reduced propensity for young people to marry over this period and that those who marry do so at later ages' (Kiernan and Eldridge (1985) p. 1).
10. See Inter-Rail 1987 brochure *Making Tracks*, where concessionary fares for those under 26 are advertised as 'complete freedom for the under 26s' (Central Advertising Services, British Railways Board).
11. P. L. Berger and H. Kellner, in Dreitzel (ed.) (1970) p. 63.
12. Pincus (ed.) (1973) p. 215.
13. Schofield (1968) p. 136.
14. T. L. Huston, C. A. Surra, N. M. Fitzgerald and R. M. Cate, in Duck and Gilmour (eds) (1981) p. 80.

4 The Marriage Trail

1. Blood, Jnr (1969) p. 18.
2. This was defined as 'something more than just going out for an evening occasionally'. The respondents were then probed for further details about these 'serious' relationships.
3. Dominian (1968).
4. Dunnell (1979).
5. Mori Poll published in the *Sunday Times*, April 1984.
6. See Chapter 1, Note 7.
7. J. Trost in Eekelaar and Katz (eds) (1980) p. 19.
8. *General Household Survey, 1979* (HMSO, 1981) p. 127.

5 Getting Married

1. For a review of prediction studies see C. E. Bowerman in Christensen (ed.) (1964).
2. For definitions of active and passive engagements see Chapter 3, p. 76.

3. The uncertainty over correct wedding etiquette when either the bride's or the groom's parents are no longer married to each other has been publicly clarified in the Royal Weddings of 1981 and 1986.
4. Marris (1978).

6 Setting Up Home

1. See, for example, the British Medical Association's annual publication, *Getting Married*.
2. Advertisement for the Halifax Building Society.
3. See OPCS Monitor GHS 83/2, replacement for Table 10, showing consumer durables, central heating and cars, 1972–82. For example, in 1979, 74 per cent of all British households had washing machines, compared with 86 per cent of our newly-weds.
4. Blood (1969) p. 20.
5. Knorr recipe book for young couples.
6. 'Marriage is good for men' in Bernard (1976) pp. 32 – 3.
7. Two in three husbands earned more than their wives and in over half the marriages the husbands' earnings were at least one third greater than those of their wives.

7 Working Husbands and Wives Who Work

1. Young and Willmott (1975) p. 278.
2. In 1911 only 9.6 per cent of married women could be classified as economically active. The figure had risen to 21.7 per cent by 1951 and by 1979 it was estimated to be 51.3 per cent (figures relate to married women of all ages). Source: *Equal Opportunities Commission, Fourth Annual Report, 1979* (1980) p. 70. The proportion of women in employment immediately after marriage has also been increasing, from 77 per cent of a sample of those married in 1956–60, to 86 per cent of those married in 1971–75. Much of this change may be due to a lengthening of the interval between marriage and first birth. See Dunnell (1979).
3. The Women and Employment Survey, 1980 demonstrates this: 'Almost all women who have a child have a break from employment; only 4% of the women with children we interviewed had been in the labour market continuously throughout their working lives and some of these are likely to leave subsequently to have a further child. What is striking is that very high proportions of women return to work after having a child and that contrary to popular assumptions this is not a new phenomenon. For example, 90% of women who had a first birth in the late fifties and early sixties had returned to work at some stage.' The survey also shows that younger generations of women (for example, women having

their first baby between 1975 and 1979) are returning to work sooner than comparable older generations of mothers. 'Overall, women are spending an increasing proportion of their lives in employment, though very few adopt the typical male patterns of continuous lifetime employment as a full-time worker' (Martin and Roberts, 1984).

4. R.D. Barron and G. M. Morris, in Barker and Allen (eds) (1976) pp. 46–79.
5. See 'Characteristics of the young labour force' in *Social Trends No. 8* (HMSO, 1979).
6. Oakley (1979).
7. See Chapter 2, p. 60.
8. For a fuller discussion of the plans for parenthood of the newly-weds, see Mansfield (1982).

8 Becoming a Couple: Together . . .

1. For an interesting discussion of the idealisation of the marital relationship and the consequences of privatising the marital world, see Clark (1987).
2. As quoted in Weitzman (1981) p. 1.
3. See Komarovsky (1962) pp. 32–3.
4. Sarsby (1983) p. 131.
5. Brown and Harris (1978); Brannen and Collard (1982); and Quinton, Rutter and Liddle (1985).
6. Brannen and Collard (1982).
7. Friedan (1965).

9 Becoming a Couple: . . . Yet Separate

1. Askam (1984) p. 183.
2. *Getting Married*, British Medical Association pamphlet, 1985.
3. See Note 10, Chapter 2.
4. Andy Capp is a popular cartoon figure in the *Daily Mirror*. He is the epitome of the henpecked working-class husband.
5. Of the newly-wed couples, 58 per cent kept their incomes separate. In this arrangement, each spouse typically retained his or her income but contributed to running costs of the joint household. This was achieved usually by each partner taking on the role of payee of specific items. Other joint expenses were discussed between the couple and were contributed to on an *ad hoc* basis, either with each contributing half of the cost or the partner with more money at the time paying a larger share. Incomes were pooled by 35 per cent of the couples, usually into a joint bank account. Although in this arrangement, in theory, control of expenditure was equally shared, in practice it was often more acceptable for only one partner (the husband) to draw money out from the common pool.

6. 'Typically, individuals in our society do not divorce because marriage has become unimportant to them, but because it has become so important that they have no tolerance for the less than successful marital arrangement' P. Berger and H. Keller in Dreitzel (ed.) (1970).

10 A Sense of the Future

1. Plummer (1983).
2. See Chapter 3.
3. Rose (1984) p. 5.
4. J. M. Eekelaar in Eekelaar and Katz (eds) (1980) p. 454.
5. Hart (1976) p. 195.
6. Zicklin (1968) pp. 236–49.
7. Parkes (1971) pp. 101–15.
8. P. L. Berger and H. Kellner in Dreitzel (ed) (1970) p. 63.
9. Parkes, (1971).
10. As part of the Life Events section of the interview, respondents were questioned in detail about the impact and effect changing circumstances and events had for them.
11. William Shakespeare, *As You Like It*, act II, scene vii.
12. A single stereotypical progression through the 'natural' predetermined order (Shakespeare narrowed his typology to the life of a man; his successors in the 1960s modelled theirs on contemporary middle-class urban American families); an emphasis upon the stages rather than the transition from one stage to the next; the explicit notion of a cyclical sequence, when individual lives follow a linear sequence which end in death.
13. For a comprehensive review of the family life cycle approach, see M. Murphy and O. Sullivan, 'The Rise and Fall of the Family Life Cycle', a paper presented at the 1986 Conference of the British Sociological Association on the sociology of the life cycle.
14. Two books which provide a useful introduction to the life course approach are Plummer (1983) Hareven (1978).
15. Berger and Kellner in Dreitzel (1970).
16. Morgan (1975) p. 216.
17. Ibid. Here Morgan is referring to Seeley, Sim and Loosley (1956).
18. Morgan (1975): here Morgan is referring to Komarovsky (1967).
19. See 'The Concept of Action', pp. 67–72, in Alfed Schutz, *Collected Papers*, ed. M. Natamon (Martin Nijhoff 1962).
20. Berger, Berger and Kellner (1974) p. 72.
21. For a definition of 'marriage seeker' see Chapter 3, p.68.

Bibliography

ASKHAM, J., *Identity and Stability in Marriage* (Cambridge University Press, 1984).

BACKETT, K. C., *Mothers and Fathers* (London: Macmillan, 1982).

BARKER, D. L., Ch. 4, ALLEN, S. (eds) *Dependence and Exploitation in Work and Marriage* (London: Longman, 1976).

BARRETT, M. and McINTOSH, M., *The Anti-Social Family* (London: Verso Editions, 1982).

BARRON, R. D. and MORRIS, G. M., 'Sexual Divisions and the Dual Labour Market' in Barker and Allen (eds) (1976).

BERGER, P. L., BERGER, B. and KELLNER, H., *The Homeless Mind* (Harmondsworth: Penguin, 1974).

BERNARD, J., 'The Adjustments of Married Mates' in Christensen (ed.) (1964).

BERNARD, J., *The Future of Marriage* (Harmondsworth: Penguin, 1976) (1st published 1972 by Wales Publishing, New York).

BLOOD, R. O., Jnr, *Marriage*, 2nd edn (New York: Free Press, 1969).

BLUMER, H. S., *Symbolic Interactionism: perspective and method* (Englewood Cliffs, New Jersey: Prentice Hall, 1969).

BOTT, E., *Family and Social Network* (London: Tavistock, 1957).

BOTTOMLEY, A., GIEVE, K., MOON, G. and WEIR, A., *The Cohabitation Handbook: a woman's guide to the law* (London: Pluto Press 1981).

BOULTON, M. G., *On Being a Mother* (London: Tavistock, 1983).

BOWERMAN, C. E., 'Prediction Studies', in Christensen (ed.) (1964).

BRANNEN, J. and COLLARD, J., *Marriages in Trouble: the process of seeking help* (London: Tavistock, 1982).

BROWN, A. and KIERNAN, K. E., 'Cohabitation in Great Britain: evidence from the General Household Survey', *Population Trends*, 25 (1981).

BROWN, G. W. and HARRIS, T., *Social Origins of Depression: a study of psychiatric disorder in women* (London: Tavistock, 1978).

BROWN, G. W. and RUTTER, M., 'The Measurement of Family Activities and Relationships: a methodological study', *Human Relations*, 19 (1966) pp. 241–63.

BURGOYNE, J., *Cohabitation and Contemporary Family Life* (London: Economic and Social Research Council, 1985).

BURGOYNE, J., 'Material Happiness', *New Society* 10 April 1987, pp. 12–14.

BURGOYNE, J. and CLARK, D., *Making a Go of It* (London: Routledge & Kegan Paul, 1984).

BURR, W. R., HILL, REUBEN, NYE, F. IVAN AND REISS, L. (eds), *Contemporary Theories about the Family* (New York: The Free Press, 1979).

BUSFIELD, J. and PADDON, M., *Thinking about Children: sociology and fertility in post-war England* (Cambridge University Press, 1977).
BUTTERWORTH, E. and WEIR, D. (eds) *The New Sociology of Modern Britain*, 3rd edn (London: Fontana, 1984).
CHRISTENSEN, H. (ed.) *Handbook of Marriage and the Family* (Chicago: Rand McNally, 1964).
CLARK, D., 'Wedlocked Britain', *New Society*, 13 March 1987.
DELPHY, C., 'Women in Stratification Studies', in Roberts (ed.) (1981).
DOMINIAN, J., *Marital Breakdown* (Harmondsworth: Penguin, 1968).
DREITZEL, H. P. (ed.) *Recent Sociology No. 2: Patterns of Communicative Behaviour* (New York: Macmillan 1970).
DRYDEN, W. (ed.) *Marital Therapy in Britain, vol. 1, Context and Therapeutic Approaches* (London: Harper & Row, 1985).
DUCK, S. and GILMOUR, R. (eds) *Personal Relationships 2: Developing Personal Relationships* (London: Academic Press, 1981).
DUNNELL, K., *Family Formation 1976* (London: HMSO, 1979).
EDGELL, S., *Middle-Class Couples: a study of segregation, domination and inequality in marriage* (London: George Allen & Unwin, 1980).
EEKELAAR, J.M., 'Postscript: Crisis in the Institution of Marriage: an overview' in Eekelaar & Katz (eds) (1980).
EEKELAAR, J. M. and KATZ, S. N. (eds), *Marriage and Cohabitation in Contemporary Society* (Toronto: Butterworths, 1980).
FLETCHER, R., *The Family and Marriage in Britain* (revised edn) (Harmondsworth: Penguin, 1966).
FRIEDAN, B., *The Feminine Mystique* (Harmondsworth: Penguin, 1965).
GAVRON, H., *The Captive Wife: conflicts of housebound mothers* (London: Routledge & Kegan Paul, 1966).
HAREVEN, T. K. (ed), *Transitions: The Family Life in Historical Perspective* (New York: Academic Press, 1978).
HARRIS, C. C., *The Family and Industrial Society, Studies in Sociology: 13* (London: George Allen & Unwin, 1983).
N. HART, *When Marriage Ends* (London: Tavistock, 1976).
KERCKHOFF, A. C. and DAVIS, K. E., 'Value Consensus and Need Complementarity in Mate Selection', *American Sociological Review*, 27 (1962) pp. 295–303.
KIERNAN, K. E. and ELDRIDGE, S. M. *A Demographic Analysis of First Marriages in England and Wales: 1950–1980* (Centre for Population Studies Research Paper, 1985).
KOMAROVSKY, M., *Blue Collar Marriage* (New York: Random House, 1962) (as published 1967 by Vintage Books 1967).
LEWIN, B., 'Unmarried Cohabitation: a marriage form in a changing society', *Journal of Marriage and the Family*, 44 (1982) pp. 763–73.
LEMERT, E. M., *Human Deviance, Social Problems and Social Control* (Englewood Cliffs, New Jersey: Prentice Hall, 1972).
LEONARD, D., *Sex and Generation: a study of courtship and weddings*

(London: Tavistock, 1980).

MACDONALD, P. and MARS, G., 'Informal Marriage' in Butterworth and Weir (eds) (1984).

MANSFIELD, P., 'Getting Ready for Parenthood: attitudes to and expectations of having children of a group of newly-weds', *International Journal of Sociology and Social Policy*, 2 (1982) p. 28.

MANSFIELD, P., *Young People and Marriage*, Scottish Marriage Guidance Council Occasional Paper, No. 1 (1985).

Marriage Matters, A consultative document by the Working Party on Marriage Guidance set up by the Home Office in consultation with the Department of Health and Social Security (London: HMSO, 1979).

MARRIS, P., *Loss and Change*, paperback edn (London: Routledge & Kegan Paul, 1978).

MARTIN, J. and ROBERTS, C., *Women and Employment: a lifetime perspective* (London: HMSO, 1984).

MORGAN, D. H. J., *Social Theory and the Family* (London: Routledge & Kegan Paul, 1975).

MORGAN, D. H. J., *The Family, Politics and Social Theory* (London: Routledge & Kegan Paul, 1985).

MURGATROYD, L., 'Gender and Occupational Stratification', *Sociological Review*, 30 (1982) pp. 574–602.

NATANSON, M. (ed.) *Alfred Schutz: Collected Papers*, vol. 1 (The Hague: Martinus Nijhoff, 1962).

OAKLEY, A., *Housewife* (Harmondsworth: Penguin, 1974a).

OAKLEY, A., *The Sociology of Housework* (London: Martin Robertson, 1974b).

OAKLEY, A., *Becoming a Mother* (Oxford: Martin Robertson, 1979).

OAKLEY, A., 'Interviewing Women: a contradiction in terms' in Roberts (ed.) (1981).

PARKES, C. M., 'Psycho-Social Transitions: a field for study', *Social Science and Medicine*, 5 (1971) pp. 101–15.

PINCUS, L. (ed.) *Marriage: studies in emotional conflict and growth* (London: Institute of Marital Studies, 1973).

PLUMMER, J., *Documents of Life* (London: George Allen & Unwin, 1983).

QUINTON, D., RUTTER, M. and LIDDLE, C., 'Institutional Rearing, Parenting Difficulties and Marital Support', *Psychological Medicine*, 14 (1985).

RAPOPORT, R., 'The Transition from Engagement to Marriage', *Acta Sociologica* 8 (1964) pp. 36–55.

RAPOPORT, R. and RAPOPORT, R. N. with STRELITZ, Z., *Leisure and the Family Life Cycle* (London: Routledge & Kegan Paul, 1975).

RICHARDSON, S. A., DOHRENWEND, B. S. and KLEIN, D., *Interviewing: its forms and findings* (New York: Basic Books, 1965).

ROBERTS, H. (ed.) *Doing Feminist Research* (London: Routledge & Kegan Paul, 1981).

ROCK, P., *The Making of Symbolic Interactionism* (London: Macmillan, 1979).

ROSE, P., *Parallel Lives, Five Victorian Marriages* (London: Chatto & Windus, 1984).

RUTTER, M., and BROWN, G. W., 'The Reliability and Validity of Measures of Family Life and Relationships in Families Containing a Psychiatric Patient', *Social Psychiatry*, 1 (1966) pp. 38–53.

SAFILIOS-ROTHSCHILD, L., 'A Macro- and Micro-examination of Family Power and Love: an Exchange Model', *Journal of Marriage and the Family*, 38 (1976) pp. 355–362.

SARSBY, J., *Romantic Love and Society* (Harmondsworth: Penguin, 1983).

SCANZONI, J. and SCANZONI, L., *Men, Women and Change: a sociology of marriage and the family* (New York: McGraw Hill, 1976).

SCHOFIELD, M., *The Sexual Behaviour of Young People*, Harmondsworth: Penguin, 1968).

SEELEY, J. R., ALEXANDER, R. and LOOSLEY, E. W., *Crestwood Heights* (Toronto University Press, 1956).

THORNES, B. and COLLARD, J., *Who Divorces?* (London: Routledge & Kegan Paul, 1979).

TROST, J., 'Cohabitation Without Marriage in Sweden' in Eekelaar and Katz (eds) (1980).

TURNER, B., *Family Interaction* (New York: Wiley, 1970).

WEITZMAN, J., *The Marriage Contract* (New York: Free Press, 1981).

WINCH, R., *Mate Selection: a study of complementary needs* (New York: Harper & Brothers, 1958).

WRIGHT MILLS, C., *The Sociological Imagination* (Harmondsworth: Penguin, 1970).

YOUNG, M., and WILLMOTT, P., *Family and Kinship in East London* (Harmondsworth: Penguin, 1962).

YOUNG, M. and WILLMOTT, P. *The Symmetrical Family* (Harmondsworth: Penguin, 1975).

ZICKLIN, G., 'A Conversation Concerning Face-to-Face Interaction', *Psychiatry*, 31 (1968) pp. 236–49.

Name Index

Subject Index

Unless otherwise indicated (e.g. marriage (in general)) all entries refer to the newly-wed study.